DEMOCRATIC TRANSITIONS IN CENTRAL AMERICA

DEMOCRATIC TRANSITIONS IN CENTRAL AMERICA

Edited by
Jorge I. Domínguez
and
Marc Lindenberg

UNIVERSITY PRESS OF FLORIDA

Gainesville ■ Tallahassee ■ Tampa ■ Boca Raton
Pensacola ■ Orlando ■ Miami ■ Jacksonville

02 01 00 99 98 97 6 5 4 3 2 1

Library of Congress Cataloging-in-Publication Data
Democratic transitions in Central America / edited by Jorge
   I. Domínguez and Marc Lindenberg.
        p. cm.
   Includes bibliographical references and index.
   ISBN 0-8130-1486-7 (alk. paper)
      1. Central America—Politics and government—1979– 2. Democracy—
Central America—History.   I. Domínguez, Jorge I., 1945–   .
II. Lindenberg, Marc.
   F1439.5.D45   1997
   972.805'3—dc20   96-21369
                                                    CIP

The World Peace Foundation supported the development and publication of this project, and
Harvard University's David Rockefeller Center of Latin American Studies provided a publication
subvention.

The University Press of Florida is the scholarly publishing agency for the State University System of
Florida, comprised of Florida A & M University, Florida Atlantic University, Florida International
University, Florida State University, University of Central Florida, University of Florida, University
of North Florida, University of South Florida, and University of West Florida.

University Press of Florida
15 Northwest 15th Street
Gainesville, FL 32611

TO THE PEOPLES OF CENTRAL AMERICA

CONTENTS

List of Figures viii

Foreword
  Richard J. Bloomfield ix

ONE Democratic Transitions in Central America and Panama
  Jorge I. Domínguez 1

TWO The Political and Economic Transition of Panama, 1978–1991
  Nicolás Ardito-Barletta 32

THREE Revolution and Democratic Transition in Nicaragua
  Jaime Wheelock Román 67

FOUR Democratic Transitions in Nicaragua
  Silvio de Franco and José Luis Velázquez 85

FIVE Political Transition in Guatemala, 1980–1990: A Perspective
  from Inside Guatemala's Army
  Héctor Alejandro Gramajo Morales 111

SIX Guatemala 1978–1993: The Incomplete Process of the Transition to Democracy
  Rodolfo Paiz-Andrade 139

SEVEN Democratic Transition or Modernization?
  The Case of El Salvador since 1979
  Rubén Zamora 165

EIGHT Recent Central American Transitions: Conclusions and Policy
  Implications
  Marc Lindenberg 180

Contributors 195

Index 197

FIGURES

4.1. Nicaragua: gross national product, 1940–77 (millions of 1970 dollars)   86

4.2. Nicaragua: evolution of the gross domestic product by sectors, 1980–86 (millions of 1980 córdobas)   90

4.3. Index of agreement between the USSR and Nicaragua in the United Nations General Assembly, 1965–89 (percentages)   96

4.4. Soviet bloc economic and military assistance to Nicaragua, 1982–86 (millions of U.S. dollars)   96

4.5. Nicaragua: gross national product, 1979–89 (percentage rate of growth)   98

4.6. Nicaragua: evolution of the average real wage, 1978–88 (1978 = 100)   99

4.7. Nicaragua: consumption per capita, 1980–89 (1989 dollars)   99

4.8. Nicaragua: rate of inflation, 1980–89 (percentages)   100

4.9. Nicaragua: external gap, 1977–87 (millions of U.S. dollars)   100

6.1. Guatemala: political regimes and prevailing influences   145

6.2. Guatemala: economic, social, and military indicators   146

6.3. The paradigm transition map   150

6.4. From the old to the new paradigm   152

8.1. Central American regime transitions, 1978–90   182

8.2. Barriers to consolidating transitions   187

8.3. Policies for consolidating transitions   190

FOREWORD

RICHARD J. BLOOMFIELD

In the late 1970s, Central America, which had been a backwater of international politics, exploded onto the front page. For the next decade, this small underdeveloped area, containing barely 22 million inhabitants, was the focus of the most acrimonious foreign policy debate that the United States had seen since the Vietnam War. For the Reagan administration, Central America was a major battleground in the contest with the Soviet Union and the defeat of Central American revolutionary movements was a top foreign policy priority. For the administration's critics, the revolutions were the result of age-old social injustice and political repression; unless those wrongs began to be righted, revolutions would be a permanent part of the landscape—"inevitable," as one critic put it—and attempts to repress them would be doomed to fail.

Surprisingly, given the distance between their starting positions, the two sides in the debate ultimately agreed on the solution to the problem of Central America. The way to cut the ground out from under the revolutionaries, said the Reaganites, was to defeat the communist insurgencies and create democracies in the region, which would offer the masses the possibility of a better future in a climate of freedom. Opponents of the Reagan administration had all along insisted that the cause of the upheavals in the region was the absence of democracy. Although they argued that democracy meant more than elections, the opponents could hardly disagree that democratic institutions were essential to enduring social and economic reform. Where the two sides continued to be at odds was on the way in which democracy could best be achieved in Central America. Moreover, the administration's opponents questioned its sincerity, charging that its newfound support for democracy was a cover for its unrelenting reliance on force to defeat the revolutionaries. If anything, the debate increased in vehemence as the decade wore on.

As a result, both sides advanced very different versions of what was happening in the area. The Reagan administration made exaggerated claims about the speed at which democracy was being achieved in most of the countries—

with the exception of Nicaragua, in spite of elections held in that country in 1984. Many of the administration's critics belittled what was being achieved in the region, at times denying that there was any real change at all, except in Nicaragua, where many felt the 1984 elections were reasonably free.

What is now apparent, with the benefit of a longer-term perspective, is that a process of transition to democracy did get under way in Central America and Panama in the 1980s and that, however haltingly and precariously, the process continues today. It is also obvious that, with the achievement of settlements of the conflicts in El Salvador and Nicaragua, the process has entered a new phase: the crisis of war has given way to the long haul of building the peace.

Accordingly, the World Peace Foundation called for a study aimed at discerning the patterns in the transition process in the region and at drawing from the experience some broader lessons that would be relevant for the future. The foundation endeavors to be a bridge between the broad insights offered by the scholar and the practical concerns of the policy practitioner. It was hoped that a study of this kind would help those attempting to consolidate democratic gains in Central America and Panama and would bring some new evidence to the debate about the democratization process generally.

Just as it was in the end the Central Americans themselves who were the architects of their own peace, so too it was the Central Americans who were ultimately responsible for whatever progress toward democracy has been achieved in their countries. While support for democratic transitions from the United States and other foreign powers was helpful in creating the political space in which democratic leaders needed to act, it was those leaders who took the risks, both political and physical, of acting. With this personal element in mind, the foundation and the editors decided to ask some of the principal actors in these events to perform the analysis that is usually left to academics in projects of this kind.

The decision to enlist practitioners as authors brought with it some complications and trade-offs. For one, these people are still active in the public affairs of their countries; as a result, several people who were at first enthusiastic about participating found themselves unable in the end to devote sufficient time to the project and dropped out. They left some gaps in country coverage. Nevertheless, the study includes four of the original six countries in which the transition to democracy has been the most difficult and accompanied by the most violence—El Salvador, Guatemala, Nicaragua, and Panama.

Relying on principal actors as analysts also raised the question of objectivity. One way to deal with that problem was to recruit from Guatemala and Nicaragua two authors each, who held opposing, or at least diverging, political views. Moreover, the foundation and the editors avoided censoring the authors even when they flatly contradicted one another, nor did we seek to de-ideologize them; on the contrary, we felt that it would have defeated the purpose of our approach to do so. The editors did, however, provide the other authors with a common set of questions to address and asked them not to be merely descriptive or anecdotal.

It is my belief that the introductory and concluding chapters by the editors of this book provide the detachment that may be lacking in the intervening chapters. It was the editors' task to draw out of the firsthand accounts of the other authors those common patterns and causal relationships that turn the trees into a forest.

Everyone recognizes that, except in Costa Rica, the transition process in the region is fragile, and the progress that has been made is not necessarily irreversible. Nevertheless, the fact that it is now taking place in a climate of relative peace that was for so long absent, and that it is a peace fashioned by the very parties to the conflict, gives cause for hope that it will endure. That hope has inspired all those who contributed to this book.

*   *   *

The World Peace Foundation expresses its appreciation to the U.S. Agency for International Development (AID) for a grant to cover the costs of translating the manuscript for this book and the publication of a summary report on the study issued by the foundation in January 1993. The editors also thank the David Rockefeller Center of Latin American Studies at Harvard University for its support and Debra-Lee Vasques for her work on the tables and figures.

Outlines of the papers were first presented at a workshop sponsored by the foundation in Cambridge, Massachusetts, in May 1991. The papers were first published in Spanish in Jorge I. Domínguez and Marc Lindenberg, *Transiciones democráticas en Centro América* (San José, Costa Rica: Editorial Instituto Centroamericano de Administración de Empresas, 1994). The papers have been translated into English, shortened, and edited for this book.

ONE

DEMOCRATIC TRANSITIONS IN CENTRAL AMERICA AND PANAMA

JORGE I. DOMÍNGUEZ

From the late 1970s to the early 1990s, revolutionary wars broke out in Nicaragua, El Salvador, and Guatemala and a revolutionary movement reached power in Nicaragua. These countries also became the object of international competition, drawing the attention of the Soviet Union, many European countries, Canada, Japan, and many Latin American countries including Cuba. The United States deepened its involvement in the domestic politics of Central America and Panama, actively supporting military efforts to overthrow Nicaragua's Sandinista government and eventually invading Panama to overthrow its government. At the same time, Central America and Panama suffered an acute economic crisis, caused in part by these wars; the crisis worsened as a result of sharp drops in the international price of coffee that occurred in the late 1970s and again in the late 1980s. In the early 1980s, the U.S. economic recession had a severe negative impact on these countries, which depended greatly on the U.S. economy.[1]

Since 1980, Central America and Panama have made serious strides in transforming their politics and their economies. In the late 1970s, there were society-led transitions in Nicaragua and, at least at the outset, in El Salvador: Social forces—with guns—overpowered the government and other elite actors. In the next decade, Nicaragua and El Salvador engaged in another regime transition that involved intensive negotiations between government and opposition as well as violence and the broad mobilization of social forces. On the other hand, throughout the 1980s there was a slow-moving, regime-led political transition shaped by the elite in Guatemala (and, in different ways, in Honduras).[2] Panama began with a similar kind of transition in the 1970s, but in the 1980s there was a turn to a society-led effort to overpower the military, culminating in a U.S. invasion in 1989. All these countries (including Honduras and Costa Rica)[3] made moderate to major transitions in the organization of their respective economies.

In order to shed light on the perhaps surprising but now clear trend toward freer politics and freer markets throughout these countries, this book features the reflections, analyses, and recollections of direct participants in many of these processes. In this introductory chapter, I weave together themes from the chapters that follow in order to propose a way to think about the still imperfect but ongoing processes of democratization and political and economic liberalization in these countries.

Following Guillermo O'Donnell and Philippe Schmitter, "by [political] liberalization we mean the process of making effective certain rights that protect both individual and social groups from arbitrary or illegal acts committed by the state or third parties."[4] By economic liberalization, we mean a turn toward market-oriented economic policies. By democratization we mean the shift to free, fair, and competitive elections, held at regular intervals, in the context of guaranteed civil and political rights, responsible government (i.e., accountability of the executive, administrative, and coercive arms of the state to elected representatives), and political inclusion (i.e., universal suffrage and nonproscription of parties). The guarantees of rights and institutions would be embodied in a "convention of constitutionalism, that is, the presumption that political change should only occur in accordance with rules and precedents."[5]

Several questions guide this analysis. Why do the powerful yield their power? How do conscious actors construct political liberalization and democratization? What rules or arrangements do they design to bring these things about? What is the behavior of economic elites in political and economic liberalization?[6]

THE CONTEXT FOR THIS BOOK

This book focuses on the four countries of the region in which the transition to democracy has been the most difficult and accompanied by the most violence: El Salvador, Nicaragua, Guatemala, and Panama. As explained in the foreword, our approach has been to engage those who have been, and remain, major actors in the politics and economies of their countries. Most of these authors have differed profoundly in their approaches to their nations' politics and economic policies; they still differ in this book. The following paragraphs situate their positions in the wider debates.

Nicolás Ardito-Barletta writes about Panama. He was president of Panama in 1984–85; before that, he served as World Bank vice president for Latin

America. In 1985, he was deposed by General Manuel Antonio Noriega, Panama's strongman. Ardito-Barletta had been Noriega's candidate in the 1984 presidential elections; Noriega turned against him when Ardito-Barletta launched an investigation of a murder allegedly ordered by General Noriega. As Ardito-Barletta explains, in the early 1980s he took a calculated risk that Panama's democratization could be fostered most successfully by working within the political regime first established in 1968 by Panama's military. His goal was to make it possible for the regime to move toward democratization by returning the military to its professional role and by reactivating the economy in accordance with market principles.

Rubén Zamora describes the division that occurred in El Salvador's Christian Democratic Party in the early 1980s. According to Zamora, some Salvadoran Christian Democrats, led by José Napoleón Duarte (who would be elected El Salvador's president in 1984), chose to work with the military in order to democratize the political regime from within; other Christian Democrats, Zamora prominent among them, aligned with the revolutionary insurgency to overthrow the Salvadoran military's long-standing grip on power. Salvadoran Christian Democrats differed also over economic policy, but they tended to agree that the government should have a major role in the regulation of the economy, the provision of social welfare benefits, and the management of certain enterprises; they differed mainly over their political strategies.

Jaime Wheelock Román was a commander of the Sandinista National Liberation Front (FSLN); in the 1970s, he took up arms in the revolution against General Anastasio Somoza Debayle's dictatorship. Afterward he served as a member of the Sandinista National Directorate. Upon Somoza's overthrow in 1979, Wheelock became minister of agricultural development and agrarian reform, a post that he held for most of the following decade. As he explains, in the early to mid-1980s he sought to foster the social and economic empowerment of poor rural Nicaraguans, but he focused less on the maintenance of the conditions that permit public contestation and that provide the political guarantees for the electoral opposition to prevail at the polls. He expresses pride in the Sandinista government's accomplishments in democratizing Nicaraguan society. By the late 1980s, he notes, the Sandinista government had revised its previous policies and created a political climate more favorable for electoral competition. In 1990, he participated in the decision to hold fair elections and to honor the results, turning power over to the opposition.

Silvio de Franco and José Luis Velázquez disagreed sharply with the Sandinista government and became exiles. For them, the Sandinista government was authoritarian, abusive, and arbitrary in both the political and economic arenas. They hold the Sandinista government responsible for Nicaragua's economic decline and for the difficulties encountered in the subsequent re-construction of the nation's economy and cooperative civil politics. In 1990, de Franco became minister of the economy and development; in January 1992, he became Central Bank president, until his resignation in September 1992. (Velázquez served as his adviser.) As minister and bank president, de Franco sought to reorient the economy in line with market principles, to break the legacy of hyperinflation, and to foster the privatization of state enterprises within a liberal democratic regime.

Our two Guatemalan authors served as ministers of government in President Marco Vinicio Cerezo Arévalo's cabinet. Rodolfo Paiz-Andrade joined the first Cerezo cabinet in January 1986 and served until October 1989. General Héctor Alejandro Gramajo Morales served as minister of national defense from 1987 to 1990; he had served in important military posts throughout the 1980s. Clearly, they share many economic and political objectives and supported many of the same policies. As defense minister, General Gramajo's defeat of two coup attempts made it possible for Finance Minister Paiz to raise taxes and to remain in office.

Paiz and Gramajo differ subtly, however. With pride in the accomplishments of the Guatemalan army, Gramajo describes a long-range strategy within the military to arrange for the transfer of government to civilian politicians as a means to ensure the modernization of Guatemala's polity and economy, the country's successful insertion in international relationships, and the defeat of a long-lived insurgency. In contrast, Paiz focuses more on the manifold efforts of civilians during the military and civilian governments to reshape policies and to construct new institutions to consolidate democracy, render markets effective, and address the much-neglected social agenda.

The differences among the authors, therefore, are sharpest in the essays on Nicaragua. Those differences endure, though they are no longer backed by the force of arms. The differences are important though more subtle in the case of Guatemala, where they illustrate the various strategies for and perspectives toward accomplishment of shared goals.

Because of these significant differences, we found it noteworthy that these authors often agree in the main aspects of their analyses. Therefore, in the remainder of this chapter, I seek to bring out the shared analytical points among authors who otherwise often disagree, while noting plainly those differences that still remain.

LAUNCHING DEMOCRATIZATION

Central America and Panama share important similarities in their recent political processes—despite key structural differences among them—that jointly set their experiences apart from those of other countries. (Unless otherwise specified, in this chapter Central America will refer only to Guatemala, El Salvador, and Nicaragua.) In exploring these similarities and differences, we find four common factors that help to explain the beginning of democratization: force, rational choices in response to a state of war, international pressure, and severe economic crisis.

The Necessity of Force to Begin Democratization

At key junctures in the 1970s and 1980s in these four countries, the powerful yielded power only because military force defeated them. The starting points of the processes of democratization that, with gains and setbacks, have been under way in these four countries since 1979 were the defeats at war of General Somoza in Nicaragua in 1979 and of General Noriega in Panama in 1989, as well as the military coups that deposed General Carlos Humberto Romero in El Salvador in 1979 and General Fernando Romeo Lucas García in Guatemala in 1982. In each of these cases military force did not merely depose a ruler; it also ended a regime. The personal dictatorships and tight oligarchies that had governed these countries would not be reconstituted; the rules of authoritarian imposition were replaced by a greater pluralism.

Despite their different histories, the use of force was necessary to begin democratization in all four countries because tenacious rulers clung to power. Prior to 1968, civilians had played an important and continuous role in Panama's government whereas the Somoza dynasty and military officers had played such roles in the other three countries. Somoza and Noriega, however, showed few signs of surrendering power unless forced to do so. In Guatemala, as Paiz and Gramajo remind us, the fraudulent "election" of Minister of Defense General Angel Aníbal Guevara in March 1982 signaled an intention to continue with an unchanged regime and triggered the coup that overthrew President Lucas. In El Salvador, President Romero's exacerbation of the use of force and his unresponsiveness to reform preceded the October 1979 coup.

At various moments in the late 1970s and in the 1980s, in Turkey, Nigeria, Peru, and Ecuador, military officers willingly and peacefully turned power over to civilians. The same pattern of a military government negotiating its exit from power was evident in Honduras in 1980 and in Guatemala in 1985; this might have occurred in Panama if General Omar Torrijos had lived. The critical point to be made here, however, is that in Guatemala, El Salvador, Nicaragua, and Panama, democratization required the use of military force at a key juncture.

Military force has been used outside this region, of course, to initiate processes of democratization. In the late 1950s in Colombia and Venezuela, and in 1974 in Portugal, for example, military coups opened the way to eventual democratization. Defeat in war is also an important part of the explanation for the democratization of the Axis powers after World War II and, in more recent times, in Greece and Argentina. The reason to call attention to the role of military force in opening the path toward democratization in the four countries we study is to identify some shared characteristics of these four transitions that situate them at one extreme of the spectrum of paths toward democratization. The more peaceful transitions toward democracy evident in the past two decades in India, Spain, Czechoslovakia, Hungary, Brazil, and Chile are different from those found in the four cases we analyze, where politics in recent decades has been played with unusual roughness by comparative standards.

From a State of War to a Democratic State

In Thomas Hobbes's *Leviathan*, political order is established as individuals recoil from a state of war that is "nasty" and "brutish." Though it is doubtful that Hobbes had Central America in mind, the decades-long civil wars in Nicaragua, El Salvador, and Guatemala surely meet his standards of wars that civilized people would wish to end.

Whereas in Hobbes's writing an authoritarian state is founded to end the state of war, in Central America the authoritarian state fueled the war. This outcome occurred, Wheelock reminds us, even when those who made the decisions to limit democratic liberties might perhaps have preferred to do otherwise. Wheelock notes that the Sandinista government responded to U.S. policy in the early to mid-1980s by limiting the opposition's liberties and political space and by subordinating all aspects of the Sandinista government project—including democratic changes—to the need to fight the war. In the long term, however, these antidemocratic policies strengthened the opposition and led more people to take up arms against the government.

Panama never faced such a civil war mainly because the opposition chose a strategy of nonviolence.[7] Nonetheless, Panama's stark economic decline in the late 1980s as the United States imposed sanctions on the Noriega regime, and the increased repression of the opposition by the regime's forces, mark Panama also as a "hardship" case prior to regime change.

In all four cases, a key reason for democratization was the decision of significant elites that the state of war or the state of hardship had to end. The elites reached this decision for various reasons, to be sure, including their inability to repress the opposition successfully and the international pressures and economic collapse to which the next two sections make reference. In the 1980s in Guatemala and Nicaragua, and in the early 1990s in El Salvador, as all authors make clear, those in government agreed with the axiom that Robert A. Dahl identified well in advance of their decisions: "The more the costs of suppression exceed the costs of toleration, the greater the chance for a competitive regime."[8] In Panama, the opposition to Noriega made the calculation that the state of hardship had to end; the opposition preferred U.S. intervention to Noriega's continued rule.

In Guatemala, as Gramajo makes clear, the decision of the army to move toward democratization featured an intermediate step: democratic politics was more likely to generate the political backing necessary to obtain resources from abroad and to defeat the insurgent left. Nonetheless, this very strategy required moving away from the pure reliance on Hobbesian force and the deliberate shift, albeit gradually and imperfectly, toward democracy.

Central Americans, therefore, sought to solve their Hobbes problem with a Dahl solution. For Hobbes, the solution to the state of war was to install an all-powerful Leviathan. Citizens of Guatemala, El Salvador, Nicaragua, and Panama had experienced such would-be Leviathans and had found them wanting. For them, the solution was to democratize power as a means to end the violence and the hardship.

Nevertheless, extensive political violence has been a part of the recent history of Guatemala, El Salvador, and Nicaragua; substantial violence was perpetrated in Panama by the Noriega forces and also during the U.S. intervention. Is such violence the midwife of democracy? To the contrary, Samuel P. Huntington reminds us; since the early 1970s successful democratization has been associated with low levels of violence. This has happened for a variety of reasons, but one is especially important: "The resort to violence increased the power of the specialists in violence in both government and the opposition."[9] Huntington's argument leads us to consider the possibilities for the future of the countries studied in this book.

Democratization in these countries remains incomplete. Although in place since 1989, Panama's government has yet to prove that it can govern effectively. In Nicaragua, the degree of contestation between government and opposition remains too acute, with recurring and severe incidents of political violence (though far short of civil war); the government is constrained in its capacity to implement its policies, as de Franco and Velázquez note. In Guatemala, civil war has yet to end. As Paiz especially makes clear, the concentration of power in the military institution and in the presidency and cabinet remains far above what might be expected in a democracy. In May 1993, President Jorge Serrano Elías staged a coup against the Congress, the Supreme Court, and other independent civilian institutions. Although the attempt failed and constitutional government was preserved, the attempt and its aftermath underscore the fragility and limitations of Guatemala's democratization. In El Salvador, though, the January 1992 agreements that ended the war have been effective; only the future can tell whether it will complete its transition to democracy.

More pessimistically, these four countries may experience a reversal of democracy. Since the restoration of civilian rule, there have been several military coup attempts in Guatemala and Panama against civilian presidents, and in Guatemala civilian President Serrano led one of those. Although these attempts failed, they indicate that much work needs to be done to secure civilian control over the military and even civilian allegiance to democratic practices. In all four countries, many people—former soldiers in all cases and former insurgents in three—have many weapons that can be and, to some degree, are used for private purposes but that could be used to destabilize the governments.

In any case, Guatemala, El Salvador, Nicaragua, and Panama stand at one end of the spectrum of countries that no doubt have made significant political openings. They have experienced war and hardship to a degree that is rare in recent times among countries that have democratized successfully. All four countries have witnessed elites seeking to make rational choices, however, with the hope that the experience of long and brutal wars and sustained hardship would indeed be the midwife for a democratic peace.

International Pressures: Induced to Be Free

In the recent past, international factors have had a persistent and pervasive role in regime transitions in these four countries.[10] All the authors indicate that Jimmy Carter's presidency (1977–81) and its policies in favor of human rights and democratization greatly weakened the support for established autocracies in the region. Somoza, Romero, and Lucas (see the Wheelock, Zamora, and Gramajo chapters, respectively) were undermined in ways that led to their eventual forcible removal from power. In Panama an important political opening can be traced to General Torrijos's decision to create a domestic political environment that would facilitate U.S. Senate ratification of the Panama Canal treaties.

The Reagan administration's eventual turn to support human rights and democratization in this region, Wheelock reminds us, derived in part from the need to build an ideological consensus to oppose Sandinista Nicaragua. By late 1983, the Reagan administration had dropped its allergy to, and instead embraced, many of Carter's policies on human rights and democratization. Curiously perhaps, its support for the turn from military to civilian rule in Central America may have been caused by the Sandinista revolution.

Historically, several authors note, the United States has had an important presence in the domestic politics of these four countries. In Panama, the U.S. government ran the canal and occupied the large Canal Zone area in the heart of the country, necessarily becoming involved directly or indirectly in the country's politics in ways that were at times adverse to democracy. U.S. troops occupied Nicaragua earlier in the century and, upon their repatriation in the early 1930s, left dynasty founder Anastasio Somoza García in command of the U.S.-created National Guard. In 1954, the United States was a major factor in the overthrow of President Jacobo Arbenz in Guatemala. In El Salvador, the United States has also played an important role at key junctures in the twentieth century, though it did not assume as powerful a role as in the other three countries until the late 1970s.

Most recently, political openings evident in Nicaragua, Panama, and El Salvador are related to the end of the Cold War. By 1989 Nicaragua's governing party, the FSLN, decided to advance the date of the constitutionally scheduled national elections from November to February 1990 and to negotiate with the opposition an extensive set of mutually acceptable guarantees to ensure full fairness and participation. These Sandinista decisions aimed to change Nicaragua's domestic political environment in the hopes that the new Bush administration would not continue the U.S. policy of war on the Nicaraguan government. The Sandinistas lost these elections, however. De Franco and Velázquez make the international argument a centerpiece of their explanation for the change in Sandinista policies that led to these elections. They argue that Sandinista policies toward the opposition and toward the United States changed because the Sandinista leadership realized that it could not count indefinitely on Soviet economic assistance and that it could no longer count on further Soviet military aid.

By December 1989, the United States could invade Panama to remove Noriega without fear of Soviet retaliation. By late 1991, El Salvador's insurgent coalition, the Farabundo Martí National Liberation Front (FMLN), knew that it could no longer count on material assistance from the former communist countries of Europe or from the government of Nicaragua, thereby increasing the likelihood that it would agree to a settlement. Similarly, by late 1991, the U.S. government had made it clear to the Armed Forces of El Salvador that they would not get continued military aid to fight a war in which the United States was no longer interested.

"Historically," Laurence Whitehead has written thoughtfully, "Washington's most memorable experiences of promoting democracy overseas took place at the end of successful wars (1898, 1918, and 1945) when, of course, international forces were in a position to overwhelm domestic political tendencies."[11] The collapse of the Soviet Union is an international earthquake comparable to those victories—a point in common between the recent experiences in Central America and Panama and Whitehead's analysis. The main point of Whitehead's study, however, and of the series of which it is a part, is that international factors were rarely so important in promoting democratization.

The analytical issue might be put as follows: With regard to the explanatory pertinence of international factors, the transitions in Panama, Nicaragua, and El Salvador most resemble the transitions in Eastern Europe and differ from the transitions in South America and southern Europe. Where a superpower was especially preeminent in a local international subsystem, the international shocks of the end of the Cold War had strong effects in the domestic politics of the countries in such subsystems. Moreover, where countries are small and highly dependent not just on the international market but overwhelmingly on the locally preeminent superpower, the leverage of outsiders to induce domestic change is strong. Even in the mid-1980s in Guatemala (the country most slowly affected by the end of the Cold War), Paiz and Gramajo tell us, the military government's decisions to move toward competitive elections and civilian rule were powerfully shaped by the effort to break out of the country's deep international isolation.

Thus, once again, the four countries we examine share certain common characteristics that situate them at one end of the spectrum of paths toward democratization: recent regime changes in these cases cannot be explained without reference to international pressures to induce democratization and, in the case of Panama, to force it. The powerful were pressured to give up or to share their power and to do so by means of democratic elections and bargains.

Economic Crisis: The Blessings of Failure

The economies of Central America and Panama collapsed at key moments that proved favorable for democratizing political transitions. The claims of authoritarian rulers that they deserved obedience because they had created the conditions for economic growth or for improved social welfare are familiar enough in the history of this region. As living standards fell and the economy collapsed, authoritarian regimes weakened in country after country. De Franco and Velázquez note that, among other factors, the severe economic downturn in the late 1970s contributed to the demise of the Somoza dynasty in Nicaragua—a point with which Wheelock agrees, though he emphasizes the structural problems in Nicaragua's economy. El Salvador's economy, too, collapsed in the late 1970s and early 1980s. Paiz and Gramajo agree that economics was an important (though not the preeminent) factor motivating Guatemala's initial transition in the early 1980s. And Ardito-Barletta notes the deep economic crisis that accompanied Noriega's loss of support and preceded his overthrow. These countries were "blessed" with serious enough economic failures to discredit long-entrenched authoritarian regimes and thus to permit a transition to more open politics.

In addition, economic malperformance shaped the rhythm of politics in these countries even after those initial transitions. De Franco and Velázquez as well as Wheelock again agree that Nicaragua's severe economic difficulties weakened support for the Sandinistas and increased support for the opposition leading up to the February 1990 national elections. Gramajo and Paiz note also that in the mid-1980s one factor motivating Guatemala's army to turn over power to civilians was the recognition of the country's economic troubles and the greater likelihood that civilians could gain international support to address them. El Salvador's deplorable economic circumstances contributed to the 1989 national election defeat of the governing Christian Democratic Party.

The uniformity of economic collapse as a factor favorable to political regime transition sets Central America and Panama apart from South America, where the relationship between economic crisis and political regime transition is far more variable: in the early 1980s Argentina's transition did occur in a context of severe economic crisis, but in the mid-1980s Brazil's political transition occurred during a business cycle upswing, while in the later 1980s Chile's political transition occurred in an economic boom.

* * *

Jointly, these four factors—the necessity of force to begin democratization, a severe state of war and hardship that eventually provokes rational choices toward change, international pressures to induce democratization, and a profound economic crisis—help to explain democratizing outcomes in Guatemala, El Salvador, Nicaragua, and Panama but also set them apart from the main examples of democratic transitions in South America, southern and Eastern Europe, and south and East Asia. Central America and Panama resemble only the disaster areas of the Cold War—Ethiopia, Angola, and Cambodia. And yet none of the authors considers his country in those dire circumstances because these four countries have chosen Dahl to answer Hobbes. To understand their reasons for cautious hope, we turn to other factors.

THE CONSTRUCTION OF CERTAINTIES

"The process of establishing a democracy," Adam Przeworski has written, "is a process of institutionalizing uncertainty, of subjecting all interests to uncertainty." He argues that "democratic compromise cannot be a substantive compromise; it can be only a contingent institutional compromise. It is within the nature of democracy that no one's interests can be guaranteed."[12] He notes, for example, that in democratic politics voters can support the expropriation of private property and the dissolution of the armed forces. Indeed so, but as a practical matter no one loves uncertainty, and few are prepared to take steps toward the specific form of uncertainty that Przeworski (accurately) considers inherent to democracy. At issue, therefore, is the need to construct certainties, that is, to fashion formal and informal assurances for key actors that will lead them at a given point to risk democracy's uncertainties. The construction of certainties (featuring a mix of procedural and substantive dimensions) must precede the contingent institutional compromises that establish democracy, because without some certainties democratic uncertainty becomes unthinkable.

The Injection of Reformers

The opening and undermining of authoritarian regimes, many scholars believe, often starts with a split among the high officials of the regime between hard-liners and soft-liners or between standpatters and reformers.[13] In our cases, one observes a somewhat different pattern: at a key moment outsiders to the regime are "injected" into it and become leading soft-liners or reformers. The likelihood of the success of reform by regime injection is variable.

The strategy of reformist injection was most long lived in El Salvador. The October 1979 coup by young military officers featured not the displacement of the military in power but the introduction of civilians, formerly in the opposition, into the high echelons of government. Months later, as Zamora tells us, the Christian Democratic Party, El Salvador's largest, divided over the strategy to follow to democratize the country. The party's foremost leader, José Napoleón Duarte, decided to work inside the regime; he became president of the militarily sustained junta and in 1984 was elected president of El Salvador.

A centerpiece of Duarte's strategy was to persuade the Salvadoran armed forces and the Reagan administration in its early years that civilians who had not been the historic allies of the military and who advocated important social and economic reforms could, nevertheless, be trusted to govern. In that way Duarte sought to open political space in El Salvador and to enlist U.S. support for the task of democratizing the country. Duarte sought to establish civilian authority over the armed forces and to negotiate a settlement with the insurgents. He failed at the second and succeeded to some degree at the first only because of the strong support he received from successive U.S. ambassadors. Nonetheless, as the 1980s unfolded, the likelihood of a military coup declined in El Salvador and, as Zamora notes, important institutional changes were made gradually to open up the nation's political space further. The Salvadoran armed forces discovered that they did not need to depend exclusively on the most conservative civilian forces. The injection of Duarte (the man the armed forces had prevented in 1972 from assuming the presidency he probably won in those elections) into the regime made an important contribution to El Salvador's democratization.

Duarte and the Christian Democrats constructed certainty for El Salvador's armed forces. President Duarte demonstrated that he shared with military officers a commitment to the maintenance of public order and national sovereignty; Duarte worked hard as well to secure U.S. funding for the Salvadoran military. In this way the injection of Christian Democrat reformers into what in many ways remained a military regime reduced the uncertainties once felt by El Salvador's military about the prospects of civilian supremacy over the armed forces.

The strategy of soft-liner injection was more problematic in Guatemala. The March 1982 coup installed a military junta in power but placed at its head a retired officer, General Efraín Ríos Montt, who had been the Christian Democratic Party's presidential candidate in the 1974 elections; Ríos Montt had probably won those elections but had been prevented from assuming the presidency. The Guatemalan scenario thus had some similarities with the earlier Salvadoran case. Ríos Montt, no longer a Christian Democrat, introduced some important changes into the government's conduct and its policies, as Paiz and Gramajo indicate. And yet the war was prosecuted more fiercely and with greater loss of civilian life than a parallel with Duarte might suggest. Ríos Montt also lasted in power for a much shorter time than Duarte; he was overthrown because he was unable to solve the economic problems and wanted to postpone elections to remain in power (see Gramajo's chapter). Ríos Montt turned out not to be a reformer.

The strategy of soft-liner injection was perhaps most promising in Panama, though it eventually failed. As Ardito-Barletta tells us, he had been out of Panamanian politics for nearly six years, serving as World Bank vice president for Latin America, when he was invited to lead the official party in the 1984 presidential elections. He accepted the offer in order to open the way toward democratization and economic growth. During the election campaign, he secured support from parties that had previously opposed the government; he also secured pledges from the main commanders that, once he was elected, the military would return to the barracks, removed from routine public management.

Ardito-Barletta did not realize until much later, however, that the commanders had no intention of retreating to the barracks and that they were prepared both to commit electoral fraud to get him elected and to remove him subsequently from office should he displease them. Whereas Duarte in El Salvador had his own strong political party and clear U.S. backing in dealing with the military, Ardito-Barletta in Panama had no party of his own and weak U.S. backing. Consequently, Ardito-Barletta was less successful in reshaping his country's politics.

The effect of this failed injection of reform into the Noriega regime was to accelerate the trend toward dictatorship and self-destruction that would harden until the end of the decade. Ardito-Barletta's strategy was not crazy, however. It was a calculated gamble that could have worked out but did not. It was based on the intellectual premise, mentioned earlier, that Panama's military would understand that the costs of suppression were higher than the costs of toleration. They did not, and thus Ardito-Barletta was not able to construct the institutional certainties that might have made the Panama Defense Forces (PDF) more responsive to democratization.

New Institutions and New Rules

In the three cases (Guatemala, El Salvador, and Nicaragua) where significant steps were taken toward liberalization and democratization in the absence of a U.S. invasion, one key factor in the political transition was the creation of new institutions and rules to provide assurances to all would-be voters.

Both Paiz and Gramajo report with pride the impressive accomplishments of Guatemala's Supreme Electoral Tribunal. Founded during the government of General Oscar Mejía Víctores, the tribunal prepared new rules for the election of a constituent assembly in 1984, and it oversaw that election. Its credibility was enhanced by the fact that the Christian Democratic Party, long in opposition to the military governments and a victim of electoral fraud in the past, won the 1985 presidential elections. The tribunal's credibility was enhanced again in 1990 when it oversaw the rules and the election which was won once again by the opposition, this time electing conservative Jorge Serrano to the presidency. In May 1993, the tribunal firmly opposed President Serrano's failed coup attempt and thus protected the democratic regime. As Paiz emphasizes, the establishment of this tribunal was an important innovation because its predecessor had been corrupt and had presided over repeated fraudulent elections. Since the mid-1980s it may have become Guatemala's most respected institution.

Important changes in the rules of the game occurred in Nicaragua as well. The opposition for the most part had boycotted the 1984 presidential elections. The Sandinista government knew that a repetition of that election would serve neither political stability nor the legitimacy of a renewed Sandinista government (in the expectation, eventually proven mistaken, that the FSLN would win). Wheelock notes that one mistake made by the Sandinista government had been precisely to neglect taking credible steps sooner toward providing institutional guarantees. In late 1987, the Sandinista government began complex negotiations with opposition parties, with economic and social groups, and with the United States to create certainty about procedural fairness for the February 1990 elections. Nicaragua's sovereign government even accepted extensive formal international inspection of the election. These new rules made the election possible.

Zamora details several important institutional changes in El Salvador. As the 1980s proceeded, the organs of the state—especially the Legislative Assembly and the Supreme Court—became more willing to recognize than to repress the existing social movement organizations. The mass media developed and became more professional and diverse. Political parties became permanent organizations, not merely vehicles convoked at election time, and thus became able to make agreements and to follow through on them. The procedures to administer elections were greatly improved—there was a new electoral registry, voting cards were given to citizens, and computers were introduced to make the count accurate and fast. In the late 1980s, the democratic left recognized the significance of these changes in institutions and rules and thus decided to reenter electoral contests.

In all three countries, the new institutions and rules created the necessary procedural certainties for participants to be willing to live with the uncertainties of electoral outcomes about which Przeworski has written. All three countries had a long tradition of electoral fraud prior to 1979; indeed, rational people had to act on the expectation that elections would be fraudulent unless proof was given to the contrary. The new institutions and rules had to be transparent and to embody the means to settle normal electoral disputes. In that way, they could break the expectations about electoral fraud. Where there were no such institutional guarantees, as in Panama's 1989 national election, the electoral results were not credible.

Creating a "Reliable" Opposition

These changes in institutions and in rules enabled a legal opposition to emerge. In all four countries, opposition leaders understood the utility of demonstrating to those in office that the opposition could be trusted to remain nonviolent and to abide by the laws, in that way seeking to create the certainty that an opposition campaign would not be disruptive and even that an opposition victory would not lead to revenge against defeated incumbents. An important "certainty" was to reassure those within the regime that, if they acted to bring about changes, they would not suffer.

The least successful but most far reaching of these opposition campaigns occurred in Panama.[14] Panama's National Civic Crusade adopted a nonviolent strategy and remained apart from political parties. It concentrated its protest on Noriega. By its nonviolent commitment and its focus on Noriega, it sought to reassure other military officers that they could act against Noriega without risk of eventual retribution. Instead of acts of violence, the crusade and its opposition predecessors relied on humor and ridicule aimed at Noriega. By its nonpartisan commitments, it sought to enable labor unions, professional associations, and civic groups to join it as formal members. The crusade was a gigantic, cross-class, social movement organization. In turn, its moderate actions and narrow focus on Noriega reassured Panama's elites with regard to its limited intentions: to remove Noriega as the means to advance toward democracy. In short, it sought to create certainties about its future behavior through its conduct of opposition to Noriega.

Much more successful constructions of reliable opposition occurred in the other three countries. Guatemala's Christian Democrats persuaded the army that they were reliable enough to govern. During his presidential campaign, Cerezo also gave public assurances to the military that his government would not bring officers to trial for human rights violations, nor would he curtail the high prerogatives that the army had kept for itself under the constitution and the existing laws. The Christian Democratic Party, moreover, had good prospects for a clear electoral victory, which would enhance the chances of governability. As Gramajo notes, an important motivation for the military to move toward civilian rule was to break out of international isolation; victory by the opposition Christian Democrats was an effective way to do that and, in turn, to obtain access to foreign economic and military support.[15]

Violeta Barrios de Chamorro also demonstrated her "reliability" as an opposition leader by never going into political exile, never breaking family relations with her children who had become leading Sandinistas, and being willing to publish her daily newspaper, La Prensa, under the often unfair conditions and censorship imposed by Sandinista authorities. Her conduct consistently emphasized nonviolence. She agreed to run in the February 1990 elections, accepting the constitution and the laws then in effect though, of course, negotiating over the electoral procedures to guarantee their eventual fairness. Her coalition embraced political parties and social movement organizations across the ideological spectrum; in its very constitution, the National Opposition Union (UNO) reassured many groups and currents of opinion. Perhaps the most visible act of reassurance occurred shortly after it became clear that Chamorro had defeated the incumbent, Daniel Ortega, for the presidency: in a photograph flashed around the world she was portrayed embracing Ortega warmly.

Another example of the construction of a "reliable" opposition to reduce uncertainties about the future occurred in El Salvador. Zamora describes his party's decision to participate in the 1989 presidential and the 1991 legislative elections. After the 1991 elections, the ruling conservative party, the Nationalist Republican Alliance (ARENA), and the Convergencia Democrática on the democratic left agreed to vote for each other's candidates for the assembly's presidency and vice presidency; Zamora was thereby elected vice president. Thus the democratic left reassured the military that the Convergencia could be trusted to be law-abiding and to govern, and it signaled to the insurgents that much could be gained through elections.

The construction of a "reliable" Salvadoran opposition also encompassed social movement organizations. Having been repressed harshly in the early 1980s, these reemerged during the second half of the decade, though they were deeply divided for various reasons. In the early 1990s, however, several of these social organizations began to form alliances that required them to moderate their demands and their conduct in order to search for an end to the war. Their behavior facilitated the march toward democratic outcomes.

These examples share the intent to create certainty by means of overt behavior. This strategy is consistent with making deals, which is the bread and butter of politics everywhere. In no case, however, does this behavioral strategy logically require a substantive agreement with regard to specific future policies, nor does it bar other procedural or substantive agreements that focus on more general issues. In Panama, the opposition would have liked a deal from regime leaders other than Noriega to remove Noriega, but it could not get one. In Guatemala, Cerezo's deal with the army was articulated publicly but was not part of a wider pact. In Nicaragua, the campaign behavior was the prelude to specific agreements to be reached as part of the transition of power and subsequent government. In El Salvador, the behavior of the democratic left and of social organizations may have paved the way for the complex and comprehensive agreement negotiated between government and insurgency late in 1991, but that behavior did not itself stem from a prior deal. There seems to be, therefore, no clear relationship between the existence of pacts and the movement toward, or the consolidation of, democracy.[16]

Constitutionalizing the Military

These efforts by governments and oppositions sought to create certainty for building democracy prior to a change toward a democratic regime. After a change, the most important step toward consolidating democratic politics was the construction of another certainty: that the armed forces would obey the constitution and that the president would not abuse power by means of the armed forces.

As de Franco and Velázquez make clear, a foundational task of President Chamorro's government was to reestablish civil peace. To that end, her government had to disarm the contras (more formally called the Nicaraguan Resistance), with international assistance under United Nations supervision, and establish its authority over the armed forces. The latter task had economic implications as well, for her government moved to cut the size of the armed forces by two-thirds and to reduce the military burden on the nation's budget.

18   JORGE I. DOMÍNGUEZ

But in affirming civilian authority over the military, the government also behaved pragmatically, making the first of its many deals with the Sandinistas as they moved toward opposition. President Chamorro agreed to retain the former Sandinista commander, General Humberto Ortega, as chief of the armed forces provided he would sever his partisan links to the FSLN, which he did formally. The Chamorro government, therefore, sought military reduction and constitutionalization, but it also agreed to keep important legal military prerogatives to provide assurances to the officer corps.

This and other subsequent agreements on nonmilitary issues were part of what Wheelock calls the building of a consensus across forces that disagree on many issues but that are prepared to work jointly, to a limited extent, to make Nicaragua governable. Wheelock believes that this search for consensus and specific agreements may have become the key rule of the game for Nicaragua since 1990—a rule often sorely tested, however. This pattern of sequential agreements also made it possible for the FSLN to change from being the party of the state to being a party in the opposition, though also in critical collaboration with the Chamorro government over some important issues. As de Franco and Velázquez rightly note, this outcome was greatly facilitated by the Chamorro government's strong commitment to the democratic values of toleration, respect, participation, dialogue, and the making of commitments.

In Panama, the task was conceptually the same but the means were different. The U.S. invasion in December 1989 defeated the PDF and made it possible for the new Panamanian government to transform the military into a new and much smaller civilian-controlled police force. The government concluded that it could not afford simply to disband the military, because the thousands of former officers and soldiers would be unemployed, embittered, and armed, posing a permanent threat to public order. Because the new Public Force was smaller, there were substantial savings for the national budget; because of a process of purging and retraining, the force was more likely to be loyal to a democratic regime.[17] Unfortunately, the pacification of Panama was soon dramatically threatened when an unsuccessful coup sought to overthrow the government on December 5, 1990.

Panama's pattern, like Nicaragua's, was to seek military reduction and constitutionalization; the new government gave assurances to a small fraction of officers and soldiers of the former PDF who were hired for the new Public Force. But Panama's attempted reduction of the size of the military and attempted subordination of it to civilian authority goes far beyond anything attempted in Central America outside Costa Rica. In Panama the new Public Force has none of the constitutional and legal military prerogatives still evident in Nicaragua and Guatemala.

El Salvador's January 1992 agreement focuses centrally on the fate of the armed forces. Consistent with experiences in Nicaragua and in Panama, the agreement reduces the size of the armed forces and their burden on the national budget and brings the military clearly under the constitution, the laws, and civilian authority. As in Panama, the Salvadoran agreement calls for a purge of the military, but one not so extensive as in Panama. The Salvadoran settlement on the military resembles the Nicaraguan case somewhat more in preserving the armed forces as an institution and in providing guarantees to a substantial number of its personnel. Whether the Salvadoran agreement will be fully implemented remains in question, given the various military attempts to stop the negotiated settlement.

Although it shares some commonalties with the others, Guatemala is the outlier. Paiz reminds us that President Cerezo did not call out the army to deal with labor strikes or street demonstrations, nor did he invoke state of siege provisions to deal with labor unrest. Gramajo details his efforts as defense minister to communicate to military officers and to civilians that the army sought to remain in its professional role apart from partisan politics. He describes as well the difficulties of many officers in adjusting to civilian authority. The size of the army was not reduced as much as in Panama, Nicaragua, or El Salvador, nor was the burden on the nation's budget. The Guatemalan army retains important constitutional and legal prerogatives for action, including immunity from prosecution for abuse of power (see Paiz's chapter) well beyond the region's prevailing norms. (Honduran and Guatemalan civil-military relations resemble each other to some extent, but Guatemala's army has a greater effect on its society than do the armed forces of Honduras on theirs.)

In Guatemala the unsuccessful military coups of 1988 and 1989 and, in 1993, President Serrano's failed "self-coup" (which had initial backing from the military high command) present the most serious challenges so far in the region to the constitutionalization of the military. The three attempts showed that a significant proportion of officers and troops were ready to overthrow the democratic regime. Defeating the attempts required personal courage and involved serious risks. Most disturbing for democratic consolidation was the weak response to the coup attempts in 1988 and 1989 from President Cerezo and other civilian authorities; even worse was President Serrano's orchestration of the 1993 attempt. Gramajo details how in 1988 and 1989 it fell to the army's administrative procedures to punish the plotters even though the full weight of civilian law should have been applied. Also worrisome was President Cerezo's response to the 1989 coup; from Paiz's and Gramajo's evidence, it appears as if the president stopped governing eighteen months before the end of his term.

Paiz gives us the more optimistic interpretation of recent Guatemalan history. He calls attention, accurately, to the fact that the coup attempts failed and that they elicited weak support. He notes that the Cerezo government was replaced through free and competitive elections by a more conservative government, led by President Serrano, making it less likely that economic elites would support a future coup. Indeed, Guatemala's business leaders opposed the 1993 attempt.

In all four countries progress has been made toward constitutionalizing the military, reducing its size and cost, and reducing the likelihood that the armed forces would be used by the president to abuse power; substantial efforts have been made to construct such certainties in civil-military relations. The greatest changes have been made in Panama because the United States militarily defeated the PDF. The fewest changes have been made in Guatemala because its army believes that it won the civil war and orchestrated and managed the transition to civilian rule. Intermediate changes have been made in Nicaragua; comparable intermediate changes have been agreed to in El Salvador. In the last two countries the conflicts of the 1980s ended in a tie, at all levels (as Zamora notes for El Salvador) or in ways that balanced each other (in Nicaragua, the Sandinistas prevailed in war but lost in peace).

The Strength of the Electoral Right

"Put in a nutshell," wrote Guillermo O'Donnell and Philippe Schmitter, "parties of the Right-Center and Right must be 'helped' to do well, and parties of the Left-Center and Left should not win by an overwhelming majority." This could even be done, they say, by "rigging the rules—for example, by overrepresenting rural districts or small peripheral constituencies." The reason for this suggestion, they say, is that unless "those partisan forces representing the interests of propertied classes, privileged professions, and entrenched institutions, including the armed forces . . . muster enough votes to stay in the game, they are likely to desert the electoral process in favor of antidemocratic conspiracy and destabilization."[18]

O'Donnell and Schmitter proved right in their political theory, wrong in their electoral sociology. Parties of the right and center-right have received a large proportion of the votes cast everywhere in South America (outside Argentina and Venezuela) and in several countries in southern and Eastern Europe when free and competitive elections have been held. This very strength, as O'Donnell and Schmitter have argued, has contributed to keeping the right allegiant to democracy.

So too in Central America and Panama. In El Salvador, as Zamora makes clear, the party farthest to the right, ARENA, was "helped" to win the 1989 presidential election by the disarray of the Christian Democrats, by the electoral abstention of part of the left, by the left's fragmentation and association with the insurgency, and by the delay of the parties of the democratic left in organizing to contest elections. Nonetheless, there is no doubt that the right is and has been electorally strong in El Salvador. Perhaps precisely because President Alfredo Cristiani is a conservative, he was able to lead the Salvadoran right, including the armed forces, to reach a negotiated peace agreement with the insurgent left. In the late 1980s and early 1990s, by means of elections and negotiations, the Salvadoran right-wing government protected the interests of its supporters and advanced their economic goals, while it served the nation in the pursuit of a negotiated settlement to the war. ARENA's candidate, Armando Calderón Sol, won El Salvador's 1994 presidential elections, thereby confirming the right's electoral strength.

Whereas the parties of the extreme right have not done as well in Guatemala as they would have liked, given their historic hold on that country's politics, Guatemala's parties of the right and center-right have done well, even in the 1985 and especially in the 1990 general elections and also in the 1994 (congressional), 1995 (presidential, first round), and 1996 (presidential, second round) national elections. As Paiz notes, Guatemala's elected president from 1990 to 1993, Jorge Serrano, was a conservative; his economic cabinet was in the hands of representatives of powerful business groups. The negotiations that his government began with insurgents may have been made possible by this configuration of political forces as well as by the Salvadoran example. In the January 1996 elections, a center-right candidate, Alvaro Arzú, was elected president, confirming the right's strength.

In Nicaragua, Chamorro won the 1990 presidential election at the head of a broad coalition that spanned the ideological spectrum. Nevertheless, the coalition's center of gravity and its program of government were well situated on the center-right. While the Chamorro government's coalition eventually broke up, the electoral forces of the center-right can clearly hold their own.

In Panama, the center-right had an important impact on the policies of the Torrijos regime at moments in the 1970s through the skill and clout of government technocrats. As in Nicaragua, so too in Panama: the opposition to Noriega was a broad coalition that spanned the ideological spectrum. This coalition's center of gravity, too, lay in professional associations and business groups. The organized opposition to Torrijos began with medical doctors and school teachers who were joined subsequently by business and civic organizations. Although Panama's electoral right has lacked the ferocity of pockets of the Salvadoran and Guatemalan right, within Panama's social structure and political style the center-right has done well in elections.

The right in Nicaragua and Panama knew their strength and that they could be influential and win elections; for these reasons, since the 1970s business and professional groups have pressed for free and competitive elections. The real puzzle, therefore, is why it took the right in El Salvador and Guatemala so long to realize that they could do so well in free and competitive elections. To be sure, the parties of the right have lost elections in the past and will again in the future but they are likely to have substantial influence in a great many ways. Misinformed about electoral sociology, the right in these two countries indeed believed that they could win only if elections were rigged. Exploring the intellectual and political roots of this belief is not part of our book, but its consequences for Guatemalan and Salvadoran history have been tens of thousands of people dead in civil wars, countless injured, vast destruction of property, and decades of institutional decay and corruption.

Some credit for civilizing the right in El Salvador and Guatemala must go to José Napoleón Duarte and Marco Vinicio Cerezo. They can be criticized for many failures of government, but they respected the integrity of those whom they had defeated in elections. The right began to learn that electoral defeat, albeit unpleasant, was not the end of the world. As Zamora notes, this recognition began an important change in the conception of power—from "all or nothing," which is the conceptual parent to coups, repression, and wars, to a more pluralistic conception that was more consistent with democratic norms.

The victories of the parties of the right in Central America and Panama have provided an essential certainty to the propertied and the powerful that democracy is worth the gamble. In Nicaragua and in Panama, entrepreneurs need no convincing that they do better under democratic politics than under the rule of revolutionaries or the military. In Guatemala and in El Salvador, perhaps to their own surprise, the business elites learned the same lesson in the 1990s.

In all four countries, paradoxically, parties of the right and the center-right were electorally vibrant in the late 1980s and early 1990s because at some earlier moment they had lost control of the national government. To regain power, the right had to build a strong conservative party while still in the opposition. Because democracy worked for conservatives to win back the presidency, it is more likely that they would work for democracy in the future.

Statesmanship

Returning to the question of why the powerful yield their power, much of the answer should be clear from the preceding analysis: the costs of suppression, the rational expectation that democratic regimes would succeed better against insurgencies, the pressures from abroad, economic collapse, and the construction of some certainties. And yet at specific moments real people had to decide to give up power. That is never easy to do, and it is much more difficult to explain.

The Guatemalan army designed a strategy to surrender some of their power. Their analysis, as Gramajo reports it, was based on rational expectations about the future. Clearly, however, many Guatemalan officers did not want to yield much power; that is one reason for the subsequent coup attempts against the Cerezo government. The Guatemalan officers who suppressed those attempts, led by the defense minister, showed courage and statesmanship.

The Sandinistas designed a strategy to remain in power. They believed that their leadership of the revolution against the Somoza dynasty gave them the right to rule. They believed that they embodied the nation's spirit in combat against U.S. aggression. On the battlefield, they had basically defeated the contras. The Sandinistas misjudged their political support and lost the 1990 presidential election. As Wheelock reports, on election night (February 25, 1990) the FSLN National Directorate gathered to analyze the results, which showed a clear victory for the Chamorro-led opposition. The decision to recognize the election results was unanimous. One reason was that the Sandinista commanders had fought against Somoza to enable Nicaraguans to choose freely. The Sandinista commanders who made this decision also showed courage and statesmanship.

If the Guatemalan military and the Sandinistas could give up power, civilian politicians were more accustomed to the democratic rules of the game. Nonetheless the role of the Christian Democratic parties is especially noteworthy in Panama, Guatemala, and El Salvador for its contributions to institutional consolidation and to respect for rules and for its willingness to give up power once defeated.

A partial explanation for these acts of statesmanship was the gradual creation of new institutions and rules that had a chance of providing some guarantees of personal and collective safety to those about to surrender power. Such rules and institutions may have provided the necessary foundations for democratic change. In turn the cumulative acts of statesmanship have become standard procedure. Though they are no less remarkable given the region's recent history, they are now commonplace and, as such, have created a new certainty.

From the right and the left, from the army in Guatemala to the Sandinistas in Nicaragua, the rhetoric of the past quarter of a century had prepared no one for acts of statesmanship. Not too many years ago the notion that ARENA and the FMLN would have negotiated an agreement to bring a long and bloody war to a civilized end would have been laughed at. These human beings may not have been able to make their history just as they pleased, but at key moments they certainly acted to make their own destiny.

The initiation of democratization in Central America and Panama may have been exogenous to normal politics. Democracy in these countries began from the barrel of a gun, although that very origin has limited its scope and may imperil its future. But after such ordeals in the launching of change, the construction of democracy in these four countries depended on the explicit creation of new institutions and new rules to provide formal guarantees to all participants. The construction of democracy also required the conscious action of politicians who demonstrated to the military that they could be trusted to govern as well as to oppose responsibly, thereby making possible the (still imperfect and much delayed) constitutionalization of the armed forces. If politicians of the left and center-left were important especially in El Salvador and Guatemala to construct a "reliable" opposition, politicians of the right were important everywhere to civilize the propertied and the powerful and to make them and, one hopes, keep them allegiant to democracy. Finally, for reasons that remain somewhat unclear, at key moments holders of power chose to give it up in acts of human will that deserve the label of statesmanship. In these ways the creation of certainty fostered the democratic transition and the eventual consolidation of democracy.

BUSINESS, POLITICS, AND MARKETS

In Central America and Panama the political behavior of organized business is best described around one constant and one variable. At key moments business has been a force for political liberalization in all four countries, but business has a more mixed record with regard to economic liberalization. Neither point is intuitively obvious. On the one hand, some might expect business to support economic liberalization, believing in free markets as the best way to advance its interests and values; some would also observe that business in these countries has been a bastion of authoritarian oligarchical politics, and it is hence the least likely group to support political liberalization. Our analysis focuses, however, on the effects of business behavior, not necessarily on the intentions of business elites.

Business contributed to political liberalization by opposing clearly and publicly some visible and important policies (typically key economic decisions) of governments that it and others deemed to be authoritarian. In so behaving, business elites helped to open political space. Their criticism of the government legitimized space for freedom of expression and freedom of association in opposition to authoritarian rule. Their use of the press and of other mass media to oppose the government furthered this result as well. They forced authoritarian political elites to tolerate opposition on some important issues, and thus paved the way to toleration of the opposition over other issues later on. The government's response to business opposition would not be killings or imprisonment but respect and conciliation.

Guatemala's business elites played a significant role in persuading the army to break the historical alliance between them, even though it is most unlikely that this outcome was the intention of business elites. In 1985 General Oscar Mejía's government tried unsuccessfully to implement a tax reform package and other economic policies. Despite all the powers of the bayonets, Gramajo reports with evident frustration, General Mejía could not even raise the cost of an urban bus ticket by 1.5 cents U.S. The military government also enacted a consumer protection law. Business groups carried out a well-orchestrated and well-funded mass media campaign to undermine the law. This campaign made the military look foolish and ignorant. If the generals were ignorant fools in matters of consumer protection, perhaps they were so on other matters as well. The effect, therefore, was to weaken military self-confidence and to embolden opposition action, in both ways favoring political liberalization. Guatemalan business elites probably did not intend to cause widespread liberalization, but, regardless of intentions, that was the result of their behavior.

The response of the Guatemalan army to this business opposition was equally telling: to call for a national dialogue, to make concessions, and to strike a deal. Gramajo notes that the military concluded from the experience that important economic policy changes could only be implemented by a government invested with political legitimacy—a legitimacy that a military government could not have. In the process, the army learned to bargain rather than to impose, to listen rather than to command, to yield rather than to overpower, all of which favored political liberalization.

In Nicaragua, the contribution of business elites to political liberalization combined intentions with behaviors. Wheelock notes with retrospective regret some mistakes made in the conduct of policies toward business. Sandinista government policy was resisted, Wheelock reports, not only by wealthy property owners but also by some small-scale merchants and certain sectors of the peasantry. Some policies, such as price and purchase controls over grains, had led to a wave of peasant protest, he writes. Merchants, industrialists, and owners of large landholdings, he says, engaged in such behaviors as capital flight and smuggling. One effect of such actions was to make it more difficult for the Sandinista government to govern, even in its most authoritarian moment. De Franco and Velázquez develop a similar point. The growth of the economy's so-called informal and black market sectors also made it more difficult for the Sandinista government to govern. More openly, the peak business confederation (the Superior Private Enterprise Council, or COSEP) criticized the Sandinista government's policies over a great many issues, not just economic policy.

The effect of COSEP's intentional opposition and of business (including some peasant) behavior that impeded the effective operation of authoritarian policies was to prevent the consolidation of an authoritarian regime and to sustain political space for the opposition, thereby favoring political liberalization. At a key juncture the Sandinistas responded, as Wheelock reminds us, by engaging various sectors in the opposition, including business, in the dialogue that led to some political concessions and eventually to the February 1990 national elections won by the opposition.

In El Salvador, Zamora indicates, by the end of the 1980s important business elites opened the political space necessary for an eventual settlement of the war. Continued war was not good for business.[19] Business confederations, such as the Chamber of Industry and Commerce, spoke publicly and clearly in favor of negotiations with the FMLN; in 1990, some representatives from these business associations even had formal discussions with guerrilla leaders.

In the spring of 1991, however, some business sectors linked with sectors in the armed forces and the ARENA party launched a massive attack on President Cristiani's strategy of negotiation; this campaign was lavishly carried out in the mass media and led to the possibility of a military coup. The latter, of course, remains a limitation on the constitutionalization of the military. But, with regard to business behavior, the observed split in the Salvadoran business community speaks well for the prospects for democracy. Such a split makes it less likely that homogeneous oligarchical politics based on a business-military alliance could be reconstructed and, instead, makes it more likely that cross-class dialogue can occur. The fact that a business executive turned president (Cristiani) led the government and the most conservative party (ARENA) to a successful negotiation augurs well for the politics of conciliation.

In Panama, business opposition to the Torrijos regime began in terms of business's attempted defense of some of its leaders from government arrest, harassment, and deportation. The government responded by closing the offices of the Association of Business Executives. The business community might for the first time have begun to think about their own stakes in democratizing Panama.[20] In 1980 a businessman, Roberto Eisenmann, was the most important founder of *La Prensa*, the newspaper that would help lead the opposition to Noriega. Years later, business groups and individual executives played a leading role in the campaign against Noriega. Of the four countries, it was in Panama that business groups played the clearest role as advocates of political liberalization.

In contrast to the nearly uniform effect of business behavior since the 1970s in creating circumstances favorable to political liberalization as the (often unintended) consequence of business opposition to important government policies, business economic behavior has not always favored economic liberalization.

For various reasons, including its reliance on the U.S. dollar and the lack of a central bank, Panama has had the most internationally open economy in the region. Nonetheless, as Ardito-Barletta notes, in the early 1970s the industrial sector successfully pressured the government for increased protection by means of quotas and tariffs. When Ardito-Barletta became president of Panama, he sought to reduce such levels of protection, with only modest success. This effort to liberalize the market (and especially the proposal for a new value-added tax on services) had the unintended effect of weakening political support for the new president in the business community.

In Nicaragua, as both the Wheelock and the de Franco and Velázquez analyses make clear, the Sandinista government somewhat incoherently coupled its coercive measures toward COSEP and specific business firms with complementary policies in support of particular business firms and sectors. The government gave incentives to agricultural exporters; the financial system was used to subsidize some private firms, which thereby acquired a stake in the economy's continued politicization. In turn, the Chamorro government moved to liberalize the economy. It encountered the opposition of those business firms that had benefited from high tariff protection and subsidized credit and from those that had formerly earned oligopoly rents.

In El Salvador, President Cristiani's liberalization of the economy created a complex pattern of winners and losers. For most of the 1980s, El Salvador's overvalued exchange rate, high effective rates of tariff protection, and many nontariff barriers such as import quotas were the pillars of import substitution industrialization at the expense of the export sector. The decision to devalue the exchange rate, greatly reduce tariffs and most export taxes, and eliminate most nontariff barriers helped exporters enormously but, by and large, increased pressures on business firms that had gained from the previous import substitution strategy. The results for business, therefore, were variable depending on the position of each firm.

Perhaps Guatemala's business community provided the clearest example of resistance to freer markets and to collective obligations to the nation as a whole. As Paiz makes clear, the Cerezo government adopted a strategy of economic liberalization. It freed financial interest rates, devalued the currency, and unified exchange rates. It began to dismantle the system that provided high rates of tariff protection and sought to engage Guatemala more freely in international markets. Relying upon its congressional majority, the Cerezo government raised taxes to set the nation's budget on a sound basis and to increase investment in the social sphere. Led by the Chamber of Agricultural,

Commercial, Industrial and Financial Associations (CACIF), the business community opposed the government over these measures, especially over tax reform. As Gramajo notes, however, Guatemala's popularly elected constitutional government had the legitimacy and political support that the military government had lacked to enact the tax reform. Subsequent to its enactment in September 1987, the Christian Democrats won a majority of mayoralties in the April 1988 nationwide municipal elections. In panic, business groups allied with some military sectors to launch the failed May 1988 coup.

At a more modest level, Paiz relates a telling anecdote about the response of some Guatemalan wealthy property owners to tax reform. To simplify administration of the property tax, the Cerezo government and its congressional majority adopted the practice of property value self-assessment. In response, property owners overcame barriers to collective action so that all neighbors in a particular section of a city agreed to undervalue their property to avoid paying higher taxes.

In each of these countries, as the authors make clear, there are many business firms that support and benefit from market liberalization. This is especially the case for those engaged in the production and export of nontraditional goods. But the point remains that much of the business community in Central America and Panama may have behaved in a manner contrary to canonized myth: business facilitated political liberalization while it has at times impeded economic liberalization.

MISTAKEN PATHS

"The lesson of the third wave [democratization since 1970] seems clear: authoritarian leaders who wanted to stay in power should not have called elections; opposition groups who wanted democracy should not have boycotted the elections authoritarian leaders did call."[21] So too in Central America and Panama. Citizens in these countries have often voted against incumbents in the 1980s and 1990s. Participation in elections, therefore, was likely to pay off for the opposition. Zamora considers this point explicitly. He believes that it was a serious mistake for El Salvador's democratic left to have delayed as much as it did in reentering the electoral arena, because the parties of the right thus became the only vehicles for the expression of voter disaffection. At the other end of the spectrum, it was clearly not a mistake for Panama's opposition to participate in the 1989 fraudulent elections; that fraud greatly debilitated the Noriega regime and served eventually to legitimate the government installed after the U.S. invasion. Clearly right, of course, were Guatemala's Christian Democrats to enter the 1985 presidential election and Chamorro's opposition coalition to enter the 1990 presidential election in Nicaragua, for they won in each case.

Another mistake is to govern with insufficient information about one's allies. Ardito-Barletta candidly acknowledges that there was much about military activity in Panama that he did not know until after he stepped down from the presidency. Gramajo tells us that he was surprised by the pusillanimous response of many civilians in the Cerezo government to the May 1988 coup; had Gramajo had more contact with other members of the government of which he was a part, he might have planned more effectively to stop the turmoil in the army in the late 1980s. Zamora confesses that, when he joined the government in late 1979, he did not even know how to distinguish among military ranks.

More serious were abuses of power by the Sandinista government that Wheelock honestly records; these actions seemed to stem from a mistaken judgment that the FSLN enjoyed more support than it did.

But the most serious mistake is one of a collective nature: the drop in living standards and the failure to address social questions. The Nicaraguan case is most dramatic. Wheelock notes the praiseworthy efforts of the Sandinistas to improve the living conditions of most Nicaraguans; in the years immediately following the 1979 revolution, these efforts made progress especially in the areas of health and education. By the end of the 1980s, however, de Franco and Velázquez document that the effort had not succeeded: from 1981 to 1990 Nicaragua lost over one-third of the value of its gross domestic product (GDP) per capita (most of this loss occurred after 1984, and some substantial portion of it was related to the war). Although circumstances were less stark in the other three cases, Panama, El Salvador, and Guatemala lost between 13 and 18 percent of their GDP per capita during the same decade. In the early 1990s, Panama's GDP per capita recovered well, while El Salvador's and Guatemala's recovered more slowly. Nicaragua's decline continued.[22] In each chapter, most notably in Paiz's, there is a sense of urgency about the enormity of the "social debt" that the elites in these countries have with their people and a sense of sadness that so little has been accomplished for so long.

CONCLUSION

The future of Central America and Panama is part of the discussion of the subsequent chapters and especially of the conclusions, but from the region's past one thing is certain: In the early 1980s no one would have forecast that one-time leaders of the opposition would govern all four of these countries in the early 1990s. No one would have forecast that fair and competitive elections would become routine across the region. No one would have forecast that every military coup attempted since 1984 in this region would fail. No one would have forecast the end of the region's wars. The actions of many, including the politicians, army officers, government officials, and academic leaders contributing to this book, have helped promote liberalization and democratization in Central America and Panama. Much remains to be done, but much has been accomplished as well.

NOTES

1. For a more general argument and evidence, see Marc Lindenberg, "World Economic Cycles and Central American Political Instability," *World Politics* 42, no. 3 (April 1990): 397–421.

2. Although there is no chapter in this book on Honduras, various chapters refer to it whenever appropriate.

3. Although there is no chapter in this book on Costa Rica, various chapters refer to it whenever appropriate.

4. Guillermo O'Donnell and Philippe C. Schmitter, *Tentative Conclusions about Uncertain Democracies: Transitions from Authoritarian Rule* (Baltimore: Johns Hopkins University Press, 1986), p. 7.

5. Jorge I. Domínguez, "The Caribbean Question: Why Has Liberal Democracy (Surprisingly) Flourished?" in *Democracy in the Caribbean: Political, Economic, and Social Perspectives*, ed. Jorge I. Domínguez, Robert A. Pastor, and R. Delisle Worrell (Baltimore: Johns Hopkins University Press, 1993), p. 2. This differs from O'Donnell and Schmitter, *Tentative Conclusions*, pp. 7–8.

6. Because the concluding chapter by Marc Lindenberg focuses on policy issues, this one concentrates on the recent past, identifying themes emerging in the remaining chapters and in other papers prepared for the World Peace Foundation study, "Democratic Transitions in Central America and Panama." I have also benefited from comments from Barbara Ellington, Jeffry Frieden, María Victoria Murillo, Ashutosh Varshney, Jennifer Widner, and Deborah Yashar. Views expressed here, however, are mine alone, as is responsibility for errors.

7. See thoughtful discussion by Eduardo Vallarino, "La búsqueda por la democracia en Panamá," in *Transiciones Democráticas en Centro América*, ed. Jorge I. Domínguez and Marc Lindenberg (San José: Editorial Instituto Centroamericano de Administración de Empresas, 1994).

8. Robert A. Dahl, *Polyarchy: Participation and Opposition* (New Haven: Yale University Press, 1971), p. 15.

9. Samuel P. Huntington, *The Third Wave: Democratization in the Late Twentieth Century* (Norman: University of Oklahoma Press, 1991), p. 207.

10. For the general importance of such factors as contributors to democratization since the early 1970s, see Huntington, *Third Wave*, pp. 85–106.

11. Laurence Whitehead, "International Aspects of Democratization," in *Transitions from Authoritarian Rule: Comparative Perspectives*, ed. Guillermo O'Donnell,

Philippe C. Schmitter, and Laurence Whitehead (Baltimore: Johns Hopkins University Press, 1986), p. 3.

12. Adam Przeworski, "Some Problems in the Study of the Transition to Democracy," in *Transitions from Authoritarian Rule*, pp. 58–59.

13. O'Donnell and Schmitter, *Tentative Conclusions*, chap. 3; Huntington, *Third Wave*, chap. 3.

14. See excellent discussion in Vallarino, "La búsqueda por la democracia en Panamá."

15. For a general discussion of the importance of certain policy issues and military prerogatives, see Alfred Stepan's *Rethinking Military Politics: Brazil and the Southern Cone* (Princeton: Princeton University Press, 1988), chaps. 6 and 7.

16. For a discussion of elite settlements and elite accommodation, see Michael Burton, Richard Gunther, and John Higley, "Introduction: Elite Transformations and Democratic Regimes," in *Elites and Democratic Consolidation in Latin America and Southern Europe*, ed. John Higley and Richard Gunther (Cambridge: Cambridge University Press, 1992).

17. Vallarino, "La búsqueda por la democracia en Panamá."

18. See O'Donnell and Schmitter, *Tentative Conclusions*, pp. 62–63.

19. See also Daniel H. Wolf, "ARENA in the Arena: Factors in the Accommodation of the Salvadoran Right to Pluralism and the Broadening of the Political System," *LASA Forum* 23, no. 1 (Spring 1992): 11.

20. Discussion in Vallarino, "La búsqueda por la democracia en Panamá."

21. Huntington, *Third Wave*, p. 190.

22. United Nations, Economic Commission for Latin America and the Caribbean, *Preliminary Overview of the Economy of Latin America and the Caribbean, 1994*, LC/G. 1846 (New York), p. 39.

TWO

THE POLITICAL AND ECONOMIC TRANSITION OF PANAMA, 1978-1991

NICOLÁS ARDITO-BARLETTA

Panama has come a long way toward creating a fully democratic political system. Nevertheless, democracy is not yet fully consolidated. Similarly, Panama has begun to position itself in the current, competitive global economic environment to enhance its opportunity for considerable and sustainable economic growth. Still, the nation's leaders must take important economic adjustment measures—measures they have only recently begun to implement.

The degree of political and economic transformation witnessed in Panama thus far has taken much longer than many had hoped it would, and the nation's accomplishments have been costlier than should have been necessary. This happened largely because the military and their civilian allies seized power and held onto it for too long against the wishes of the Panamanian people. Also, certain economic interest groups have insisted upon maintaining financial privileges that deny the nation's economy the flexibility required to remain competitive in the world economy. Panama lacks mechanisms and institutions to educate and inform the political process—the types of mechanisms found in effective modern democracies.

This chapter reviews the political and economic changes that have taken place in Panama since 1978. In examining various successes and failures, I assess what Panama must try to accomplish if it is to become a stable, democratic, and prosperous nation.

A CRITICAL JUNCTURE: 1978

The essential question facing Panama is how to consolidate a small nation of 2.6 million inhabitants. Because of its unique geographical position as a site for international passage, Panama has been coveted historically by the world's superpowers. Spain, Britain, France, and the United States have all sought to develop Panama's isthmus as the major point of transit between the Atlantic and Pacific oceans. Spanning the narrow isthmus, the Panama Canal greatly facilitated transit between these oceans following its construction by the United States early in the twentieth century.

Panama's sovereignty over its isthmus would ultimately be recognized by the United States in the 1978 Torrijos-Carter treaties, named after the presidents of Panama and the United States, General Omar Torrijos and Jimmy Carter, respectively. The treaties allowed Panama's ever increasing participation in canal administration, return of lands and waters, and greater economic benefits, and guaranteed full control over the canal by the year 2000. Until the close of the millennium, however, Panama and the United States are equal partners in the canal's administration, operation, and defense.

The treaties ushered in a climate of goodwill and better relations with the United States, projected a positive image of Panama abroad, made Panama a more favorable place to invest, caused a sharp increase in national income, opened political space, and consolidated development opportunities. Most of Panama's foreign debt owed to commercial banks was restructured, economic policy became more favorable to private investment, and the overexpansion of the public sector was curbed. There were dramatic improvements in social well-being, in the nation's broad physical infrastructure, and in economic opportunities funded by the additional income and the reversion of territory to Panama by treaty. The export service economy, too, prospered. However, on the negative side, controls and regulations contributed to stagnation of other sectors. Unemployment grew and it became clear that the fiscal situation had to be kept under control because the foreign debt had almost grown beyond prudent proportions. Economic regulations favored a more intensive use of capital than of labor, causing unemployment and lowering the net productivity of resources.

Torrijos had made a commitment to the presidents of the American republics to begin a degree of democratization that would culminate in direct presidential elections in 1984. In 1978, Arnulfo Arias, several times president of Panama and perennial presidential candidate, was allowed to return from exile and engage freely in political activity. The majority of exiles also returned and a political debate began on what type of democratic transition would best serve the interests of the country.

The economic policy Torrijos and his heterogeneous political supporters would define for the country was uncertain, however. The government had been polarized for several years, with a small group of professionals and members of the center-right in one camp and the populist left and Marxists in the other. The left had the upper hand and gave the initial boost toward bigger government in 1972–75, but it was neutralized in 1975–78. Policy was reoriented toward promoting freer private enterprise activity, fewer government regulations, and a less activist fiscal policy. Panama stabilized its financial situation and took advantage of numerous opportunities for economic growth provided by the areas that had reverted to the nation from the former U.S. Canal Zone and by the newly constructed, expanded infrastructure. These policy changes occurred during my term of service as minister of planning and economic policy.

In 1978, the direction of policy changed again. The government allowed state activism and populism to continue, while the foreign debt grew. Democratic openings became more defined. A social democratic incumbent party was created from within the government, while the traditional political forces—Arnulfo Arias's popular Panamanistas, traditional liberalism, and the fledgling Christian Democrats—reorganized.

With the approval of the treaties, I thought that my obligation to the country had been fulfilled. I did not approve of prevailing policies; rather, I felt that free enterprise and a flexible economy should be encouraged. However, since that was not the direction in which policy was heading, I resigned as minister and assumed the position of vice president for Latin America at the World Bank.

THE POLITICAL AND ECONOMIC TRANSITION (1978–1984)

Panama's political and economic transition has taken place in discrete but uneven stages. The transition has been characterized by changes in the leadership of the National Guard, by the upper military echelon's growing ambition to retain power (defying their pledge to the country to do otherwise), and by the inability of the growing opposition to remove them from power. The economy had suffered due to those realities, and the military lost popular support by clinging to an obsolete power base built around clientelism rather than gaining ground by making timely economic adjustments.

Political Transition under Torrijos (1978–1981)

As new advances were made in political liberalization, it became apparent that the country suffered serious political polarization—the result of ten years of strong, centralized government; of isolating groups that traditionally participated in political activity; and of uncertainty created by the leftist-Marxist presence in the government.

General Torrijos chose not to become president of Panama but remained commander of the National Guard. On his recommendation, the National Assembly of Representatives elected Dr. Arístides Royo president for a six-year term (1978–84); Royo was well liked by the leftists in the government.

With a new canal treaty in place, Panamanians had high expectations for the future. Yet the arrangements made to transfer canal administration from the United States to Panama—based on increasing Panamanian participation accompanied by a gradual U.S. withdrawal—were difficult at best. A number of political groups that had been displaced since 1968 were extremely frustrated and anxious to participate. They all questioned the legitimacy of the 1972 constitution. The more belligerent of these critics were adamant that the constitution be replaced by one similar to the liberal constitution of 1946, which would return the National Guard to its traditional subordinate position.

The new push for democracy began with the agreement to open a legislative assembly in 1980. Two-thirds of the assembly would be chosen by the Assembly of Representatives from among its members; the other third would be chosen by direct popular vote. For the first time since 1968, the organized opposition was given the opportunity to be represented in a government body.

At the end of 1979, there was a major national protest against an education reform policy considered to be Marxist influenced. Led by teachers and doctors, it was joined by the Catholic Church, private schools, and some business associations. After several marches by hundreds of thousands of Panamanians, the government negotiated a radically different education reform proposal. Subsequently, some well-known leftists would leave the government to assume positions overseas. This diluted the leftist influence in the government and marked the beginning of a more centrist orientation. Thus, the political action by professional associations—such as teachers' and doctors' groups—proved successful and would recur in the future.

I never understood completely why Torrijos insisted on including left-wing Marxists in the government. On the one hand, he may have sympathized to some extent with their demands for social justice; on the other, he had viewed them as the one group capable of standing in the way of approval for the canal treaties. Therefore, he included some leftists in the team negotiating the treaties. Evidently, Torrijos felt that by including the leftists in the government he could avoid having to deal with the guerrilla violence plaguing the rest of Central America. This may have outweighed concerns about the cost of adopting many leftist economic policies.

In practice, Torrijos sat at the center of power. However, he usually resisted any pressure to act as head of state. Instead, he respected Royo's office; decisions were actually made by the president. With its extensive contacts throughout Panama, the National Guard served as Torrijos's power base. The

National Assembly of Representatives was his link to popular support and the Democratic Revolutionary Party (PRD) was his instrument for political organization. Public administration operated under his shadow. Power was divided among these bodies, with Torrijos at the center; he did not take direct action, but rather he guided the direction of actions.

He was active in some international matters. For instance, he supported the Sandinista efforts to overthrow Somoza in Nicaragua and worked to fortify his relationship with a prominent group of international Social Democrats including Felipe González, Carlos Andrés Pérez, Daniel Oduber, and Michael Manley.

Speculation held that Torrijos would be the presidential candidate in 1984. He denied such rumors. In 1981 (before his death in an airplane crash), when I last saw him alive, Torrijos told me that before retiring as commander of the National Guard he wanted to retire the senior staff "so that they would not do what he had done." He said he wanted to leave a new generation of officers in charge and a new civilian government. Through President Royo, Torrijos offered me the 1984 presidential candidacy. But I had been away from Panama since 1978 because of policy disagreements with the populist-Marxist group; I had visited the country only on occasion. I had to look hard at the situation and needed to determine whether Panama could have the type of government that, in my opinion, would put the country's development on the right track.

Political Transition after Torrijos (1981–1984)

Upon Torrijos's sudden death in 1981, the political power structure that he had built began to disintegrate. The first power struggle was within the National Guard. General Rubén Darío Paredes replaced Commander Florencio Flores and forged a pact—secret until 1987—with Colonel Manuel Noriega and Colonel Roberto Díaz Herrera. The pact outlined an arrangement wherein they would take turns as presidents and commanders. The year following Torrijos's death, tension between the National Guard command and President Royo's civilian government reached its peak. The military forced Royo's resignation. Vice President Ricardo de la Espriella ascended to the presidency, but actual power fell back into the hands of the military command under Paredes's control. The cabinet was named jointly by both de la Espriella and the military command.

The National Guard high command then increasingly began to partake in domestic affairs. The military interfered in public administration and in rural affairs and also controlled the PRD, using this as its tool for political mobilization. The high command's relations with labor unions, transport organizations, and agrarian and student groups granted it powerful influence within those populist groups. The military, thus, had a degree of political power that matched that of the nation's traditional parties arrayed in the opposition. It was also becoming more and more apparent that high-ranking National Guard officials were engaging in business dealings with national and foreign investors; corruption and abuses of power rose rapidly.

In 1980, the newspaper *La Prensa* was founded by a group of business leaders who had been exiled four years earlier. *La Prensa*'s goals were to promote freedom of the press, democracy, and the military's return to the barracks. The newspaper insisted on transparency in government activities and lashed out at government corruption, frequently putting the military on the defensive.

Political management was mainly in the hands of Paredes and his colleagues, with input from President de la Espriella. Public administration was directed by de la Espriella, with the military's participation.

Paredes pledged to hold a direct presidential election in 1984 and reached an agreement with the opposition to reform the national constitution and to establish a government and a political environment that would be acceptable to all. A multiparty commission was formed to draft changes to the constitution. Their recommendations were approved in a national plebiscite. Among their recommendations were that the National Assembly of Representatives be divested of certain special powers, that the nation's legislative body be elected entirely by direct popular vote, that the president's term be reduced to five years, that presidential powers be strengthened, that the separation of powers be more clearly defined, that the National Guard's influence on the executive branch be reduced, and that some economic and social regulations be liberalized. A new electoral code was prepared, and the Electoral Tribunal was created to organize and supervise elections.

At the time, the judiciary and the attorney general's office were not independent enough to guarantee their impartiality. Many Panamanians viewed the justice system as corrupt. In 1982, there was a tremendous national scandal when $60 million in social security funds slated for housing construction "disappeared." This and other instances of corruption, such as those involving COFINA (a state development bank) and a contract to build a bridge over the canal, considerably lowered the public's opinion of the government, especially since members of the judicial system appeared to be delaying prosecution of those involved. An activist attorney general who sought to prosecute corruption was openly forced to resign.

General Paredes purged some leftist elements from the government and tried to maintain close ties to business groups. In 1983, he began promoting his potential candidacy for the presidency. Meanwhile, Colonel Noriega was apparently solidifying a large base of support within the National Guard. When General Paredes retired in August 1983 to seek the presidency, Noriega rose to become commander of the National Guard.

To win the presidential nomination, Paredes tried to form a coalition of parties led by the PRD. However, his colleagues in the military and President de la Espriella did not support him. Personal friction, resentments, and fear of a strong Paredes presidency existed among the groups who would not support Paredes. He was finally obliged to abandon his quest.

President de la Espriella and the commanders were left without a presidential candidate. There were several possibilities within PRD ranks, but because the government had a badly tarnished image while its opposition was relatively strong, the government needed a broad coalition of parties to win the elections.

There was an economic recession in 1983. To the public, the military government appeared exhausted and corrupt. The country wanted a change. The military realized this. They approached Fernando Manfredo, Panamanian deputy administrator of the canal, and offered him the candidacy. He refused. President de la Espriella then phoned me in Washington to ask that I consider the candidacy.

Because I had been working at the World Bank, outside the country and the government for almost six years, I acquired experience as an international economist and a reputation as an honest man. This, and the international contacts I had, made me a promising candidate for president. Also, because a coalition of parties was needed to secure an election victory, I had the advantage of being the only non-PRD candidate acceptable to the PRD and the only person linked to Torrijos acceptable to the parties not closely tied to his government.

In conversations with de la Espriella and the commanders (Noriega, Díaz Herrera, and Justine), we agreed on several points. First, if I were elected, my government would press for true democratic reform. Second, the military would return to the barracks and resume their professional function of backing the civilian government; the government would in turn support the military's institutional functions. Third, the government's platform in the electoral campaign would be prepared by the full coalition of parties. Finally, our government would continue the program of economic stabilization and adjustment already in process.

Upon beginning to build our coalition of parties, I sought out Arias, eighty-two years old; he had previously sent me a conciliatory and friendly message. I invited him to form a large national front with us to secure the return to democracy, with the blessings of de la Espriella and Noriega. I proposed that Arias be the nation's "great patriarch" of politics and assume a special place in our government to help strengthen democratic institutions. I also suggested that he choose a candidate from his party to be vice president in our coalition. Arias did not accept my proposals, however.

I approached the leaders of all the other parties with the national front proposal. Two parties not associated with the incumbent government agreed to join us. We nearly received the support of a third opposition party—a liberal party—but, divided internally, it eventually aligned itself with Arias.

Our final coalition, the National Democratic Union (UNADE), consisted of the PRD, which headed it, three other parties identified with the government, and two opposition parties (the National Liberal Party and the Republican Party). The rest of the opposition united around Arias, forming the Opposition Democratic Alliance (ADO), which included the Panamanistas, the National Liberal Republican Movement (Molirena), and the Christian Democratic parties. With the UNADE coalition, however, we would involve new groups in an orderly transition to democracy. The country wanted a change; ours would be the "constructive change."

The Economic Transition (1978–1984)

The economic transition that Panama witnessed from 1978 to 1984 began with the resurgence of growth stimulated by additional income Panama received from its part in operating the canal, from the transisthmian pipeline, and from private investments. The period ended, however, with a massive accumulation of foreign debt, a regulated economy in an inflationary stranglehold, and decreased foreign financing sparked by a regionwide crisis in 1982. As a result, from 1984 to the present, Panama has had to adopt a strategy of stabilization and adjustments.

The 1978–82 period. During the 1975–78 period when Panama suffered "stagflation," the public sector played an important role in pushing forward wide-ranging public investments. Public investment programs continued in subsequent years but with two negative consequences. First, the availability of banking credit to the private sector was seriously reduced. Second, an ever increasing percentage of Panama's foreign debt was used to pay for current expenditures and interest payments rather than used for investments.

The new annual revenues generated after the approval of the canal treaties were used entirely to enlarge the bureaucracy and fund current expenditures, not to retire the external public debt as I had recommended. The public employee roster increased by 50 percent between 1978 and 1984. State enterprises, such as the sugar mills, had substantial deficits that were financed by the foreign debt. The mortgages due from the massive state-financed popular housing program of 1975–78 were not collected. In 1981–82, the steeper interest payments on the foreign debt prompted the servicing of debt through incurring additional debt. By 1982, the government's deficit had climbed to almost 16 percent of the nation's gross domestic product.

On the positive side, once public investment projects—like the fishing port, the airport, expansion of the free zone and the tourist industry infrastructure, and the opening of Darién and feeder roads—were finished, they offered promising opportunities for export-oriented private investment. The free zone and, to a lesser degree, the fishing port were best utilized for that purpose. On the whole, however, the government failed to adopt policies that facilitated private investment, nor was there an appropriate rate of return on infrastructure capital expenditures.

The transisthmian oil pipeline is one of Panama's largest projects. Construction began in 1978 and ended in 1982; the pipeline began adding considerably to Panama's income by 1983. A joint venture between Panama, whose government possesses partial ownership, and the United States, which provided the majority of the private capital, it carries the bulk of the Alaskan petroleum being transported from the Pacific via the Caribbean to the east coast of North America. Panama's economy reaped significant benefits from its construction; the pipeline continues to add to the country's exports and fiscal revenues.

The Ministry of Planning recommended instituting the Canal Authority to coordinate the different components of Panama's growing participation in canal administration and to plan for the effective use of the former Canal Zone after it reverted to Panama. Unfortunately, the institution became too bureaucratized and engaged in conflicts with other government offices. It was eliminated in 1982.

The increase in international oil prices, rising global interest rates, and Panama's 17 percent loss in its international terms of trade worsened its balance of payments by at least $650 million from 1978 to 1983. This was compensated for by income from the canal, pipeline revenues, and additional debt financing, thus avoiding a drastic crash in the economy. However, the economy was made much more vulnerable in the process.

By 1982, the economy appeared to be recovering but increasing vulnerabilities became evident. Panama was burdened by considerable foreign debt, especially that accumulated by the public sector. Little use was being made of an infrastructure that had been strengthened and expanded in the late 1970s to attract private investments and to increase exports. Private investment in the reverted Canal Zone areas was moving ahead at too slow a pace. Labor market regulations remained rigid and favored only capital-intensive investments. The capital investments that had been made yielded low rates of return because they were managed ineffectively. There was a real reduction in the total productivity of Panamanian resources, which damaged the competitiveness of the nation's exports. There persisted an imprudent bevy of import quotas and tariffs, giving excessive protection to a small group of industries. All in all, Panama consumed more than it produced and imported more than it could export. Adjustments needed to be made.

Yet from 1978 through 1982, the reorientation of economic policy to promote exports and private investment was not made. Instead, the economy slid into a more precarious position.

The 1983–84 period. Panama was forced by its shaky financial situation and the drying up of foreign financing to embark on a stabilization and structural adjustment program under the aegis of the International Monetary Fund (IMF) and the World Bank. The program called for a gradual but considerable reduction of Panama's fiscal deficit (a task made somewhat easier by the income flowing in from the pipeline). Deficit-reduction measures included shutting down some state-owned and poorly run sugar mills, converting import quotas into tariffs, easing price controls, and improving state administration. At a later stage, the government would change labor legislation, reduce import tariffs, and reform agriculture and livestock policies.

The recession that was felt throughout Latin America wounded Panama in its most prosperous sectors: the export of transport services through the canal, free zone exports, banking and reinsurance services, tourism, and regional commerce. Economic growth halted and unemployment figures rose. The balance of payments adjustment occurred automatically because Panama operates on an open financial system and a fixed monetary exchange rate (the U.S. dollar is Panama's domestic currency). The effects of the recession were felt mainly in Panama's fiscal situation. Nonetheless, matters began improving as the adjustments were made and the international banking community lent its support.

There were two fundamental aspects of the Panamanian economy that the military did not understand. First was that an automatic adjustment in the balance of payments can take place, given that Panama has a fixed exchange rate and an open financial system, and that such an arrangement has powerful fiscal repercussions. Second was the vital necessity to stimulate the real productivity of resources, given that Panama could not maintain the competitiveness of its exports through currency devaluations.

From 1983 to 1984, stabilization went relatively well, although it did not enhance the government's image. However, various groups still retained special economic privileges, such as the transport unions, public employees who received automatic salary increases mandated by law, labor organizations, professional groups such as doctors and teachers, and manufacturers. This limited the country's capacity to adapt to the changing international economic situation.

POLITICAL TRANSITION AND ECONOMIC ADJUSTMENT, 1984–1985

The 1984 elections ushered in my administration, the goal of which was to promote the transition to democracy and to continue the economic adjustment program. Unfortunately, the military upper echelon wished to continue ruling and obstructed our work. In doing so, they precipitated their own destruction and severely damaged the nation.

I had agreed to run for president because I wanted to set a course for democratic transition and economic development. With the support of the Torrijos contingent, my numerous friends, and my personal acquaintances in the opposition, I thought I could create an atmosphere of reconciliation and stability and institute the necessary political changes and economic policies.

Some factors worked to my advantage, while others did not. As my candidacy was backed by the government, our campaign labored under the shadow of sixteen years of military government, an economic recession, the past several years of corruption, and strong opposition from Arias, the ever popular leader and octogenarian. Yet I benefited from being part of a "new generation" of leaders and from having an image as an honest and respected economist, a supporter of private enterprise, and an effective promoter of social development, well linked to the international economic community. On balance, this record compared favorably to Arias's rash and erratic management style.

To the casual observer Arias may have appeared to be the odds-on favorite. However, professional polls showed that Arias's "Panamanianism" had the support of a solid 25 percent of the electorate. Torrijos's PRD held an equally solid 26 percent. The remaining parties had 5 to 7 percent each. These surveys indicated that the electorate divided evenly between us.

UNADE supporters included a broad spectrum of the business community, labor unions, professionals, agricultural and livestock groups, public employees, and people who had benefited from the projects of the Torrijos administration. We had a broad base of support.

Unfortunately, on the day of my return from Washington, after I resigned from the World Bank, President de la Espriella was forced out of office by the military. Although he had suggested that I seek the candidacy, he did little to help me consolidate my support. In fact, he had been in frequent contact with Arias. Apparently, he had other ambitions that conflicted with the goals he and the National Guard had agreed upon. In any case, the matter took me by surprise and boded ill for the political campaign and the future. Vice President Jorge Illueca, who had served as president of the United Nations General Assembly, took de la Espriella's office.

We developed an intensive political campaign that relied on solid professional advice and heavy television coverage to reach and recruit as many voters as we could for our cause. We would gather and show powerful popular support, working to reach a peak of enthusiasm on election day. I campaigned vigorously, visiting every region, going house-to-house, and shaking the hands of more than 300,000 voters. Attendance at our rallies in the closing days of the campaign exceeded that at Arias's. Final polls showed a tight race, which it eventually was, with perhaps 2 to 3 percent in our favor.

The slogan of our campaign was "constructive change." The UNADE political platform was based on consolidating democracy; regaining economic growth through exports and promoting social development; establishing honest and efficient public administration; and developing an international policy commensurate with Panama's interests. Rarely had such elaborate yet professional and pragmatic positions as ours been presented during a political campaign. We talked constructively about many economic adjustment policies while remaining realistic about the costs of making the transition. The campaign was civil and courteous but intense, for we were debating critical issues.

The main difference between ADO and UNADE was more tactical than strategic. Both coalitions wanted democracy and withdrawal of the military from politics. Both knew that economic policies needed to be revamped and public administration improved. UNADE's tactic, however, was to negotiate the military's withdrawal; ADO's was more confrontational and even vengeful.

In the last month before the election, it became clear that the race would be close. Realizing this, the opposition began "predicting" a fraudulent victory by the government, even while UNADE was calling for national reconciliation. Unfortunately, UNADE did not win a resounding electoral mandate; the results were too close. I have collected and preserved the most reliable information and proof of the results. They show that UNADE won by 4,500 votes. When the opposition declared fraudulent 3,000 votes cast in a remote mountain district—inhabited by an indigenous population—we asked the Electoral Tribunal to investigate; the outcome of this investigation did not alter the national election results. Thus, we accepted victory, convinced that our win was real. However, because of the clumsiness of some military personnel who provoked acts of violence at the start of the official ballot counting, the opposition proclaimed to the international community that an "enormous" fraud had taken place. This made the transition appear illegitimate.[1] We wanted to cooperate with the opposition parties to strengthen democratic and civilian institutions and return the military to their barracks, but these allegations hurt our chances of working well with the opposition.

The possibilities of reconciliation were also damaged when the Electoral

Tribunal awarded our coalition five legislative seats that had been subject to dispute in a move that the opposition called fraudulent. I did not intervene in the matter, hoping to avoid the problems encountered by Arias when, in 1968, his opposition lost ten previously confirmed legislative seats.

The country, then, was divided into two large camps. I appealed for national reconciliation and, as president-elect, worked diligently to achieve it. I formed sixty working commissions made up of one thousand citizens representing all political persuasions. The commissions were to draw up recommendations for government action on every conceivable issue. I continued meeting with independent and opposition groups to maintain cooperative ties as well as initiating contact with other more resistant elements among the opposition parties. With my labor union friends I discussed the need for possible labor legislation reform. Based on those discussions, we agreed to conduct private negotiations first before taking action in the Legislative Assembly. I made the same overtures to the Industrialist Union, offering to engage in prolonged consultation to reach a conciliatory position on industrial protection policy before acting.

With the help of the dean of the Central American Management Institute (INCAE),[2] a specialist on the subject, we conducted separate seminars on development policy with political parties and legislators, the military, labor unions, the media, and the business community.

I traveled extensively to renew contacts in the United States, Japan, other East Asian countries, Europe, and Latin America. We invited many renowned investors and bankers to my inauguration. Surveys at the time showed my popular support increasing, despite the vocal opposition.

In private talks with opposition leaders, I asked for their vote of confidence for democratization. They said they would support me only to the extent that I publicly demonstrated that I was returning the military "to its place." I asked for their trust and patience.

My Government of Democratic Transition

When I assumed office, the nation had high expectations for economic progress. My cabinet was peopled with professionals and a representative mix of the parties that had made up the UNADE coalition. One of our immediate tasks was to strengthen the governing political coalition, which included a range of actors from the intellectual left and labor groups to well-known business leaders. Naturally, there was friction among the coalition's varied groups, but the benefit of having a coalition that could unite many different actors in pursuit of the structural changes needed in Panama—provided everyone could be convinced—made our efforts worthwhile. We enjoyed a two-thirds majority in the Legislative Assembly, the support of the newly named Panama

Defense Forces (PDF) and most of the media, and the sympathy of the Catholic Church for our democratic goals.

We had to put into effect a good part of the structural-reform program during our first year in government to ensure foreign financing, to restructure Panama's foreign debt, and to prepare the economy for accelerated and efficient growth. This meant that various groups had to make sacrifices because we had to introduce new taxes, reduce current public expenditures, stop automatic salary increases mandated by law, change the labor code to stimulate productivity, reduce some industrial quotas and protective tariffs, and make more flexible some agricultural operations. The changes were needed to help the economy grow at a better pace in order to generate more employment. This could only be accomplished by reducing the public sector and making it more efficient, stimulating more private economic activity, increasing and diversifying exports, and improving the nation's capacity to generate employment and social well-being. Part of this strategy also called for a tourism program and an accelerated containerport project; for inviting export-manufacturing industries based in Panama to take advantage of the U.S.-sponsored Caribbean Basin Initiative (CBI), which lowered U.S. tariffs on exports from Caribbean and Central American countries and Panama; and for stimulating beef exports.

Our goal was to gain enough credibility at the beginning of our term to be able to ask for sacrifices. Because we possessed sufficient political power to make the adjustments, we could spend political capital in our administration's first year and a half. After that, we planned to push forward with the more positive and popular programs in the following three years of our term. In doing so, we needed to win over the center of the political spectrum and isolate the opposition.

Twenty laws were approved during our first month in office in order to give us a credibility boost. Some of the laws provided incentives to help spur recovery in our healthier economic sectors, such as construction, tourism, reinsurance, and banking. Other laws promoted integrity and efficiency in public administration by reforming bidding on public contracts, improving the audit and control law, reducing smuggling, protecting state property, and creating an export institute. Still other laws improved the judicial system by installing a new Judiciary Code and expediting trials in a Social Security scandal. We scaled down the bureaucracy by reducing paperwork and removing superfluous employees—people on the payroll who were not actually working. And we took measures to support production and export of agricultural and livestock goods.

I tried to strengthen our relationship with the PDF by creating a National Security Council with the participation of Commander Noriega and various ministers. I had breakfast with the commanders once a week and kept them informed of the government's actions, seeking out their support and advice on many issues. Knowing Noriega's penchant for intelligence work and intrigue, I determined it best to lay my cards on the table and avoid generating any distrust which might motivate the army to invade the turf of the civilian government. It was particularly difficult, however, to make them see the need to cut back various subsidies. The military were starkly aware that such changes might create friction between them and the organized groups to whom they had granted economic concessions in the past in exchange for political support.

My constant goal was to show them a vision of the need for real change. The public had fervent expectations for a new direction for Panama's politics and economy. I had to make the military see that the economic and political path they had followed for so many years had reached a dead end. Now was the moment when they should withdraw honorably to their professional role, as we had jointly promised the country. Otherwise, the government could not hope to maintain credibility in the eyes of the public. It was time to close the door on the past and to open a new chapter in Panamanian history. Initially, they fulfilled their commitment. However, they were unhappy that I had named my cabinet after consulting the parties but not the military. I gave them some posts in the diplomatic corps and protected public employees they had previously appointed, with the proviso that such employees do their jobs. I underscored the need to maintain public faith in the government's honesty since we would be asking the people for sacrifices. The military replied to this with "We are honest."

I was not aware of Noriega's illicit international activities. Had I been, I would have declined the candidacy. I did know that he and other military officers participated in business dealings and that they were not "chemically pure," but I did not realize that they were doing so to such an alarming and grotesque extent. The risk of failing in our political and economic transition was great enough without the military's involvement in arms and drug trafficking, money laundering, and contraband. Our administration was committed to cooperating with other nations in restricting drug trafficking and money laundering. Prosperity depended on nurturing Panama's image as a successful center of legal, internationally accepted, and lightly regulated international business services. I had the military's assurance that they agreed with this criterion. In fact, Noriega showed me letters from the U.S. government congratulating him for his efforts on antidrug campaigns. The military also pointed out that, in 1984, it had shut down a Colombian drug laboratory along the border with that country. I did not grasp the extent and highly developed nature of the network of intelligence contacts the military had with their counterparts in countries like the United States, Cuba, and Israel—beyond what I deemed normal and necessary collaboration with such international intelligence services.

The PRD had the absolute majority in the Legislative Assembly. The question was whether its political loyalty lay with the president and the civilian government or with the military. We tried very hard to win and keep the support of the PRD and the UNADE legislators, which was key to the success of the adjustment program. Not only did I meet with them frequently, but I offered them the concessions typical in Panamanian politics, such as jobs, community projects, and public honors.

The first economic adjustment measure was a law to increase certain taxes, freeze salaries, and cut public spending. This adjustment was needed to reduce an unsustainable fiscal deficit and to secure an agreement with the IMF, obtain new financing, and restructure the debt. Because Panama has no central bank, this action was also needed to ensure the liquidity of the national treasury and the National Bank of Panama. The fiscal deficit was still 7 percent of GNP and we wanted to lower it to 3 percent in 1985 and eventually to zero.

The draft legislation was reviewed by the PRD, other UNADE parties, the cabinet, and the military commanders. There were reservations all around, but we ultimately decided to enact the law six weeks after taking office. We announced to the nation the need for a shared sacrifice. We had prepared the sectors backing the government for the controversial legislation but we did so too hastily and without extensive public debate. Once the law was approved, the affected interests (teachers, doctors, and lawyers, among others) began to organize against it. Even a minority of business groups protested the measure, though most continued to support me.

Despite efforts to explain the necessity of the law through dialogue, negotiation, and public information campaigns, 80,000 people staged a protest march in opposition to the law. This diminished our public support. We continued to negotiate; the opposition gathered a coalition of trade guilds called the Coordinadora Civilista Nacional (CoCiNa). The coalition made me an offer: come out against the military and its budget, and they would support me. The commanders and I had already agreed to a reduction of $5 million in the military budget; I did not think it prudent to press the issue further. The opposition held a second march, this time numbering 20,000 people. To avoid further confrontations and friction, we abrogated the law and began again. We had made the mistake of not debating the issue publicly and sufficiently. The UNADE organized a march of 40,000 people to show support for the government.

I appointed a commission from the UNADE parties to negotiate with the protesting groups. Three months later, we approved a tax package. It was weaker than the first one, but did raise taxes enough to improve public finances. We were also able to come to a satisfactory agreement with the IMF. The experience, however, weakened me politically and gave the military upper echelon the opportunity to challenge the civilian government's authority. The military's allies pointed out to the officers that the marches had been aimed against them and that the elected government could not be trusted.

At that point, I began an intensive campaign to try to regain my lost political ground. I visited the countryside, publicly inaugurated new projects, held dialogues with trade guilds, and so forth. We made a point of emphasizing the many positive accomplishments. These efforts began paying off. However, a small group of senior officers in the PDF and a PRD populist-Marxist group continued to challenge the authority of the president and the cabinet. The military again began pressuring some trade guilds and manipulating their connections in the media. It was a frank conspiracy to stymie the government, a practice at which Noriega and some of his colleagues were expert. Gradually, the question of who should govern—the president and the cabinet or the military—became the nation's central concern.

Only seven months into my term, the military, with the support of the PRD and its legislators, began pressuring for a partial change in the cabinet. I resisted by making other concessions and by arguing that it was preferable to wait until the adjustments were finished before replacing ministers. The opposition supported my position indirectly, though publicly they continued their attacks. The military did not ease up. Rumors began circulating that there would be a coup unless I relented. We finally agreed to change six ministers in exchange for full military support for the pending economic adjustments. The military and the PRD could recommend people for the ministerial appointments but I reserved the right to veto any selection. Although it would have increased my popularity, I felt that to act otherwise risked the collapse of the government program. The economic adjustment measures that had yet to be taken were controversial and would require full support from the political coalition and the PDF for negotiation and approval.

We had two choices: risk public finances or risk political support. Because Panama had no central bank, government finances would suffer cash flow shortages by early 1986 if the adjustments were postponed. Besides, the economic recovery already under way would abort; public support would tumble. On the other hand, pushing too quickly for adjustments would lead to increased opposition, jeopardizing our capacity to govern. Therefore, adjustments had to be made gradually and sequentially. Each measure would have to be negotiated separately to ensure fiscal and political stability and sustained economic recovery.

There was an even bigger problem, however, extending beyond the logistics of implementing reform. On the one hand, I had to be wary of the military upper echelon's renewed interest in ruling the country. To prove their strength, they made their support for me more and more costly. On the other hand, I had to change people's conception of negotiation from one of how to divide up the existing pie to one of making the pie grow for the benefit of all concerned.

Under all these pressures, the government took action. First, the cabinet and the UNADE directorate agreed to initiate a package of reforms, starting with the labor code and continuing with liberalization of industrial protection and changes in agricultural and livestock policies. Preliminary agreements were concluded with the World Bank; results were kept secret temporarily while negotiations proceeded within Panama. Once agreement was reached in Panama, the government would negotiate its final arrangement with the World Bank, mindful of the bargains struck back in Panama.

The government also worked constructively in other areas. It lent more support to private investment (especially in construction), to agricultural and livestock production, and to the export of services and industrial products. Various social development programs were announced, as was draft legislation that laid out a master plan on how to utilize the reverted Canal Zone. A trade agreement was signed with Mexico. We also worked on an agreement with Japan and the United States to study the options for the future of the Panama Canal. And, for the first time, a bank owned by drug traffickers was closed.

At the presidential level, we moved ahead with the Contadora agreement to seek peace in Central America. Several Latin American presidents joined in calling on the United States to recognize that economic adjustment without growth would adversely affect the region's newly emerging democracies. These countries needed additional foreign financing and better terms to restructure their debts. Under my leadership, Presidents Raúl Alfonsín of Argentina, Julio M. Sanguinetti of Uruguay, Belisario Betancur of Colombia, Alan García of Peru, and Salvador Jorge Blanco of the Dominican Republic spoke individually with James Baker (the U.S. secretary of the treasury at that time) in Lima about Latin America's options. I had spoken previously with Presidents Miguel de la Madrid of Mexico and Jaime Lusinchi of Venezuela. We were pleased with Baker's announcement in Korea of a new debt-restructuring plan.

Prior to my inauguration, there had been discussions between my team and labor leaders about possible changes to the labor code. It was agreed that negotiations would be kept secret and respectful. Progress looked promising; I had appointed one of Panama's most internationally respected labor leaders as my minister of labor. Thirty days after my inauguration, we had almost reached agreement on a labor bill to become law immediately. However, because of the tax and expenditure law, negotiations on the labor law were postponed. In the ensuing cabinet shuffle, the minister of labor was forced to leave. To pick up the labor reform proposals where we left off, I formed a closed-door commission to prepare and negotiate the draft legislation. When it was complete, a PRD leader presented it to the military's second in command, Colonel Díaz Herrera. Díaz Herrera, however, proceeded to have it published in one of the major newspapers. Because of this breach of trust, the following day there was a labor strike (although we managed to stop it through our alliance with Panama's largest labor federation). It had become apparent that while on the surface the military and the PRD left supported me, behind my back they were conspiring against me.

Our administration, therefore, had to open talks with labor and business to seek a consensus on new legislation. I promised to be flexible and to defend whatever agreements we reached in Panama at the subsequent meetings with international institutions.

With the specter of an internal conspiracy hanging over my government, I had to soften the government's position even further to create a climate of cooperation. Over the course of four days, I hosted luncheons with more than seventy industrialists, met several times with labor leaders, and sent the minister of agriculture to talk with agricultural leaders. I had in-depth meetings with legislators to win their support. In response to Noriega's criticisms in the international media of our economic adjustment programs, we mounted a pro-democracy demonstration of fifteen thousand farmers in a rural province. At that demonstration, I emphasized the agreement Noriega and I had reached to defend and strengthen democracy. Later, I talked with him at length to try to deepen our understanding. Arias then sent me a message suggesting that he might provide unconditional backing if I were to replace the military's upper echelon. But to do so at that moment would have invited a coup. Instead, we continued the tripartite dialogue among labor, business, and the government.

Those conspiring against our efforts, however, continued looking for ways to weaken the presidency. This was evident in that labor leaders would agree to certain points at a meeting, and then later, having met privately with the conspirators, they would take the opposite stance. In an audacious and despicable move, the conspirators tried to convince Noriega that the World Bank's position was more flexible than mine. In a dramatic meeting with the military, I offered to call the president of the World Bank, my friend and former boss, so that he could inform them directly of what the bank required in order to grant a structural adjustment loan. The commanders balked. They finally understood that the adjustments were necessary because, if we postponed them and therefore had to turn down the World Bank, we risked a financial crisis in 1986.

A small group of military, labor, and leftist PRD leaders had gone to Cuba in August to participate in Fidel Castro's campaign against Latin America's service of the external debt. Upon their return, they portrayed me as a pawn of the IMF and the World Bank. They decided to try to overthrow me if I insisted on pursuing adjustment policies.

I explained to the commanders that we had only three options. These ranged from the politically risky choice of approving all the reform measures at once to the financially risky choice of postponing all the measures until the following year. Noriega supported an option that lay between these two, that of approving the agricultural and livestock laws before the end of 1985 and the labor and industrial laws in the first quarter of 1986. This option could still win Panama the World Bank loan and private bank refinancing by December, thus keeping the political situation tolerable and saving the fiscal situation. I too supported that option and presented it to the cabinet and the political parties; both accepted it. We negotiated with each pressure group; these discussions were undertaken separately and sequentially to quell the political unease.

Led by Colonel Díaz Herrera, the military's second in command, the conspirators opposed the agreement Noriega and I had reached. Nevertheless, I had neutralized the danger of a coup attempt for the moment. There was still pressure, however, from the upper echelons of the military to have greater control over government decisions. This made more difficult the long road my administration had yet to travel to institute wide-ranging adjustment programs. It would remain so until we could garner full approval (which would have to include broad participation from business and labor) of the adjustment programs and then move on to the more positive and noncontroversial parts of our long-term development plan.

Two weeks after agreement on which adjustments would be implemented on what schedule, news arrived that Dr. Hugo Spadafora had been decapitated. Spadafora had been deputy minister of health and a colorful Panamanian leader of anti-Somoza and later anti-Sandinista guerrillas. He had been a friend of Torrijos and was an enemy of Noriega, whom he accused of international drug trafficking. His murder caused a great commotion in Panama. The opposition used the incident against the military, accusing them of perpetrating the crime. I knew Spadafora; I had respected and admired him. His father, a civic leader in a prosperous city in the interior, had supported me in the elections and had been with me a week earlier at a national conference of municipal leaders. Out of personal commitment to the truth, to his father, and to public opinion, I backed an investigation into Spadafora's gruesome murder. I also agreed to appoint a special investigative commission, for which I selected three well-known Panamanians whom the attorney general swore in immediately.

At that point I had to leave Panama for a while to attend to some international matters. One stop was the United Nations General Assembly to voice support for a formula on renegotiating foreign debts that would allow Latin America's economies to grow under the framework of adjustment programs. I also met with Latin American presidents and attended the signing of the joint agreement between Panama, the United States, and Japan on the study of options for the future of the canal. Further, I met with private banking officials who had already agreed to lend funds to promote investment opportunities in Panama.

When I returned to Panama, I found that Díaz Herrera's group had used the crisis surrounding Spadafora's death and my decision to investigate the crime to convince Noriega to overthrow me. Díaz Herrera had first tried to replace Noriega but had been unable to do so. Therefore, he had turned the military's energies toward decapitating me as president, for the ostensible reasons of my having spurred the investigation into Spadafora's murder and of my being "too democratic." I pointed out that, had I not appointed the investigative commission, the whole country would consider the military guilty of the crime. And that is in effect what happened.

I was faced with the military's arbitrary power and its renewed influence in the Legislative Assembly as well as with personal threats against my family. Then, after a fourteen-hour discussion during which I was detained in Noriega's office, I was forced to "separate" myself from office—an unconstitutional action. I used the word *separation* because it allowed me to maintain that I was still constitutional president while I sought outside support.

Unfortunately, Vice President Eric Arturo Delvalle agreed to assume the presidency. With the cooperation of the Legislative Assembly, this action lent the "coup" the appearance of constitutionality. Delvalle had been in contact with the conspirators for over a month and aspired to be president regardless of how it happened.

During my one year in office, the economy had begun a recovery, experiencing 4 percent growth in 1985. The fiscal deficit had been cut and Panama's international financial circumstances had improved. Our administration had spurred the development of various export-oriented sectors. We had designed a medium-term development program to utilize Panama's transisthmian export services efficiently. And we had taken significant administrative and social development measures. All of this had been accomplished despite very adverse conditions. We had to weather constant pressure from the opposition as they questioned the government's relationship to the military and many of our actions, from the outcome of the elections to the newly initiated structural adjustment program for the economy.

Many people, including friends, thought that I should first have made a more concerted effort to consolidate political support before launching the adjustment program. However, remedies for fiscal weakness could not wait that long; it seemed a better strategy to ask for sacrifices in the beginning and end with three solid years of development, leaving the government strong and prepared for the following elections. This option was feasible because we had the political power to take action. It was the military upper echelon's desire to continue ruling, the populist-left conspiracy within the government coalition, and the opposition's efforts to weaken and neutralize the military at all costs that made it difficult to harness that apparent initial power to complete our task successfully. With hindsight, it is evident that success was impossible because of Noriega's immensely corrupt practices. He was unwilling to bargain whenever his illegal dealings were at stake.

My overthrow surprised the U.S. government, which tried only tenuously and belatedly to prevent it. Involved in the Nicaraguan conflict and according it top priority, the U.S. government preferred not to risk another crisis in the region. The United States simply sent Noriega a message to clean up his act and restore democratic government. When Noriega refused, the U.S. government backed Delvalle. Some sectors of the U.S. government did, however, attack Noriega in reputable U.S. newspapers as a drug trafficker.

After my overthrow, many senior officials in the U.S. executive and legislative branches as well as influential private citizens sought my opinion of the situation. I responded that if the military continued to control the government, Panama's stability could not be maintained.

MILITARY-CONTROLLED CIVILIAN GOVERNMENT AND ECONOMIC ADJUSTMENT (1985–1989)

Delvalle's term began with a political march up to the PDF barracks to show the new government's respect for Noriega. Despite two months' worth of rallies organized by Spadafora's brothers and by opposition groups to protest his murder, the government weakened the investigation and eventually dropped it. The de facto government was now made up of the military's upper echelon and the PRD's legislators and ministers. One of Noriega's main confidants was the minister of the presidency. Delvalle's party was given some bureaucratic posts as a sweetener.

Discovering that the fiscal situation I had warned of was real, the government resumed negotiations with the World Bank, trying to convince it to yield on certain issues. That proved impossible, so the government reopened negotiations with those groups affected by the adjustment program, just as my government had done. Six months later, in March 1986 (the same month agreed to with me), the labor, industrial, and agricultural and livestock laws were approved to ward off the financial crisis. Large protests and street violence erupted, lasting three weeks and almost paralyzing Panama's oil refinery and fuel distribution. Soldiers took control of Panama City during this whole time.

The government resorted to loans and short-term deposits, some from questionable sources, to maintain the liquidity of the National Bank while waiting for the first disbursements from financial agencies and international private banks to come through. Having experienced such difficult months, the civil-military government decided to postpone further controversial actions and instead to attempt to consolidate political support. It continued to develop some of the programs begun by my government in areas such as tourism, ports, and construction but did not continue promoting exports nor developing the former Canal Zone.

Some of Delvalle's work to establish ties with opposition sectors bore fruit but most members of the opposition remained at arm's length. They looked askance at the military's growing control over the government and its increased intervention (along with that of some political groups) in many businesses, at times in association with foreign investment.

Noriega continued to solidify his base of support in the PDF, little by little stripping Díaz Herrera of power. In May 1986, attacks against Noriega began in the U.S. press. The opposition in Panama used these to complement their own efforts to tarnish the image of Noriega and the PDF. With the full knowledge of what had occurred in the Spadafora case, the U.S. Senate Foreign Relations Committee began applying more pressure on President Ronald Reagan to investigate Noriega and to distance the administration from him. It is now known, however, that Noriega was at the time cooperating with the effort by the U.S. Central Intelligence Agency (CIA) to assist the Nicaraguan contras—paramilitary forces that sought to overthrow that country's Sandinista government.

Meanwhile, economic recovery continued at a slower pace (3 percent annually) but enough to alleviate social pressures. Toward the end of 1986, Noriega forced the resignation of cabinet ministers and directors of autonomous entities connected to Colonel Díaz Herrera. Thus the way was paved for Díaz Herrera's retirement, despite his efforts to reconcile with Noriega.

Because Panama was not complying with the adjustment plan, the IMF and the World Bank suspended disbursements. The fiscal situation again began to deteriorate slowly. The laws that had been approved at the beginning of 1986 were not enforced strictly; exceptions were granted too easily and the administration of the laws was diluted. Upon retiring, Díaz Herrera was not given the lucrative embassy and consulate in Japan as he had hoped. Resentful, in June 1987 he attacked Noriega publicly, accusing him of Spadafora's murder, electoral fraud (asserting that Arias had won in 1984), theft, and sabotaging Torrijos's airplane to cause it to crash. His announcements evidently aimed to achieve maximum impact and support from the Arnulfistas.

Díaz Herrera's accusations touched off an eruption of opposition political activity. The Arnulfistas declared themselves ready for a return to power. Business, professional, and civic associations organized themselves under the banner of the National Civic Crusade. There were daily public demonstrations.

I went on national television to announce that I had been forced from office because of my inquiries into the Spadafora murder and that I had originally accepted the presidency only because I was convinced that the victory was legitimate. However, in light of new information made public, I asked that the ballots be recounted to determine the real results. The people deserved the truth and the country needed democracy. The government responded that evening by suspending the constitutional rights of citizens.

Two days later, I accompanied the Civic Crusade to El Carmen Church for a celebration in support of democracy. The church was surrounded by soldiers. Noriega then sought to hurt me economically; in addition, the Legislative Assembly declared me, along with others, a traitor to the country. Nevertheless, I continued in my support of the democratic cause, but more quietly to avoid being exiled while making frequent trips out of the country.

The U.S. Senate announced its support for democracy in Panama. Various senators, including Senator Christopher Dodd, visited Panama to show their support. Noriega, however, unwisely launched a street protest at the U.S. Embassy, causing physical damage. This move provoked the suspension of U.S. Agency for International Development (AID) programs in Panama and spurred additional U.S. Senate resolutions supporting democracy in Panama.

Backed by the nation's opposition parties, the Civic Crusade began a vigorous pro-democracy campaign. In almost daily street demonstrations, they called for the military's withdrawal from power. This incited increased military repression in the streets. Crusade leaders were jailed, and it appeared that Delvalle had authorized these repressive actions. The international press corps began arriving in Panama in significant numbers; soon, the repression suffered by the Panamanian people and their struggle for democracy, justice, and freedom became global news. I met with the press frequently to provide my perspective. Street demonstrations continued for several months, persistently met with military repression. Some Crusade leaders were exiled. Talks were held to negotiate an agreement but neither camp would budge on its positions: the Civic Crusade wanted Noriega out while the government considered that nonnegotiable.

The economy grew at a rate of 3 percent annually during the first half of 1987 but the rate then fell rapidly over the remainder of the year. Panama's banking center began to suffer again. Public finances deteriorated because economic growth decelerated and because the World Bank and the IMF continued to withhold disbursements as long as Panama failed to fulfill its obligations. By the end of the year, the liquidity of the National Bank was once again precarious.

The opposition's strategy was to close the circle around the PDF in hopes of spurring an internal coup to dethrone Noriega. If a coup were to ensue, it would be through the combined force of street protests, the fiscal and economic crisis, international accusations against Noriega for drug trafficking, and pressure from the U.S. government and the rest of Latin America to isolate Noriega's government. I worked with Gabriel Lewis, a Panamanian businessman and a former ambassador to the United States during the canal treaty discussions. He had many contacts in Washington and was directing the Civic Crusade's strategy there. During this period, the U.S. Senate approved a series of resolutions favoring democracy in Panama and imposing sanctions against the military regime.

The Civic Crusade alone was not strong enough to initiate changes in the face of the PDF's resistance. The U.S. government had to intensify pressure on Noriega while warning him through various emissaries. Eventually, the United States charged Noriega in Florida with crimes of money laundering and drug trafficking. The State Department offered Delvalle U.S. support if he were to remove Noriega. Delvalle tried to do so in February 1988 but instead was himself removed from office by the Legislative Assembly.

The United States continued to recognize Delvalle as president. However, Delvalle did not sit well with either the Crusade or most Panamanians because he was considered an accomplice to the military's abuses. On Delvalle's order, Panama's funds in the United States were frozen. This caused a run on Panama's international banking center; banks had to shut down for two months, freezing deposits and causing a crash in the money supply and the liquidity of the economy. Protests, street violence, and a general business lockout ensued. A coup originating from within the PDF was attempted but failed; it did not receive U.S. backing. Noriega recovered and painted himself as the victim of U.S. aggression rather than of internal pressure from Panamanians. With the crash of the economy's liquidity and the two-week-long business lockout, the economic costs of the struggle to the Civic Crusade and the opposition rapidly mounted. The Latin American nations were dismayed by what they saw happening. Their governments supported Panama's democratization effort, to varying degrees, but they were also suspicious of U.S. intervention in Panama's internal affairs.

When domestic negotiations failed to displace Noriega, the U.S. State Department carried out direct and secret negotiations with Noriega to obtain his honorable retirement. A preliminary agreement, reached in May 1988, fell through at a critical moment; the United States suspended negotiations. From there on, the United States escalated its economic sanctions against the regime. The Panamanian economy continued to pay the price of the confrontation. In 1988, there was a 20 percent drop in GDP and an abrupt increase in unemployment. Public demonstrations petered out because of the increasing costs and the terror that Noriega instilled in the people. Nevertheless, the latent and quiet opposition grew all the while.

In U.S. public opinion, "Noriega" became synonymous with "drug trafficker." As the U.S. presidential elections drew near, both U.S. parties asked Noriega to leave Panama. Moreover, the January 1990 date was nearing when canal administration would be turned over to a Panamanian who would be designated by Noriega, should he still be in power. Because the United States did not want to see that happen, it was only a question of time before there was another confrontation between Noriega and the United States.

Throughout the remaining months of 1988, the Panamanian government launched a survival operation. Foreign debt service had been suspended since the beginning of the year to allow the public sector to continue functioning, albeit precariously. The Civic Crusade and the large opposition continued fighting but with greater caution, for they had been severely hit from all sides. Negotiation between the Civic Crusade and Noriega went nowhere: one side demanded that Noriega leave while the military demanded he stay.

The 1989 Elections

At the end of 1988, preparations for the presidential election began. Over the previous two years, Noriega had successfully decapitated (figuratively speaking) the leadership of two parties, the Liberal Party and the Labor Party (Pala), and had achieved a change of leadership in the Panamanista Party. Arnulfo Arias died in mid-1988; at his funeral, there was an enormous antiregime protest of over 250,000 citizens.

Noriega and his government called for elections thinking that the opposition would not participate. The government prepared a fake opposition, with Noriega allies in the leadership of the Panamanista Party. But the opposition accepted Noriega's electoral challenge and united in a coalition to defeat his candidate; the opposition slate of candidates was headed by an Arnulfista, a Christian Democrat, and a Molirena candidate. The political campaign practically became a referendum on Noriega and the military government. The United States provided the opposition candidates with financial support. Noriega's candidate, Carlos Duque, concentrated on the unjust U.S. aggression against Panama. The ADO-civilian opposition and their candidates, Guillermo Endara, Ricardo Arias Calderón, and Guillermo Ford, put forth the popular demands for liberty, democracy, justice, and an end to the dictatorship.

The opposition won the elections hands down as predicted in polls taken during the campaign; there was no room for vote fraud to change the results. The elections were supervised by large observer groups, among them one headed by former U.S. President Jimmy Carter. Noriega and his group then voided the elections because of the "imprecision of the results and foreign influences." The victorious candidates protested and were violently attacked in the streets. The picture of a bloodied Ford, candidate for the second vice presidency, was televised around the world.

The case was brought before the General Assembly of the Organization of American States (OAS). Did the OAS have the right to intervene in Panama's internal affairs to prevent electoral fraud? Led by the United States, Costa Rica, and Venezuela, members approved a resolution holding Noriega responsible for the events; a delegation was appointed to consult with the Panama government and opposition with the objective of finding a mutually acceptable compromise. Two months of talks in Panama brought no results. The opposition defined the argument as "popular sovereignty expressed at the polls," whereas the government focused on "preserving the sovereignty of the state from foreign interventions." The OAS mission tried to bring the parties together but was unable to do so. The final OAS resolution supported democratization in Panama but somewhat diluted the condemnation of Noriega's regime and did not impose sanctions.

On September 1, 1989, the day that would have marked the end of my presidential term, Noriega and his government appointed, under questionable constitutional proceedings, a provisional government under the then Controller of the Republic, Francisco Rodríguez. He was made responsible for negotiating a democratic solution to the problem in six months. The opposition was unwavering in asserting that they had won the elections and should be governing. They made the Catholic Church the depository for the voting records that they were able to rescue.

Noriega and the PDF intensified their spying on and persecution of the opposition, though without murder, which made them more effective. Noriega prepared the so-called dignity battalions made up of public employees and street people paid by the PDF. They were made to appear harmless, as if organized purely as an act of psychological warfare. In reality, they were armed and trained to act in case of U.S. military intervention. Noriega consistently tried to make U.S. oppression of a sovereign Panama the central issue. A psychological war ensued between the PDF and the U.S. Southern Command, which was stationed in its barracks to protect the canal. All contact between these two armies had been suspended, although according to the canal treaty, contact should have been respectful, frequent, and cordial.

During 1988–89, many international banks and foreign companies shut down their operations in Panama. A large number of foreigners, among them 15,000 U.S. citizens—the families of soldiers and civilians who administered and defended the canal—left Panama, emptying apartments and houses. Tourism declined drastically. The business community suspended all private investment; public investment was reduced to a minimum.

The sudden decline in fiscal income profoundly affected health and education services. Medical attention in rural hospitals conjured up a Dantean picture. Maintenance of roads and public buildings was reduced, causing profound deterioration of equipment and the country's physical assets. The economy continued to weaken and unemployment increased.

On October 3, 1989, a second military coup was attempted. Again, Noriega emerged unscathed. The perpetrators of the attempt were assassinated without trial or indictment. Noriega intensified his harassment of and spying on the opposition. The adversities Panamanians faced became more and more insufferable. U.S. public opinion the previous year had favored removing Noriega from Panama for drug trafficking; now there was criticism of the lack of response from U.S. President George Bush's government to the coup leaders' request for support from the U.S. Southern Command. The psychological warfare between the PDF and the Southern Command became increasingly risky as the number of minor incidents between the two escalated.

In December, in yet another unconstitutional maneuver, Noriega assumed full control of Panama, naming himself the head of state before a National Assembly of Representatives he had appointed. Curiously, they declared themselves in a "state of war" with the United States. That night, one U.S. soldier was killed, and two were injured. President Bush's administration, which had prepared carefully for military intervention, decided to move that weekend.

On December 20, 1989, the United States intervened militarily in Panama and destroyed the PDF. Noriega sought asylum at the Vatican Embassy but finally turned himself over to the U.S. Army. The United States installed in office Endara, Arias Calderón, and Ford, who had all been elected in the May 7 suspended elections. Despite the direct intervention of a foreign power on

Panamanian soil, U.S. actions were greeted with approval and relief by a majority of Panamanians. Noriega's dictatorship had become so insufferable that Panamanians wanted relief at any cost.

General Noriega's power in Panama was brought to an end. His boundless ambition and egocentricity had led him to forgo all opportunities for an honorable exit for himself and the PDF. The army had used their political power for their own ever more corrupt purposes. They had promoted the myth that they were continuing the nationalist-populist struggle and had created a clientele of vested interests that fed off the regime in ways that were increasingly damaging to Panama's integrity, development, and modernization. Noriega had an incredible ability to manipulate power and a strategic single-mindedness and amorality rarely seen in a government leader; in his ambition for power and money, Noriega abused Panamanian nationalism, destroyed the PDF, undermined Torrijos's legacy of social development, and corrupted national values to such an extent that it will require some time to restore them. The country lost four years in its quest to return to integrated development and to continue progress on a democratic transition begun in 1984 and aborted in 1985.

The PDF and Noriega were too powerful for the domestic opposition to confront and too intransigent to negotiate with to achieve a peaceful political transition to democracy. Thus an armed foreign intervention, though unfortunate, was necessary to prevent the country from sinking into political and institutional darkness.

A NEW DEMOCRATIC GOVERNMENT AND ECONOMIC TRANSITION (1990–1991)

The new democratic government began with high expectations. Its leaders wanted to set the course for freedom and progress, but they faced some serious institutional and economic limitations. In their favor, they enjoyed the enthusiastic support of the majority of the population. The Panamanian business community wanted to work and produce after three years of increasing uncertainty and arbitrariness. Panama could benefit from reinstituted freedoms and law. The administration had the backing of the U.S. government, which wanted to promote the success of the new democratic administration in the aftermath of military intervention.

To the detriment of the new administration as it entered office, the economy was in decline. The GDP had fallen 22 percent during the previous two years, the unemployment rate was at 25 percent in the metropolitan area, the fiscal deficit and foreign debt were enormous, and there was a freeze on bank deposits. Stores had been looted during the first three days of the U.S. military intervention. The police were demoralized, the physical infrastructure and social service system had deteriorated, and democratic institutions were feeble. Reports of drug trafficking and money laundering had tarnished Panama's image internationally; Latin America questioned the legitimacy of the new democratic government.

Nevertheless, several fundamental factors favored economic recovery—factors with deep roots in Panamanian history. The national constitution remained consistent with the country's economic base. Without a central bank, the monetary system is based on fixed parity of the balboa and the dollar. Panama's laws governing corporations are favorable to international business. Panama can also serve as a tax haven for international businesses. It has a profitable service economy based around the isthmus, which also extends its benefits to other related businesses. Its urban population is trained to take advantage of these economic activities. These factors were not altered even by the most arbitrary actions of Noriega and the military.

There were, however, some serious and fundamental limitations. Regulations and subsidies make the economy inflexible. They work in favor of certain economic groups only and distort the labor market. They impair the efficient allocation of investments, favor import substitution, and discriminate against exports. The policies have resulted in public expenditures and a bureaucracy far larger than advisable if one is to create effective economic growth and employment.

The new government, made up of a coalition of four ADO parties, represented liberal, Panamanian, and Christian Democratic strains. They divided the responsibilities of public administration among them. The vice presidents were given leadership roles in the fields of national security and the economy. The government's program became the product of interparty negotiations to identify the nation's goals, the means to achieve them, and the role of each of the coalition parties.

Landmark steps were taken to achieve democracy in Panama. There was a new and independent Supreme Court, responsible for reorganizing the judicial system. The PDF was transformed into a demilitarized public police force under civilian control; more than 3,000 military personnel and officers were retired. The Legislative Assembly was reorganized. Those who had legitimately won the elections in May 1989 took their seats; new elections took place in districts where the results had been inconclusive. New municipal governments were established throughout the country, safeguarding the functions of the local representatives in counties and in the municipalities.

Seven political parties survived the May 1989 elections. Four of them were involved in the new government, while three others were either in the opposition or independent. Torrijos's PRD won a significant minority of seats in the legislature, and successfully made its presence felt. The government began with an overwhelming majority in the Legislative Assembly. The Civic Crusade did not transform itself into a political party, but it continued to contribute to the government, demanding fulfillment of the objectives that had been the reason for its founding. Nevertheless, the great majority of trade associations (which had previously united in the crusade to overthrow the military dictatorship) returned to their normal tasks.

Freedom of the press was fully restored; one of the largest newspapers, commandeered by the military-controlled government, was returned to its rightful owners. Through the media, an enormous amount of energy, repressed for so long under military rule, broke to the surface and dispersed in all directions. Demands mounted that former officials of Noriega's government who had committed specific crimes be brought to justice. Also, there was pressure to discredit those who had participated in the military-controlled governments, to achieve instant improvements in various aspects of national life, to condemn indiscriminately everything done during the years of civil-military administrations, and to bring back the traditional values—virtues and vices—of the democratic governments prior to 1968.

The new government officials were more representative of upper- and middle-class educated citizens than of the populist groups nurtured by Torrijos and the military. Initially, the government had significant accomplishments in administrative, fiscal, and monetary areas. It unfroze bank deposits without sparking negative consequences for the international banking center; in fact, the center began to grow again. The 1990–91 budgets were balanced, with substantial increases in revenues along with effective controls over expenditures. Smuggling and corruption decreased; the efficiency of many public services improved. There was timely legislation to increase the efficiency of the judicial system, administrative services, and certain economic activities, such as efforts to create industrial export parks.

The economy recovered with 5 percent growth, based on renewed confidence in the private sector in response to the reintroduction of freedoms and the rule of law. Another contributing factor was the renewed spending by U.S. citizens in Panama on apartment rentals, tourism, and sales to military installations and to the canal administration, all of which had been standard sources of Panamanian income. In 1991, the economy gained momentum; it posted growth of 9 percent, spearheaded by a construction boom and by growth in some traditional services. Yet it would take all of 1992 to recover the level of production of December 1987.

On the other hand, the urban and rural popular majorities have not yet witnessed significant improvement in their situation. Unemployment dropped slowly; it was still at 14 percent in 1995. Social services to the poor have not yet returned to 1986 levels. Street crime rose because of unemployment and the decreased efficiency of a police force that had not been fully rebuilt. There were signs of unrest throughout the country.

Two widely shared goals were the democratization of the country and the improved functioning of a social market economy. The long-delayed government programs for economic structural adjustment and improved financial management were in place in 1991, and these were followed by agreements with the IMF and the World Bank that opened the door for new loans and the renegotiation of the external debt. Nevertheless, subsequent implementation during 1992 was sluggish and haphazard. Broad sectors of the population began to question the government's effectiveness in leading the country's recovery and in providing jobs and street safety. They worried over increasing old-style "politicization" of government actions.

No government could avoid a weakening of its public support when faced with such high expectations and such serious limitations as confronted the government that took power in Panama in 1990. The majority of Panamanians pointed to errors of style and substance in the new government that weakened its capacity to act. In April 1991, the governing coalition broke up, the departure of the Christian Democrats leaving it without a parliamentary majority. Although the government unquestionably made advances in many sectors, it still lacked a well-defined agenda to mobilize citizens so as to direct their energies toward achieving democratization and a sustained economic recovery.

During the years of political upheaval, both the military government and the successor civilian government used organized social groups (workers, transport unions, the business community, and professionals) to defend their claim to power. Neither believed that it had the political strength to impose on the population the initial costs of economic adjustment in exchange for potential benefits for everyone that would have resulted from sustained growth in the medium term. Those in the government in the early 1990s knew in 1985 that the adjustments had to be made, but earlier they had opposed such adjustments in order to break the power of the military. In turn, the military was weakened politically and the government fell into a fiscal crisis. Military leaders chose not to demand the sacrifices required to rekindle the economy and to return to democracy. In the early 1990s, the democratic government found itself in the same political difficulties with organized trade associations, which did not understand or want to pay the initial cost of adjustment. In the meantime, the country had paid a high price for the political and economic transition.

Most Panamanians supported democracy and the general direction the government took in the 1990s. However, they questioned its slowness, ineffectiveness, and lack of decision-making ability. In view of the long-term challenges of the 1990s, various groups and political parties questioned whether the government had the energy and capacity to organize and rally public opinion in order to foster the country's economic, social, and institutional development. Panama's embryonic democracy will grow stronger to the degree that this democratic questioning prompts the government to improve its performance and focus public attention on the essential issues facing the country. The experiment will grow weaker to the degree that it contributes to more groups seeking more radical solutions.

Panama's long-term goals can be outlined as follows:

1. *Political goals.* To promote the effective functioning of democratic institutions to educate public opinion, facilitate negotiations, and foster compromise. To make timely decisions while maintaining civility and public freedoms.

2. *Economic and administrative goals.* To implement short-term structural adjustment programs and orient the economy toward increasing and diversifying exports. To take timely advantage of the canal and its administration (which is being turned over to Panama), modernize the canal, maintain the effectiveness of the transisthmian pipeline, make better use of the Canal Zone areas turned over to Panama in the late 1970s, and prepare for the negative economic effects when the United States withdraws its military bases by the year 2000.

3. *Social goals.* To promote economic growth that generates enough jobs and provides for basic human needs and infrastructure investments, incorporating the poor and marginal population into national development efforts and benefits.

Panama's transition to a democracy with a more flexible and dynamic economy is at a decisive stage. A democratic spirit of coexistence, negotiation, and accommodation of dissimilar interests should pilot the nation toward its modernization objectives. Nevertheless, it would be premature to predict the outcome.

THE OUTLOOK FOR PANAMA AS THE YEAR 2000 APPROACHES

Panama finds itself in an especially important decade in its history, poised to gain increasing control over the Panama Canal. The country's long, historic struggle to consolidate itself as a nation-state will finally bear fruit. Its partner in governing the canal, the United States, is preparing to turn over to Panama the entire canal infrastructure—its administration, operation, maintenance, and defense. Partly for that reason, the United States intervened militarily in Panamanian affairs to eliminate General Noriega's regime and his military command who were blocking the transition to democracy and a modern economy. The intervention, unfortunate in certain ways, had the support of the majority of Panamanians and of the U.S. population.

The canal transition opens transcendental opportunities for development. If Panama fails to modernize and remain competitive, it can lose its potential for development. Sixty percent of the population lives in Panama's metropolitan international transit area where 80 percent of the country's economic activity occurs; 75 percent of all economic activity is made up of services. Given the small domestic market, exports play a key role in economic growth. Panama already exports 37 percent of its GDP, which gives it a higher degree of prosperity than many of its neighbors. Of total exports, almost 70 percent come from international transport services and related commerce.

The canal, the transisthmian oil pipeline, the international airport, and the maritime ports lend Panama's geographic position its commercial value. The related commercial services and activities (the Colón Free Trade Zone, the international banking center, international financing, insurance, and communications) broaden the international economy of the country. A symbiotic relationship exists among all of these economic activities. If the canal, the ports, and the airport remain competitive, the development of the commercial free zone, tourism, the banking center, and the budding industrial export parks will benefit. If these develop, they will in turn increase the transit volume through Panama.

A well-planned and unified strategic vision, based on current studies and information, is needed to develop and modernize these resources optimally. Such a vision would guide the proper policy making to encourage private, free, and flexible transit-related economic activity to reach its fullest potential. For such policies to be implemented satisfactorily, the various government agencies must coordinate their efforts—for example, the airport and port authorities must work together with people in charge of tourism, the commercial free zone, the banking center, and the communications industry.

When the United States withdraws from the canal's management, it will leave the large canal infrastructure. It will fall to Panama to incorporate this infrastructure in an orderly fashion into its plans for economic, urban, and social development. This involves careful planning, factoring the new canal responsibilities into a strategic vision in order to reduce transition costs and broaden opportunities for national development. Panama's situation is similar to that of Singapore in the 1960s when the British withdrew from their military bases. Some of that country's successful experiences would be useful to Panama.

These opportunities present a far-reaching challenge to Panamanians and their institutions. Unfortunately, precious time was lost during the critical decade of the 1980s because there was not sufficient consensus about the transition toward democratic institutions and an open, flexible, and competitive economy. As a result, Panama entered the 1990s with weak institutions and a lack of preparedness. It will need to use its best people in order to advance development and strengthen institutions.

There is sufficient complementarity to make coherent various policies, such as democracy based on broad freedoms, an open and flexible economy built mainly around the transit economy and the canal, economic development based on private activity, and social development oriented toward preparing the Panamanian people to participate in the international opportunities open to the country. However, Panama's institutions must be strengthened, and structures based on favoritism and concessions to pressure groups must be modified because they reduce the country's capacity both to prosper on a more efficient and productive basis and to compete internationally. Time will reveal whether democracy will help Panama achieve the optimal and practical objectives supported by the groups that stand to benefit the most from the transition to a more modern and globally integrated Panama, and whether such groups will successfully neutralize or absorb other groups whose current benefits impose high costs for the rest of the nation and impede its fullest potential for growth.

NOTES

1. The Christian Democratic Party published a book concluding that they had won by 2,300 votes. No evidence was presented to support this claim.

2. Dr. Marc Lindenberg and colleagues from the Instituto Centroamericano de Administración de Empresas (Central American Management Institute [INCAE]), located in Costa Rica.

THREE

REVOLUTION AND DEMOCRATIC TRANSITION IN NICARAGUA

JAIME WHEELOCK ROMÁN

The 1980s proved to be a decisive decade for Central America, a decade of transition. The Sandinista revolution in Nicaragua, as well as armed uprisings and popular struggles witnessed elsewhere in the region, were reactions of a populace seeking greater freedom and prosperity and protesting years of political oppression and economic marginalization. The decade of the 1980s proffers numerous lessons to those currently responsible for shaping the region's future—lessons they should study and apply.[1]

The forces that gave rise to the changes of the 1980s had been building for decades. Most Central American nations suffered an acute, structural weakness: a majority of the population suffered economic and political repression at the hands of a powerful minority. This situation reached a critical point in the 1970s and 1980s, however, when government power began to erode and, eventually, to collapse, sending a wave of change across Central America. Although El Salvador and Guatemala also experienced radical challenges to their traditional political structures, only Nicaragua broke with its past in 1979. Profound transformations of economic structures accompanied the political changes in Nicaragua. Other countries saw only limited liberalization, stopping short of fundamental change.

Nevertheless, every country was suffering the legacy of decades-long deterioration in terms of trade along with typically predatory foreign investment. The region was also wracked by recurring economic crises, the result of factors internal and external to the region, leaving Central America beset by burgeoning debt, inflation, economic downturns, and impoverishment. Although there has been evidence of some progress in liberalization and democratization in recent years, there still remain significant economic hurdles to overcome.

Of the many changes witnessed in Central America during the 1980s, those in Nicaragua are perhaps the most dramatic. In the relatively brief period of ten years various events took place. The Somoza dictatorship was overthrown, and Nicaragua's economic base and property rights were transformed. There was reform of the state's structure and function; political institutions grew around powerful social and labor organizations. The government vigorously combatted illiteracy and health problems. General elections were held in 1984. In 1987, a new constitution instituted political pluralism, a mixed economy, and nonalignment. And a major conflict broke out across the country when domestic forces hostile to the revolution and supported by the United States took up arms against the government. That period ended in 1990 when the Sandinista National Liberation Front (FSLN) lost the national elections, and the war came to a close. Nevertheless, the types of historic events and changes that usually occur over long periods played themselves out in Nicaragua in just ten years, deeply transforming Nicaraguan society.

The changes of the 1980s have left Nicaragua with much more room for real democratization. There is a more democratic distribution of property, and the country has stronger social organizations and political parties, each with its own agenda. There are now a constitutional body, laws, and institutions protecting pluralism and the independence of state powers, and there is respect for individual freedoms, human and civil rights, and freedom of the press. And with the end of the war and the transformation of the armed forces—now reduced in size, disassociated from politics, and more professional—political power has been, in effect, more equitably distributed throughout Nicaragua. There exists now, as probably at no other time in the nation's history, the opportunity to move forward, combining achievements made in social justice with newly evolved political freedoms.

The type of balanced transition that needs to be made poses numerous risks, however. To sustain democratic stability, the obstacles to be overcome are a persistent economic crisis, deep polarization of certain groups in society, and insufficient international cooperation aimed at helping Nicaragua recover its strength following the devastation and impoverishment wrought by the contra war and various other crises.

BACKGROUND

The history of Nicaragua's development exhibits characteristics common to many Central American countries. First, Nicaragua was late to enter the world market as an exporter of raw materials, such as coffee, wood, bananas, and minerals. It has essentially a primary economy. Second, it preserved the pattern of exploitation typical of the Spanish colonies, namely, lordly masters and large estates, marked by the exploitation of labor through various bonds of servitude. Third, too many of the most productive sectors of the economy were controlled by foreign enclaves, which wielded considerable influence over the economy, the government, and political events; these sectors included the extraction and exploitation of natural resources such as wood, minerals, and rubber. Finally, due to cyclical fluctuations in prices of raw materials on the world market, Nicaragua experienced short periods of accelerated growth followed by periods of prolonged stagnation. The nation's economy was dependent and cyclical, based on wealth extraction. Widespread poverty, marginalization of some of the populace, illiteracy, and unemployment coexisted with small pockets of modernization.

Situated in the middle of the Central American isthmus, close to the Panama Canal, Nicaraguan territory was always strategic to the colonial powers in their plans for expansion and geopolitical control. In the twentieth century, Nicaragua suffered two prolonged armed occupations by the United States, the second of which gave rise and continuity both to the National Guard and to the Somoza dictatorship.

In 1934, as authoritarian regimes solidified elsewhere in Latin America, a military and dynastic dictatorship also took power in Nicaragua. The military dictatorship was the political model of choice of the United States and dominant local groups, for it met their strategic interests; and local groups were unable to establish the alternative—civilian, republican government—in societies wracked by violence and economic and social inequality.

However, during the 1950s, the flaws in the classic agro-export economic model and its supporting political structure, the military dictatorship, became clear. Although in some instances political, economic, and social reforms emerged, particularly in Guatemala, Honduras, and Costa Rica, these ended in frustration or reversal; in Nicaragua, the Somoza dictatorship remained unchanged. At the end of the 1950s, however, two events altered the dynamics of Nicaraguan society: the Cuban revolution and the Central American Common Market (CACM).

In the face of the Cuban revolution, movement toward regional economic integration to modify the traditional (now exhausted) agro-export economic model and toward agrarian reform, modernization, and reformist political changes looked more like superficial alternatives than real change. The sectors rooted in the estate system, as well as people in the military with control over government, erected barriers even against demands for modest change.

Although after 1950 there had been comparatively high and stable economic growth in Nicaragua and in Central America in general, social inequality and poverty were increasing. Forty percent of the income was concentrated in the hands of just 5 percent of the population. The country's main resource, land, was controlled by 1,200 families. The Somozas alone owned 20 percent of the land. Meanwhile, 56 percent of the population was illiterate, the infant mortality rate was 120 per thousand live births (in 1976), and basic utilities, such as water and electricity, barely reached 26 percent of the population. The unemployment rate was over 35 percent.

Insurrectional activity increased in at least three countries of the region, particularly in Nicaragua in the 1970s. This activity coincided with weakening of the CACM, breakdown of the regional economic integration model, and growing economic crisis. Having begun with isolated guerrilla encampments, armed rebels moved into areas where people were the most dissatisfied. They offered the type of organization and leadership that had been lacking and represented a new alternative to traditional parties. These armed rebels would eventually overthrow the military dictatorships and drastically change the economy and society.

In the mid-1970s, the Somoza dictatorship began to deteriorate rapidly. The repression, social injustice, and abuses had grown intolerable, causing open dissension among most of the nation's impoverished population. There was also opposition from the business community, provoked by the monopolistic and illegal incursions of the Somoza family into industry, finance, and real estate sectors.

Under President Jimmy Carter's administration, U.S. policy promoting human rights was a major factor in weakening, delegitimizing, and isolating the Somoza dictatorship, whose main backer before Carter had been the United States. With the heightening of the armed struggle, the opposition's organizing around and announcing a platform of national unity, and the expansion of the popular struggle, the Somoza dictatorship was finally defeated after nearly forty-five years in power.

THE DECADE OF THE SANDINISTA REVOLUTION

Two factors are largely responsible for the political and economic evolution of Central America—and Nicaragua in particular—during the 1980s: the Sandinista revolution and U.S. foreign policy. The Somoza regime disintegrated in the face of emerging, discontented sectors protesting unmet political demands, an economic system skewed in favor of a wealthy few and excluding the majority (workers, peasants, youth, and professionals), growth of labor and other social movements, and the regime's own illegitimacy. The Nicaraguan people began to unite to overthrow the Somoza regime.

From the outset, the Carter administration promoted not the violent over-throw of the Somoza regime but rather a relaxation of authoritarian control through reinstating freedom of the press, free elections, and other democratic rights. Successful pressure on the Somozas from the United States made it possible for some members of the traditional political and economic opposi-tion to reactivate a search for options to replace the regime peacefully. Such were the efforts of the conservative coalition composed of the Democratic Liberation Union (UDEL; Unión Democrática de Liberación) and the Broad Opposition Front (FAO; Frente Amplio Opositor) that had tried to replace the dictatorship since the early seventies.

Yet, while the traditional opposition formed the FAO, demands for change through armed revolution continued to grow. The armed struggle was gaining much support and legitimacy. Offensives launched periodically by the FSLN weakened the National Guard. Meanwhile, the democratic changes the FSLN offered were winning it support and legitimacy from broad sectors. FSLN actions began to have the effect of isolating the dicta-torship and neutralizing the FAO alternative.

By the end of 1978, most social organizations and several leftist and cen-trist political parties and movements supported the armed struggle, at the forefront of which stood the FSLN. Early in 1979, faced with the advancing armed struggle, attempts were made to negotiate a transfer-of-power arrange-ment that would amount to Somocismo without Somoza. That option, backed by the FAO and the United States, failed. The conservative coalition weakened, and several other parties and movements then joined the insurrec-tion; the National Patriotic Front (FPN) was formed. In March, the three fac-tions of the FSLN were united, and a final offensive was launched. The non-revolutionary reformist options were still backed only by local financial capital, a small group of traditional politicians, and elements within the Roman Catholic hierarchy.

In June 1979, after the United States unsuccessfully pressured General Anastasio Somoza Debayle to resign and after international consensus to in-tervene militarily—with Organization of American States (OAS) support—dissolved, the United States was forced to compromise. This meant pre-serving a purged National Guard and forming a coalition government under conservative control. However, the U.S. search for replacements for the So-mozas was erratic and too late. The insurrection had become the most viable option for change; there were no true political parties to serve as alternatives; the business sector was weak and lacked cohesion; and until the bitter end the Somozas were reluctant to relinquish power.

The popular struggle coalesced in the form of armed guerrilla action in the countryside, uprisings in the cities, and a general strike. The struggle was further bolstered by the FSLN's announcement of a "political platform of national unity." This announcement strengthened the international legitimacy of the struggle and contributed to the gathering of forces against General Somoza. On July 17, 1979, Somoza left the country, the National Guard fell apart, and, two days later, the new Government Junta for National Reconstruction assumed power.

Cuba, Costa Rica, and Panama played important roles in supporting the insurrection. In addition, Venezuela advocated the violent removal of Somoza, followed by the formation of a centrist government. Mexico encouraged the international isolation of the Somoza government.

The 1979 Sandinista Revolutionary Government

Profound changes took place after July 1979. Agrarian reform was initiated. All the goods usurped by the Somoza family, high-ranking military officials, and landowners linked to the regime were expropriated. Mines and natural resources were nationalized. Approximately 40 percent of the industrial and wholesale trade sectors formerly monopolized by the oligarchy came under state control. The government's National Reconstruction Plan began its work with financial support from the international community.

On an institutional level, the government was reformed to promote socioeconomic change and a new social support base for the revolution. The government took control of the most important social and economic management entities; banks and foreign trade were nationalized and fiscal reform enacted. New military institutions were established to carry out national defense and preserve the new revolutionary order.

Important social changes took place. A national literacy campaign was launched and the new government offered free education through the college level. The health care system was extended to guarantee free and universal medical attention to all citizens; one of its key features was a national program of preventive medicine that involved direct popular participation. Popular housing projects were begun in different parts of the country, with priority given to rural workers. Electric energy, potable water, and new roads reached communities in the interior for the first time.

In the political arena, one of the government's first actions was to proclaim a Statute of Rights and Guarantees. It declared freedom of political association without discrimination for the first time in Nicaragua. Large labor and other social organizations were formed. The total of 160 established unions in 1979 grew to over 2,000 in only a few months. Peasants, women, workers, youth, professionals, and others formed their own organizations at the national and local levels, paving the way for grassroots democratization.

These transformations generally resulted in economic change benefiting the marginalized sectors of society. Also, these changes affirmed national independence and sovereignty. Broad channels for popular participation were opened, and new democratic institutions were created to replace the old structures of the Somoza regime.

The Gains of the Mass Movement

During 1979–84, mass popular movements developed vigorously, thus shaping a revolutionary dynamic. This was the period of greatest legitimacy for Sandinismo, when extraparliamentary fora prevailed, enabling the government to turn into policy the popular demands to deepen reforms. These informal fora also facilitated government dialogues with the Superior Private Enterprise Council (COSEP), political parties, and others. The government acted through decrees and other administrative acts.

For example, when the Nicaraguan Institute of Agrarian Reform was founded in August 1979, hundreds of thousands of acres were occupied spontaneously by local peasant movements, which began to organize with their own styles of management such as "agricultural blocks," "agrarian reform councils," "peasant self-sufficiency units," and "Sandinista agrarian brigades." There was an agrarian movement in every part of the republic. Even the indigenous communities invoked their ancient rights to the lands ceded by the Spanish Crown.

During this period, legislation was formulated to help advance the revolution. A national consensus crystallized around Sandinismo. While the FSLN accumulated more and more support, less attention was given to institutions and rules. Although directed from above, the changes in this period unleashed labor, peasant, and other social movements of great autonomy, participation, and authority.

Nicaragua began a transition toward a mixed economy, seeking to improve the distribution of gains from economic growth. However, the socioeconomic reality of the time was that individual peasant producers, a large class of craftsmen, and numerous small businesses dominated the economy, making it impossible to move swiftly toward collective forms of production. Also, efforts to give priority to the least-favored sectors of society were soon blocked by the war. Ultimately these efforts were thwarted, because a mixed economy was so foreign to the current socioeconomic reality.

Nevertheless, from the beginning the traditional Nicaraguan political sectors had no support. Social and economic forces tainted by the Somozas lost their moral and political strength, were removed from power, and were excluded from important decisions. The more modernized, liberal middle-class sectors (the National Patriotic Front) shared in and endorsed the changes, though from an ancillary position.

The FSLN exercised unopposed hegemony; it made the major decisions for change. This did not seem to jibe, however, with the FSLN's declared desire to govern based on broad and effective citizen participation. But the FSLN's strength lay primarily in the fact that it had been the architect of the overthrow of Somoza. It had accumulated, if not a consensus, at least the support of the most numerous and best organized of the popular sectors. And, of course, the FSLN represented, in a more radical sense, the mission to bring the significant change Nicaragua demanded. The Sandinistas' right to assume a high degree of control over the state came from the overwhelming political legitimacy acquired by Sandinismo, not only in massive support from its social base but also from support offered early on by other actors, such as the church, the business community, the middle sectors, and professionals.

Initial opposition to democratic change was not significant, and Sandinismo governed without major obstacles. Perhaps for this reason, not much emphasis was given to legal and normative aspects of governance during this period. In fact, while supported by a strong and authoritative mandate, Sandinismo showed traces of intolerance in its commitment to transformation. Conflicts erupted, for example, with the church and the press. Political allies were not treated well; opposition parties and Somoza-era politicians were treated with contempt. Sandinismo dealt inconsistently with the business community. On the one hand, it was compelled to break up property concentration within certain economic groups; on the other hand, it encouraged the business community to incorporate itself in the plans for reconstruction and economic rehabilitation.

Although somewhat ambiguous, the move toward democratization was part of the same revolutionary project geared toward socioeconomic transformation. At the beginning of the period of revolutionary change, some Sandinista leaders assumed that the democratization of Nicaraguan politics would serve as a tactic to reduce support for, and thereby to prevent, U.S. aggression against the Sandinista government. Later, in 1984, democratization in the political arena would become a substantial part of the Sandinista project, and ultimately it would be an essential component of the revolution.

The delays in setting up the rule of law were, in one way or another, related to the disproportionate growth of the state and its institutional incoherence. These factors were not considered very important at first and were dealt with only when the necessity of confronting the war required it. The government was Sandinismo's main instrument for achieving its objectives, and the government tended to grow as the responsibilities of the FSLN multiplied.

Among the changes promoted after 1979, at least three gave rise to substantial contradictions or problems from early on. First, Sandinista foreign policy was inclined to seek alliances with the Soviet Union and Cuba, enemies of the United States. Second, solidarity with insurgent movements in Central America, particularly in El Salvador, struggling to overcome centuries of oligarchic domination, was a defined commitment of the Nicaraguan revolution. Finally, transformations in property and commerce met resistance not only from the sectors linked to large landholders but also from conservative members of the rural class of smallholders and from small business owners.

In 1981, U.S. President Ronald Reagan's ultraconservative administration began promoting and financing economic, political, diplomatic, and armed aggression against the Sandinista government. Using the arguments that Nicaragua endangered U.S. national security because of its links to the USSR and Cuba, that it threatened the stability of its neighbors by supporting insurgent movements, and that it was a dictatorship, the Reagan administration isolated Nicaragua. The United States sought to legitimize this aggression and worked to gain the support of other Central American states for this policy. By 1983, Reagan had obtained use of territories in Honduras, Costa Rica, and El Salvador as launching pads for counterrevolutionary and U.S. Central Intelligence Agency (CIA) military operations. These U.S. actions precipitated a hardening of the Nicaraguan political process, including new limitations on the opposition's political freedoms.

CIA plans to build an "internal front" drove the Sandinista government to place controls on the newspaper La Prensa, which was allowing itself to be used as a vehicle for destabilizing propaganda. It became necessary to decree a state of emergency and to restrict activities and demonstrations organized by the right-wing political parties aimed at weakening and isolating the government. Political and business leaders from COSEP were detained on several occasions for their connections to the armed contras, as the members of the militarized counterrevolution came to be known.

The implementation of democratic reforms, which now ceased to have even tactical functions, was limited because of both foreign aggression and extreme internal polarization. When the dilemma arose in the FSLN National Directorate whether to continue democratic freedoms or to limit them to defend the revolution, we inclined toward the latter because at that moment all of Sandinismo's major achievements hung in the balance. The government believed that the temporary suspension of certain freedoms would help to secure global stability.

The Sandinista regime viewed U.S. policy as the main obstacle to achieving its overall plan. Once U.S. aggression began, the entire Sandinista project, including democratic reform, became subordinate to the nation's military defense. From 1982 to 1983, the military became the center of gravity for economic, domestic, and foreign policy.

Institutionalizing the Revolution in the Midst of War

From 1984 to 1987, a movement to institutionalize and legalize the revolution began, arising largely from concerns within the country itself. The five years of provisional government had passed; the broad economic, social, and political transformations that had taken place needed to be institutionalized. There had to be an end to actions taken via "de facto routes"; this de facto process had become unacceptable to many different economic groups and emerging political organizations. The decision-making framework and actions under which the Sandinistas operated were creating instability; few people knew with certainty where the FSLN was really headed. At the same time, some countries and groups in the international community opposing the Reagan administration's aggressive strategy demanded the effective institutionalization of political space for liberalization and democratization.

During this period, a number of critical events took place. The 1984 elections inaugurated a civilian presidency. A National Assembly was established which, since 1985, has been responsible for legislation. Independent electoral and judicial bodies were created. The nation's constitution was promulgated; the government enacted laws to guarantee personal rights and to decentralize public administration.

In short, the Sandinista government continued to take steps toward democratization even in the midst of war. In July 1979, at the height of its popularity and power, the FSLN, unlike other contemporary revolutions, renounced the single-party system, promoting political pluralism. In 1984, as fierce fighting spread in Nicaragua, the government kept its promise to hold elections; they took place at the end of that same year. The constitution, based on democratic principles, was proclaimed in 1987.

During these years, however, the war began to interfere with the government's political and socioeconomic policies. In fact, from the very beginning the aggression was directed at undermining and destabilizing the economy. Mining of ports, sabotage of petroleum distribution routes, destruction of productive centers and of the economic infrastructure—all were precursors of what later became a generalized war, backed by the U.S. commercial embargo and financial blockade.

In 1984–85, in part to battle the growing contra aggression, the government found it necessary to adjust economic and other policies in the war zones, including policies toward specific economic sectors. Established as policy priorities were the need to confront U.S. aggression, to correct inconsistencies in policy regarding internal alliances, and to guarantee fully and strengthen property rules. Also, the principle of a mixed economy was elevated to constitutional status.

One of the most important achievements of the government, agrarian reform, had introduced new social and productive forces. The agricultural sector helped by the agrarian reforms included agroindustrial state enterprises, cooperatives, and small producers. With 50 percent of all land, this sector reported increased production: by 1985 production had grown to 60 percent of total export production and 89 percent of the production for domestic consumption.

Nonetheless, agrarian reform also brought counterproductive political results. For example, initially, land was distributed predominantly to cooperatives or to create state farms. Peasants, however, favored a more traditional allocation of land as individual property; hence, it became politically imperative to respond to their concerns. Material and financial resources were distributed to favor the state sector. Even though peasants had received credit and technical assistance since 1979, the government did not formulate a consistent economic plan to assist them. In titles issued during the early years of the Sandinista government, restrictions were placed on the right to transfer property, generating distrust. The government expropriated land belonging to a number of relatively well-off peasants as well as land owned by several efficient producers, which led to widespread uncertainty and a subsequent loss of investments. The adoption of these economic, trade, and price policies in the countryside created tensions with the peasantry which, along with the military draft and military abuses, fed the ranks of the counterrevolution. Prices for products from the countryside increased more slowly than did prices for industrial products; rural producers were thus at a disadvantage. In 1983 and 1984, there were also shortages of essential products in the rural areas, reducing peasant consumption. These factors combined to incite uprisings in this sector.

One major problem was the government's coercive style of political and administrative management, widely resented by most rural classes. The mandate that they organize themselves politically, economically, and socially severely disrupted the peasants' traditional rural social structure, further fanning disagreement and distrust toward the revolution.

Government leaders realized that they had to take action to correct these (perhaps inevitable) errors and failures in the implementation of the revolutionary program. So, in 1984, a political and economic rectification program was developed to improve rural attitudes toward the revolution. Packaged as a general plan to confront the war in the northern zones of the country, several initiatives were begun under the rectification effort. First, emphasis on growth of the state sector of the economy, which affected large and some small and midsized private producers, gave way to a new policy of freezing state expropriations and seeking to establish credible and reliable policies toward private rural producers.

Also, the pattern of land distribution shifted from the cooperative model to one that favored requests for individual land. State price controls and grain purchasing practices—established to foil private speculators—were discontinued in the war zones. The abandonment of these policies was intended to counter the discontent they fostered among peasants, which worked to the contras' advantage. Rationing policies for basic products and the strict state-distribution channels (originally imposed to protect urban consumers) were softened. Modifications were introduced to reform the military draft, which had met massive peasant protest. Military crimes and abuses against the population were punished.

Many of the policies mentioned above had first been introduced to protect the poorest classes or to fight against the effects of aggression. And yet, these same policies had negative consequences in broad sectors of the countryside and city, with people resenting the policies as abusive interference with traditional economic activity or peasant customs. That is why the policies were changed.

Nevertheless, it was not just these domestic policies that negatively affected the revolutionary agrarian program of the FSLN. Several external and objective factors also had serious political repercussions for the Sandinista revolution. First, there was U.S. government aggression. In addition, the main war theater was the vast agrarian region in the north and east of the country where Sandinismo had weak political links and where the revolution's social and economic programs were just beginning to develop.

Further, material production began to decrease, largely because of systematic destruction of production centers and of the economic infrastructure and because of assaults and forced recruitment carried out by the counterrevolution against the cooperatives and the peasantry. Between 1983 and 1986, close to 250,000 people were displaced. Thirty thousand war victims were recorded, of whom 18,000 died. The revolution gave rise to centers of resistance and fear in rural areas. The expropriated Somocistas and the idle landowners who were affected by the agrarian reform supported U.S. aggression. Many agricultural and industrial company owners as well as merchants depleted capital, smuggled, and ultimately abandoned their companies. When the revolution responded by expropriating them and engaging in other intervention measures, the conflict was heightened.

After 1979, the revolution's agrarian program began to fulfill its promises, and the revolutionary government began to exercise hegemony in rural areas. But these gains were undermined by the war that began in the rural areas in mid-1981 and prevented the new government from completely fulfilling its goals there.

The Esquipulas Talks and Opening Civic Freedoms to End the War
The period 1987–90 was characterized by liberalization aimed at strengthening the revolution's credibility and countering the policy of foreign aggres-

sors. It was also directed at negotiating an end to the war and at normalizing relations with Central American neighbors. This period was framed by the Esquipulas agreements of the Central American presidents and the internal Sapoá agreements with the contras.

The contra and foreign aggression stymied democratization and economic progress. But, not wanting to close all channels for political expression, Sandinismo had to find alternative solutions to resolve the armed conflict. First, the government engaged in direct negotiations with the United States in Manzanillo, Mexico, and later it negotiated through the Contadora initiative. The Sandinistas' objective was to negotiate a commitment to nonaggression and to guarantee a security framework, which would allow them to continue with plans to transform Nicaragua, including full democratization. But ultimately both the Manzanillo and Contadora talks were virtually sabotaged by the U.S. administration, which was more intent on overthrowing the Sandinista government than on reaching any agreements with it.

By the end of the 1980s, after several years of war and counterinsurgency, the situation in Central America had worsened, while support for U.S. policies was declining. At this point, the Central American presidents, led by Oscar Arias of Costa Rica, began several rounds of talks at Esquipulas (Guatemala). These talks would become a key factor in opening political space and in generating accords to end civil wars; these accords, although aimed at Nicaragua, were to be implemented by all the Central American nations. It was in this sense that the Sandinista revolution was crucial to inspiring a political solution to armed conflicts. It made electoral promises, reconciliation commitments, and civil liberties and human rights commitments, granted amnesty, and made efforts to reduce the armed forces and to open up dialogues between political forces.

The international balance of power was unfavorable to the U.S. administration's aggressive policy toward Nicaragua, and thus it had a positive influence on the Nicaraguan democratization process, even in the midst of war. In addition, economic cooperation from European and socialist countries helped to avoid an economic breakdown, which could have closed political space in Nicaragua. It was equally clear that Nicaragua had sought (since 1987, and more insistently in 1989) to end the internal war which it could not sustain economically or in human cost.

The liberalization efforts that the Sandinista government promoted were evident following the Esquipulas and the Sapoá agreements. As in the previous three years, the Sandinista government resisted any inclination to clamp down politically, despite the temptation to do so because of the war. La Prensa was reopened; there was wide latitude for freedom of expression; effective steps were taken to ensure open participation of the political parties; the state of emergency was lifted; a gradual, and later general, amnesty was decreed; prisoners of war were freed.

With a new U.S. administration, which had not yet decided the course of its foreign policy toward Nicaragua, the FSLN strategy shifted to create an environment conducive to ending the aggression and advancing political solutions. It was crucial to bring the bloody and prolonged war to an end through elections. For that reason, the FSLN moved the elections forward to February 1990 to replace bullets with ballots.

To end the war by political means required other steps to foster the holding of elections. Thus a process of domestic reconciliation began to improve the climate for elections. The FSLN negotiated with business producers around the themes of economic incentives and respect for property. An effort was made to get all political parties to agree to participate in elections. The government negotiated actively in the Esquipulas regional forum while also working to improve relations with the United States. Finally, the Sandinistas agreed to international supervision of new elections to avoid any questions about the results, as the United States had raised during the 1984 elections.

THE REGION'S BALANCE OF TRANSITIONS

Beginning in the 1980s, the Central American countries entered into a process of transition from military regimes to civilian governments, though the scope and depth of these changes varied from country to country. During this period, democratic freedoms increased throughout the region and governments changed through elections. In Guatemala, El Salvador, and Honduras, civil governments were restored through elections, though severe restrictions remained on democratic practice. In Nicaragua, there has been a profound democratization inspired by socialism, though I have noted imperfections in terms of achieving liberalization. In Costa Rica, the process of democratization begun at the end of the 1940s has been modified by trends toward concentration of capital and the weakening of its sovereignty.

Similar to the reforms the region experienced in the sixties during the Kennedy administration, democratic reforms were implemented throughout Central America in response to the anti-Sandinista focus of the Reagan administration. The low profile of military personnel, the promotion of superficial electoral processes, the emergence of civilian governments, and economic aid—all of these appeared to be a response to the fear that a radical transformation, such as Nicaragua's, might be repeated elsewhere in Central America. Avoiding revolution was the agreed-upon goal of the United States, the conservative political class, and the traditionally dominant economic groups.

Decisions to democratize in other Central American countries did not originate from within the countries, as they had in Nicaragua, but were part of a strategy directed by the United States to confront the Sandinista revolution. In these countries, the military—traditionally defiant in the face of transition to civilian regimes—did not have the strength to oppose such transitions because the United States promoted these changes in order to combat the advance of communism. The U.S. government and its allies in the region perceived Sandinismo as communist and feared its expansion throughout Central America. For these reasons, in Guatemala, El Salvador, and Honduras there was no organic link between the political transitions and changes in the economy. The only exception may be some of the reforms initiated during the government of José Napoleón Duarte in El Salvador, but they lacked both depth and fulfillment. Nowhere in Central America outside Nicaragua were there serious efforts based on democratic transitions to correct injustices in the economic system.

Apart from its counterinsurgent intent, U.S. policy did facilitate the opening up of democratic expression and respect for civil and human liberties, which relieved some of the accumulated social and political pressures. Elections, respect for institutional and legal structures, mechanisms for dialogue, diminished political influence of the military, more empowered political parties (including the perpetually persecuted parties of the left)—all were advances of this period.

There still remain, however, certain obstacles. The U.S. government and international financial institutions insist on imposing conditions that constrain the processes of domestic social change. The democratic processes are precarious, limited, and inconclusive. Except for Nicaragua and Costa Rica, the countries concerned lack a well-regulated, modern political system. Even the electoral processes, their most developed institutions, relatively speaking, need further development. The military in each country has been an obstacle to varying degrees; in Guatemala, some military officers have attempted coups while in El Salvador many officers have been reluctant to accept a political solution. Nevertheless, the military certainly does not have the power it did ten years ago. The right wing greeted the democratic process with reticence and little conviction. This sector was more involved in counterinsurgent efforts and was timid about rallying around a national consensus.

In Nicaragua, democratization and liberalization intrinsically required basic transformations in society, including a radical modification of economic strategies. Sandinismo sought to transform the government by moving away from the aggressive and dictatorial leadership style of the Somozas, while carrying out long-overdue redistributive economic reforms. Although in terms of economic growth the result was rather tenuous because of the contra war, there were profound structural transformations that resulted in a broad redistribution of property. This was a basic objective of real democratization in Nicaragua.

In fact, after the agrarian reforms, peasants who had owned just 3 percent of the land came to own 35 percent of it. More than 120,000 families, a majority of whom were landless peasants and unemployed "semiproletarians," benefitted from the property reassignments. Half the arable land in Nicaragua, which had been concentrated in the hands of large landholders—the Somoza family and its allies—was transferred to the peasants. The estate system, which had been the basis of the local oligarchy's authoritarian regimes, was reduced from 40 percent of all land holdings to 6 percent over a ten-year period.

A number of conditions facilitated such political and civic fulfillment among the citizenry: the creation and strengthening of labor and social organizations; the promotion of political parties following forty years of tyranny; the development of the constitution and the rule of law; periodic elections of public authorities with equal suffrage and fair elections; respect of individual rights; freedom of expression; and the right to unionize. These conditions evolved and matured in Nicaragua only after the fall of the Somozas in 1979.

Equally tangible, social improvements in ten years included the reduction of illiteracy from 56 percent to less than 13 percent; a decrease in infant mortality from 120 to 52 per thousand live births; and an increase in average life expectancy from forty-five to sixty-four years. All are truly substantial contributions to democracy and stability.

On February 25, 1990, democracy in Nicaragua was put to the test. The governing FSLN party, the undeniable leader of the revolution, was defeated. The society had reached the limit of its endurance; there was no end in sight to the war. The majority of the people believed that the war and severe economic difficulties would continue if the FSLN were to remain in power.

The FSLN government had moved the elections forward from November to February 1990 to bring an end to the war. But in doing so, it lost the elections. Nevertheless, the early elections fortunately brought early peace to the people. In accepting the election results, not only did the FSLN take a step toward achieving peace, but it reaffirmed its long-standing (pre-1979) goal of creating an opportunity for democratic development with social equality in Nicaragua in the wake of the Somoza dictatorship. Sandinismo lost the battle over the election, but nonetheless it won the real war—the achievement of peace.

On the evening of February 25, with the first election returns showing certain victory for the National Opposition Union (UNO), the National Directorate of the FSLN held an emergency meeting to analyze the situation and take a position. The opinion was unanimous—to respect the popular choice unequivocally and acknowledge electoral defeat. For us, it was much preferable to accept a bitter defeat and what that would demand from us than to resist the will of the majority, who had withdrawn their support. After all, we had long struggled in order to secure for our people the right to express themselves with complete freedom. We had guaranteed a fair electoral process, but the FSLN had for so long suffered from systematic attrition that we came to the elections at a disadvantage.

From a Central American perspective, it would appear that only in Nicaragua did profound and lasting political regime changes occur. However, in taking this route to democratization, the FSLN made some poor decisions which created obstacles to progress. Because of the weakness of opposition parties, the FSLN often acted without having sought a consensus. During 1979–1984, it neglected to strengthen institutional and legal processes and, instead, took executive action on a de facto basis. In some cases, it adopted political strategies and organizational methods observed in countries that were not in comparable circumstances. The FSLN used coercive tactics, especially during times of intense warfare, which at times severely limited individual freedoms and civil rights, including the freedom of expression.

Nevertheless, the net outcome of Sandinismo on Nicaragua has been positive. Even if we consider just three achievements of Sandinismo, a positive mark will be left on the pages of Nicaraguan history: (1) the overthrow of the Somoza regime, (2) the democratization of property, and (3) the establishment of an electoral system—the very foundation of representative democracy—that furnished Nicaragua with the first "clean" elections in the country's history. When the FSLN lost in 1990, it became the new civic opposition.

Despite these achievements, there still remain some worrisome factors threatening the continuation of democratic progress. A minority of Nicaraguans linked to the Somozas and the radical sectors of the traditional right are determined to restore the pre-1979 political and socioeconomic order. Also, the rearming of the contras and incidents of persecution of the FSLN and its members make building a national consensus for stability and the common good more difficult. Threatening questions are being raised concerning the status of property rights reforms, which have benefitted thousands of citizens. And lastly, there have been smear campaigns to undermine the achievements of the revolution and its leaders.

Nevertheless, Nicaragua may still enter a stage where peace, stability, economic recovery, and democratization become paramount considerations sought through agreement. My hope is that the more conscientious political and social forces in the country, including the government and the opposition, take this path. Among disparate forces, a shared vision could be forged for the future of democratic development in Nicaragua. Even now, as we try to construct a democratic, civilian regime, we see efforts to establish consensus among political actors; if these efforts continue, they may isolate and discredit the extremists.

There has been progress from the taking up of arms to solve problems in 1979, to de facto rule in 1979–1984, and ultimately to the movement toward institutionalization—prompting the 1990 elections. The search for consensus and the making of agreements has become the key rule of the game. If this search is successful, the 1979 revolution will have achieved its true goal: democracy built on stable social transformations, where the future direction of the nation is increasingly decided by the citizens and their representative institutions.

NOTES

1. The opinions expressed in this paper are my own. Nevertheless, they represent a collective experience—mine and those of my colleagues and collaborators, whose contributions I include, and alongside whom I have lived during years of intense political upheaval and government service.

FOUR

DEMOCRATIC TRANSITIONS
IN NICARAGUA

SILVIO DE FRANCO AND
JOSÉ LUIS VELÁZQUEZ

Since its earliest days as a Spanish colony, Nicaragua has been governed by authoritarian regimes that have embraced such widely different ideologies as conservatism, liberalism, and Sandinismo to justify their rule. Yet Nicaragua's ruling power structure has consistently been an oligarchy, run by either a handful of individuals or by groups sharing power through political pacts. Under such a system, Nicaragua has experienced intermittent moments of peace and economic growth, only to see them followed by periods of conflict and economic crisis.

The oligarchic structure was so entrenched in Nicaragua that not even two revolutions—a liberal revolution in 1893 and the Sandinista revolution in 1979—could uproot it. Rather, these violent episodes only expanded, readjusted, and rearranged the compact oligarchy governing the country.

Under the paternalistic rule of General Anastasio Somoza García after World War II, Nicaragua began to experience increasing tension between its growing economy on the one hand and its stagnant political system on the other. As illustrated in figure 4.1, Nicaragua's gross national product (GNP) increased eightfold from 1940 to 1980. The economy had begun to diversify in the 1940s, and the structure of society began to change with it. At the same time, however, political power was increasingly concentrated in the hands of the president's family and colleagues.

Under the Somoza dynasty, as during periods of foreign military intervention, much of the Nicaraguan population became profoundly alienated. Such prolonged concentration of power in a single governing family—from 1936 to 1979—stunted the political development of the ruling class, deepened the nation's social inequities, and further concentrated the national wealth in the hands of a privileged minority. By the late 1970s, the political system was

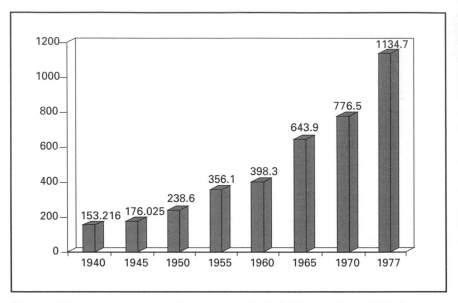

Fig. 4.1. Nicaragua: gross national product, 1940–77 (millions of 1970 dollars). *Source:* Víctor Bulmer-Thomas, *The Political Economy of Central America since 1920* (Cambridge: Cambridge University Press, 1987), pp. 308–9.

strained to the breaking point. A series of events aggravated the Somoza regime's problems, and the increasingly explosive situation finally detonated.

First, the government proved itself impotent at managing the disastrous aftermath of the 1972 earthquake in Managua. Second, General Anastasio Somoza Debayle and his colleagues inexcusably violated the rules of the game when they engaged in unfair economic competition; the family made incursions into fields such as banking and trade, traditionally reserved for the independent private sector. Third, the economy was hit with the oil crisis, which drove up the price of imports and accelerated inflation, and a worldwide recession adversely affected the terms of trade. Fourth, the Somozas' grip on power was threatened by changes in U.S. foreign policy, specifically President Jimmy Carter's human rights policy, which, by criticizing human rights abuses in Nicaragua, seemed to open a breach between the Somoza dynasty and its presumed protector, the U.S. government. Finally, a crisis in the Central American Common Market (CACM) resulted in a reduction in the flow of investments and the level of regional trade.

The rigidity of the status quo under General Somoza did not permit political measures that might have been taken to release the tensions building up within Nicaragua. Thus, as the proposed presidential succession of the last member of the Somoza dynasty neared, a power struggle began.

On July 19, 1979, the regime fell victim to the economic modernization process that had occurred under its reign. The economy grew rapidly from 1963 to 1968 and with it the pressure from the newly emerging middle classes for greater political participation. The tensions that had built up within Nicaragua led to an abrupt attack on the regime by a multiclass, multiparty coalition, actively supported by the international community. However, this event was by no means a classic example of the unfolding of a class struggle in a semifeudal or "primary" society, as it has been characterized by some. Rather, it was the product of the considerable distortions that an accelerated modernization process—accompanied by profound imbalances in economic growth, by social mobilization, and by lack of political institutionalization— is capable of producing in a traditional society.[1]

Nicaraguan society in the 1970s was far from the popular caricature of a feudal society in which the aristocracy exploited the labor force and dominated the economy. On the contrary, a money economy thrived throughout the nation: Nicaragua had the most dynamic financial sector in Central America. Agricultural exports, particularly cotton and sugar, were produced using the most advanced technological and administrative methods

Another misconception concerns the degree of inequality that prevailed in the country. Undeniably, there was a high concentration of income in a few hands. However, the income was not as concentrated as it was in El Salvador, Guatemala, or Honduras. For example, in Nicaragua, there were 42,000 coffee producers, while in El Salvador there were only 300; in Nicaragua there were 6,000 cotton producers, while Guatemala had only 80. Nicaragua's basic grain production, covering an area of close to 618,000 acres, was in the hands of small producers and peasants.

The CACM had initiated an industrialization process (for better or worse) that brought complexity and vigor to the country's economic and social structure, paralleling the expansion and modernization of the state apparatus. This economic growth and diversification fostered social differentiation, promoting the emergence of new socioeconomic groups such as a middle class and a bourgeoisie. These two classes became highly radicalized and politically mobilized and demanded participation in the political process.

The Somoza dictatorship stood in the way of the country's modernization. By mid-1979, radicalization of the middle class and bourgeoisie led to a burgeoning popular opposition movement, stimulated by the regime's indiscriminate repression. One of the three competing groups within the Sandinista National Liberation Front (FSLN)—the Tercerista faction—skillfully outmaneuvered its more extreme rivals within the Sandinista Front[2] as well as within the Broad Opposition Front (FAO), which represented the majority of the democratic opposition.[3] As a result, the Sandinista Front was able to assume the leadership of a broad alliance of political forces to overthrow the Somoza dictatorship. This alliance coalesced around two focal points: a statute to replace, de facto, the constitution, and a government program based on the principles of political pluralism, a mixed economy, and nonalignment.

On July 19, 1979, the dictatorship collapsed, and the army—the regime's mainstay—was formally disbanded. This collapse was unexpected even by the FSLN. The path was now open for the insurgent forces to take power immediately. Their sudden ascension to power disoriented the Sandinista leaders. The internal differences and conflicts that had afflicted the organization in the past were mostly over different strategies for overthrowing Somoza. However, once the Sandinistas were in power, they had to shift their focus abruptly to the only differences remaining, namely, what shape their political program should take.

Because the Tercerista faction wielded the most influence within the Sandinista leadership, the new government initially moved in the direction this faction favored—that of a social democratic project called the "Third Way." But last-minute realignments among the Sandinista factions and early exclusion of advocates of democratic procedures from the decision-making process led to abandonment of the Third Way. Instead, the focus shifted to establishing an Eastern European– and Cuban-style regime in Nicaragua.

Once the Tercerista leadership became aware of the realities of power, which they had previously underestimated, they realized that sufficient political space had opened up to allow the group to go beyond a simple social democratic experiment. This was the beginning of the attempted "transition to socialism" project. Once the transition project had been chosen as the course to follow, the only discrepancies that would arise within the Sandinista National Directorate[4] would be related not to the goals of the process but to its details; namely, questions of pace, procedure, and opportunity. The radicals wished to advance the collectivization of the country rapidly. The moderates advocated a slower pace, taking into account political calculations and "objective conditions of the moment."

Sandinista leaders made their decisions unilaterally, without consulting the Nicaraguan people in matters shaping their own destiny. Moreover, the decision to initiate a transition to socialism contradicted the original government program, which emphasized majority consensus and support from key social sectors, among them the unions, the Church, business organizations, political parties, ethnic minorities, and other sectors of public opinion.

THE TRANSITION TO SOCIALISM PROJECT

During the first half of the 1980s, the Sandinista Front tried to carry out their transition to socialism project. The project's goals were the nationalization of private property; replacement of market forces with centralized planning and direct government intervention in production; creation of a centralized nucleus of power based on a united government, the Sandinista party, the army, and the newly created mass organizations;[5] the application of Marxist-Leninist principles in order to bring about the homogenization of the population and create a proletarian society; establishment of a strategic alliance with the Soviet Bloc; and the active support of Third World radical-left movements.

This socialist program began with a strong push in 1979 but ran up against a series of obstacles that had been underestimated by the Sandinista leadership. In order to understand how these obstacles caused the transition to fail, we will examine the FSLN program and its evolution.

Nationalization of Property and Production

The first five years of Sandinista government witnessed an accelerated process of nationalizing property and production. During the period 1980–86, the public sector's share in GDP increased steadily to the point that, in 1985, the public sector share of national productive activity surpassed that of the private sector (fig. 4.2) The impact of nationalization fell most heavily on banking, foreign trade, natural resources, transportation, and properties and businesses that the Sandinista regime considered strategic for implementing its project.

The indicators presented in figure 4.2 suggest that the transition project's economic model was based on the assumption that the capital accumulation needed for development would be supplied predominantly by the public sector. However, in practice the public sector assumed responsibility for large portions of national economic activity without having the ability to manage production efficiently. This caused national production to shrink. During this initial period, the Sandinista administration put roughly 60 percent of the country's economic resources into the hands of the government while exercising iron control, through legislation and government policies, over the 40 percent that remained in private hands. Nevertheless, the public sector was unable to become a significant source of capital accumulation.

The increased government presence in production had a devastating impact on private activity. Confiscations and expropriations extending beyond the property of General Somoza and his colleagues, accompanied by flagrant violations of the rules of the game, profoundly affected government relations with business. This provoked the breakup of the Sandinistas' broad alliance, forged in the struggle against the Somoza dictatorship. This alliance was replaced by a tactical alliance with elements of the private sector, intended to gain the time needed to create sufficient technical and administrative capacity in the public sector for the transition.

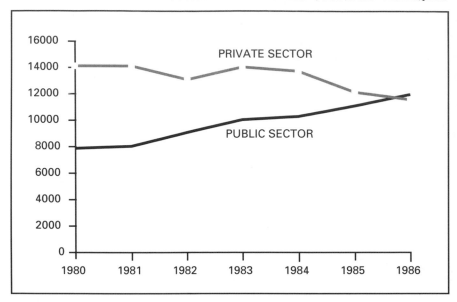

Fig. 4.2. Nicaragua: evolution of the gross domestic product by sectors, 1980–86 (millions of 1980 córdobas). *Sources:* International Monetary Fund (IMF) and INIESEP.

The business executives who survived the confiscation process became mere government functionaries. In practice, they administered their companies and properties on behalf of the government, given that the government made most decisions concerning the production of goods and services.

The nationalization of the economy had direct political consequences, accelerating the centralization of power in the hands of the FSLN. By increasing its influence and state ownership and undermining the institution of private property, the FSLN acquired overwhelming political power, which it used to weaken and exclude other sectors of national life from the decision-making process. The government's economic monopoly was the key (combined with political and ideological controls) to subordinating and controlling citizens and intermediary organizations, putting them in a vulnerable position.

Substituting Government Intervention
and Centralized Planning for Market Forces

The attempt to establish a centrally planned economy was frustrated by the constraints of the Nicaraguan economy. It was impossible to establish a planned economy when the country's income was subject to the vagaries of the international market and to domestic sociopolitical factors. Consequently, it was impossible to plan expenditures, especially because these included a gigantic and increasing military budget that absorbed 62 percent of state income.

Later attempts to bring planning and the market in line failed not only because of fluctuations in export income but also because of the ideological aversion of some Sandinista leaders toward a market economy. The free-enterprise beliefs of the country's medium and small producers could not be reconciled with the official ideology of nationalization.

The attempt to replace market forces with government decisions resulted in large economic distortions, both at the level of production and at the level of distribution of goods. The disproportionate growth of government at the expense of private production and the government's inability to meet the economic and employment needs of the population ironically gave rise to economic phenomena outside the government's control. Among them were the emergence of the informal sector or underground economy, the appearance of hoarding, speculation rooted in hyperinflation, currency devaluation, rationing, and total distortion of the market. Subsidies, credit cancellations, and unproductive labor policies reduced economic efficiency, leaving the system unable to respond to the challenges of reconstruction. The upsurge in the war and the subsequent massive displacement of the peasant population from affected areas—a strategy designed to deny the counterrevolution a social base—destroyed the country's key grain production base, drastically reducing the grain supply, inflating prices, and making Nicaragua more dependent on foreign aid.

As a result of the government's political manipulation of resource allocation and its inefficient administration, the black market became an essential part of the national economy, a part the government was unable to control and which benefited the small group that participated in it. In short, at the beginning of the second half of the 1980s, the Sandinista economic program hung in limbo, with neither the centrally planned economy nor the so-called mixed economy in place. What had really come about was a bureaucratized economic system based on arbitrariness, its primary objective not to satisfy the needs of the people but to suit the political goals of the regime.

Creation of a Subsidy Economy

The regime was unable to transform the government into a mechanism for new capital accumulation capable of financing the Sandinista administration's distribution and expansion policies. Therefore, the regime came to be financed initially by donations from the international community. Later, when the flow of international money dwindled while government revenues were absorbed by military expenditures, public spending was financed by foreign debt, which increased from $1.6 billion to $11 billion by 1990.

Far from being invested efficiently and productively, income from credits, donations, taxes, and government enterprise earnings was used to subsidize the Sandinistas' political clientele, which led to further expansion of inefficient public spending and production. This political clientele was subsidized by sustaining the activities of the new mass organizations and by placing party members and sympathizers in government enterprises and in the bureaucracy. The government grew from 35,000 employees (including the army) in 1979 to 187,929 employees in 1989.

Expanded public spending was earmarked for the government's social programs to subsidize consumption, to cover growing military expenses, and to finance unproductive public investments. The most damaging long-term policy, however, was the subsidizing of production. From the beginning, the Sandinista leadership showed an inconsistent attitude toward the nation's business community. On the one hand, they expanded confiscations of businesses and restrictive regulations governing enterprises, proclaimed the imminent demise of private enterprise, and persecuted business organizations such as the Superior Private Enterprise Council (COSEP).[6] On the other hand, they made concessions and deals with business individuals and groups to continue to generate foreign currency from agroexport activity. The resulting climate was one of insecurity and instability because productive property was constantly threatened with arbitrary expropriation by the government, which needed to maintain the flow of currency and employment sources. Such a climate fostered a reciprocal blackmail between the business community and the Sandinista leadership whereby the government threatened the entrepreneur with confiscation if the business did not produce while the entrepreneur threatened not to produce if the government did not make credit available.

This modus operandi caused the degeneration of credit into an instrument for subsidizing production. This inverted logic meant that the entrepreneur no longer sought income to make profits, out of which a debt could be paid; rather, the objective was to lose money, request the government to forgive the debt and, from that, deduct earnings. The situation created a vicious cycle: Each year at the end of the harvest, producers unleashed political pressures to force the government to forgive their debts and open new credits to them for the upcoming season. In this climate, the nation's banks became mere distribution centers for subsidies. And when the resources from foreign grants became scarce, access to international credit was closed, and military spending increased, the government had to resort to printing more money to maintain the credit privileges it had created. This fed hyperinflation, which ultimately reached a record 23,833 percent monthly in 1988 (see also fig. 4.8).[7]

The subsidies were especially valuable to companies in the public sector called People's Property (APP) enterprises. The government allowed these companies to buy input supplies at far below market value and arbitrarily to fix the sale prices of their products at above market prices. Basically, these firms had a monopoly.

Additionally, this policy of subsidizing enterprises resulted in a highly inefficient apparatus heavily dependent upon government perquisites. The policy changed the expectations, values, and behavior of both entrepreneurs and workers, who came to believe that there was indeed a free lunch. Among other things, the subsidy policy reinforced the rent-seeking mentality of private business operators; they became accustomed to avoiding risk and seeking government protection and privileges.

Political Implications of the
State–Party–Army–Mass Organizations Axis

In order to concentrate economic resources within the government, the transition model was built on four linked elements: the FSLN as a party operating under so-called democratic centralism; the Sandinista Popular Army (EPS), the military arm of the party made up of its leaders and militants; the government administrative apparatus made up of central and municipal government agencies, autonomous entities, and the public sector (APP) enterprises; and mass organizations created by, and as an extension of, the ruling party. These elements were run by the Sandinista National Directorate.

Building the social base to support this framework as well as concentrating power in a central government involved a prolonged process of destroying civilian society and excluding important sectors of the population from the decision-making process. There was a distinct pattern to this exclusionary process. First, the governing party deliberately weakened intermediary groups and organizations that had maintained their independence of the government. The government undermined their political support, their base of legitimacy and, in particular, their economic resources.[8]

At the same time, the Sandinistas created new, parallel organizations—which were, in some cases, dismembered versions of the organizations described above—to give the appearance of new groups being formed by the revolutionary process. In reality, many of these "new" groups were mere extensions of the governing party's structure, disguised as intermediary organizations to give an impression of grassroots influence on the decisions adopted by the party leadership. These groups had no concrete roots in society and were merely façades.

While Sandinismo was reducing actual participation by civic organizations at all levels of society, it simultaneously founded an array of military and paramilitary organizations (e.g., the army, the militias, compulsory military service, the voluntary police, the Defense Committees, and the shock forces called *turbas*). The purpose of these groups was to "defend the revolution." Citizens were drafted into these organizations, hence militarizing society. In addition, scarce resources were manipulated for political purposes and the populace was permanently mobilized for the "defense of the revolution." The Sandinistas implemented these actions progressively, following criteria laid out by their leadership and taking advantage of favorable conditions and opportunities.

The emasculation of civil society and its replacement by sham organizations controlled by the regime, accompanied by militarization and rigid social controls, opened the way for an exercise of power unchecked by legal counterbalances. With political, economic, and social power concentrated within the governing elite, the government (citing defense of the "revolutionary process") suppressed basic freedoms—especially freedom of expression—and closed the political space vital to the democratic participation of intermediary organizations responsible for defending the interests of social groups. The state–party–army–mass organizations axis, supported by the gigantic government's economic machinery, reduced basic individual and social freedoms. Political pluralism became mere rhetoric.

Proletarianization and Ideological Homogenization

The transition to socialism project implied an effort by the regime to convert the majority of the population into "proletarians" or wage earners. Indeed, the nationalization of productive goods and private property transformed property owners who had remained in the country into wage-earning employees of the government.

Agrarian reform, which in the first years of the transition project was part of the process of nationalizing productive agricultural units and proletarianizing the peasantry, became instead an instrument of counterinsurgency when, in 1985, the regime began to feel the effects of a peasant rebellion in the northern and central parts of the country. In any case, land distribution was not meant to transform the peasants into farmers but rather to incorporate them into a framework of military cooperatives, similar to the "strategic villages" of the Vietnam War. In the country's western agro-export region, the conversion of cotton and sugarcane lands to peasant agriculture severely reduced exports, which plummeted from $700 million in 1977 to $250 million in 1989. Following the February 1990 elections, agrarian reform took a new slant, toward benefiting members of the ruling party and its political clientele.

The proletarianization effort was accompanied by an attempt to homogenize the population ideologically by imposing Marxism-Leninism on them. The government ran a national literacy campaign to implant this new creed among literate people and those learning to read. To the same end, the government retooled its ideological apparatus—the educational system and cultural, propaganda, and media outlets. This spawned intolerance for, and persecution of, other ideologies, reinforcing the regime's antidemocratic slant.

A STRATEGIC ALLIANCE WITH THE SOVIET BLOC AND THE NATIONAL LIBERATION MOVEMENTS

The transition to socialism project was supported by strategic and tactical international alliances. Knowing that the "anti-imperialist" nature of the project conflicted with the interests of the United States, the Sandinistas struck a strategic alliance with the Soviet Union and its allies in order to obtain the international political support and economic resources needed to carry out their project in the face of opposition from the United States. Other governments and organizations of the radical left that called themselves "national liberation" movements, especially those in neighboring countries like El Salvador's Farabundo Martí National Liberation Front (FMLN), were anti-imperialist by definition, and thus natural allies. The regime placed special emphasis on support from these nearby groups because it needed to secure allied government support in the Central American region as well as to expand the influence of its "revolution without borders." The ideological affinity and alliances of the Sandinista regime, Soviet Bloc, and the national liberation movements were based on Marxism-Leninism and anti-imperialism.

The strategic alliances of the transition were complemented by a tactical alliance with the social democratic governments and political parties of the Socialist International. These groups were captivated by the Sandinista rhetoric proclaiming that the Nicaraguan experiment blended the principles of nonalignment, mixed economy, and political pluralism.

The strategic alliance with the Soviet Bloc and national liberation movements put the national problem into the context of the East-West conflict in the closing years of the Cold War. This unwise decision to align strategically with the Soviet Bloc brought grave consequences for Nicaragua. First, it delivered the coup de grace to any possibility of maintaining a nonalignment policy. Figure 4.3 represents the index of agreement between Nicaragua and the Soviet Union in United Nations General Assembly votes; it shows that the percentage of agreement between the two countries jumped from 30 percent in 1979 to 85 percent in 1983, and to 92 percent in 1988.

Second, the Soviet-Nicaraguan alliance provoked direct interference by both the USSR and the United States in Nicaragua's internal affairs. This

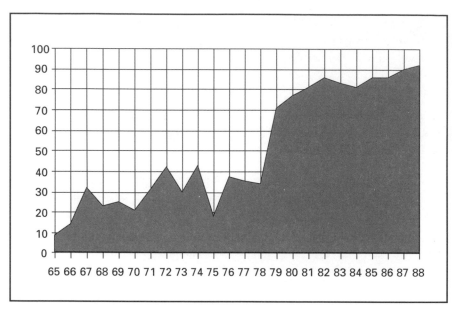

Fig. 4.3. Index of agreement between the USSR and Nicaragua in the United Nations General Assembly, 1965–89 (percentages). *Source:* UN Department of Public Information.

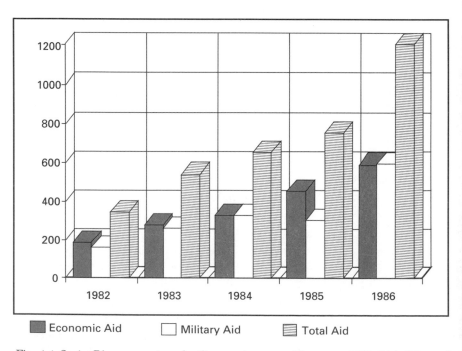

Fig. 4.4. Soviet Bloc economic and military assistance to Nicaragua, 1982–86 (millions of U.S. dollars). *Source:* U.S. Department of State.

interference precipitated a civil war and continued to make it extremely difficult to negotiate a solution to the war. Third, the alliance gradually isolated
Nicaragua from other nations in the hemisphere, resulted in a U.S. trade embargo, and increased levels of economic and military dependency on the
Soviet Union (see fig. 4.4).

BREAKDOWN OF THE TRANSITION
TO SOCIALISM MODEL

In 1979, the Sandinista leadership rose to power under optimal conditions:
the Somoza dictatorship was over and had been rejected throughout Latin
America, social forces that had emerged during the modernization process
were pushing for change, a large anti-Somocista alliance was forming, and social democratic parties were ascending worldwide.

These favorable conditions prevailed until mid-1983, when they began to
change in part because of management errors within the Sandinista leadership. Changes were also brought about by other factors: the surge of armed
and civilian opposition in Nicaragua's interior, the sharp fall in national production levels, the Republican Party's victory in the United States, signs of international economic recession, limited support from the Soviet Bloc for the
transition program, the refocusing on European countries of social democracy's attention to international issues, and stagnation of the so-called liberation struggle throughout the world. These factors magnified the leadership's
errors and helped to end the transition.

In 1984, the regime began to feel the effects of international isolation and
the adverse changes in the internal political situation. The leadership felt they
had to develop an "opening" to provide some democratic space within the
system. One element of this strategy was a call for general elections. Goals
were to reduce internal and external political pressures, reestablish the eroding
support of old allies in Western Europe and Latin America, and neutralize
U.S. policy toward Nicaragua. The maneuver failed. The nod toward democracy by Sandinista leaders was not convincing, nationally or internationally.
The Sandinista opening failed to block military assistance to Nicaraguan
rebels from the U.S. Congress or to reestablish the past levels of assistance
from Western Europe.

After this failure, the Sandinista leadership again turned to the Soviet
Union to salvage its transition to socialism. However, the USSR was interested in using the Nicaraguan conflict only to facilitate the withdrawal of its
own troops from Afghanistan. Also, it was busy concentrating on internal
transformation (*glasnost* and *perestroika*) while maintaining a détente with the

United States. Consequently, all the Sandinista leadership obtained from the USSR was arms—not badly needed economic assistance.

Meanwhile, national liberation movements reemerged in the region due to the stagnation of the Nicaraguan transition. This liberation fervor dampened the possibility that the revolution would take hold or that it would gain new regional allies. The U.S. Republican administration actively opposed pro-Sandinista movements, especially in El Salvador. In Guatemala, Honduras, and El Salvador, popularly elected governments took office. Various Central American presidents became quite active in searching for negotiated solutions to the region's conflicts.

By the middle of 1987, the Sandinista leadership was faced with the dilemma of choosing between abandoning the transition to socialism project to retain power or abandoning power to preserve the project. The negative effects of Sandinista policies and the war had inflicted upon the country the greatest disaster it had ever known. Miscalculations in economic policy and a decision to take a confrontational stance against the United States had degenerated into a war of attrition between the two countries, preventing Nicaragua from regaining production levels that had existed before the fall of Somoza. Figure 4.5 shows the fall of GNP growth rates during the period from 1979 to 1989. Figure 4.6 shows the evolution of the average real wage, which in 1988 was one fifth of what it had been ten years earlier. And, as illustrated in figure 4.7, consumption per capita fell from $1,401 in 1980 to $504 in 1989. Figure 4.8 depicts how the rate of inflation shot to unheard-of levels, reaching 23,833 percent in 1988.[9]

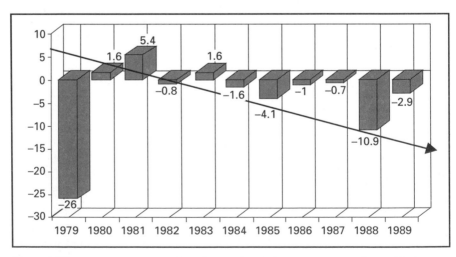

Fig. 4.5. Nicaragua: gross national product, 1979–89 (percentage rate of growth). *Sources:* IMF and INIESEP.

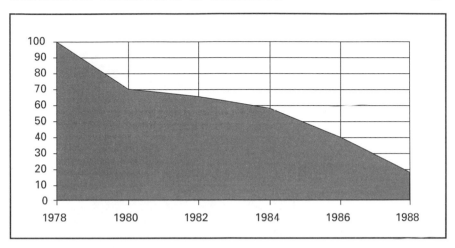

Fig. 4.6. Nicaragua: evolution of the average real wage, 1978–88 (1978 = 100). *Sources:* IMF and Consejo Superior de la Empresa Privada (COSEP).

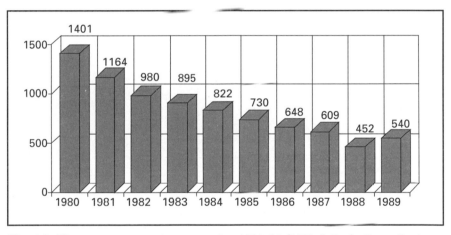

Fig. 4.7. Nicaragua: consumption per capita, 1980–89 (1989 dollars). *Source:* Instituto Centroamericano de Administración de Empresas (INCAE), Managua.

A decline in the country's export capacity, coupled with increased imports to compensate for the lack of internal production of basic consumer goods, caused the external gap to widen to an average of $400 million annually. This had to be filled with foreign credit and donations, as shown in figure 4.9.

By 1987, eight years of transition to socialism had left 500,000 Nicaraguans (16 percent of the population) in exile as refugees or émigrés; 300,000 displaced due to the war; 10,000 political prisoners; 30,000 dead; the great majority of the population living in misery or suffering shortages and political

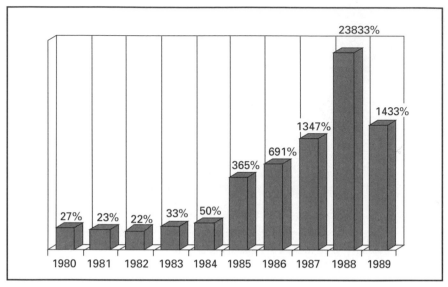

Fig. 4.8. Nicaragua: rate of inflation, 1980–89 (percentages). *Source:* INCAE, Managua.

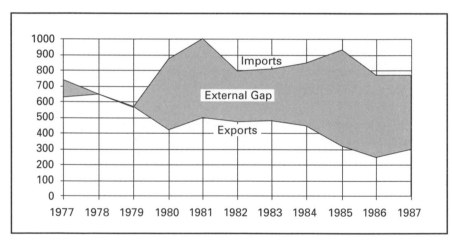

Fig. 4.9. Nicaragua: external gap, 1977–87 (millions of U.S. dollars). *Sources:* IMF and INIESEP.

persecution; and 20,000 peasants enrolled in the ranks of the Nicaraguan Resistance as contras.

In sum, under the Sandinistas the Nicaraguan economy became based not on the country's productivity but on resources solicited and obtained from abroad by exploiting the East-West conflict and presenting the country as a victim of "imperialist aggression." Foreign resources were critical in sustaining the economy. These foreign resources were distributed among the Sandinista leadership and the state bureaucracy; a rent-seeking economic sector which benefited from production subsidies; the elite working class of the state enterprises and the unions; and the military apparatus.

Additionally, insulating the economy from market mechanisms, on top of the regime's corruption and inefficiency, accelerated the collapse of internal production, which left foreign resources increasingly insufficient as compensation. Even if there had been massive and dependable foreign resources, the system would still have plunged into crisis because of inefficiency, corruption, war, and uncertainty, which hobbled the regime's domestic political support. The coup de grace was the reform policy of Mikhail Gorbachev in the former Soviet Union. Perestroika changed the Soviet Union's "regional conflicts" focus, its relations with the United States, and its priorities in allocating resources, with more resources focused on the Soviet Union itself. This policy change meant a substantial reduction in resources for the Sandinista regime. Hence, the regime was compelled to change its policies abruptly.

What happened between the USSR and Nicaragua is just one of the many examples of how changes in foreign economic and political influences can decisively condition the domestic situation within dependent countries and limit the political will of peripheral ruling groups. In Nicaragua, the presence of economic resources from abroad helped to insulate the regime from domestic dangers.

With the deterioration of the domestic situation, the Sandinistas' power base fell away. Then, as tension between the superpowers relaxed, the Sandinista leadership was compelled to abandon its program and seek a negotiated settlement through the Esquipulas process. It did not do this before rushing through a new constitution that would provide it with a strong negotiating position against its domestic and international opponents. The change from arbitrariness, which predominated in the first seven years of the Sandinista regime, to governance based on the rule of law resembling the standards of civilized nations was a victory for the Nicaraguan people.

The search for a negotiated settlement to the contra war continued to move forward, driven by the rapid changes taking place in Eastern Europe in 1988. The collapse of the socialist bloc and the profound change in U.S.-Soviet relations—with all their ideological, economic, and political implications—completely reversed the situation that had previously supported the Sandinistas' economic plan. These changes bankrupted the Sandinistas' *Weltanschauung*. The Sandinistas were moved from the offensive to the defensive. In this context, Nicaraguan democratic forces that joined together under the National Opposition Union (UNO) would triumph in the elections of February 25, 1990.

THE TRANSITION TO DEMOCRACY

After a decade-long dictatorship, the Nicaraguan transition to democracy began with the settlement among the Sandinista leadership, the civic opposition parties, and the contra forces. They agreed to move the elections ahead and to adhere to the results.

Confident of their popular influence and the persuasive ability of their electoral machine, Sandinista leaders expected to win an easy and resounding victory, thus legitimizing their right to power. They could then establish a government, retaining the largest share of power and co-opting the country's most important political and economic sectors. The Sandinista philosophy was simple: Something had to change for everything to remain the same. In the end, the Sandinistas had come to believe their own propaganda proclaiming the complete unification or "oneness" of the people and Sandinismo; this was the reason they were confident that they could hold a clean election and not lose it.

Democratic procedures are full of uncertainties and surprises. On February 25, 1990, Sandinista leaders faced a brutal reality: by an overwhelming majority the Nicaraguan people rejected their administration and elected UNO candidate Violeta Barrios de Chamorro as president. A new, long, and difficult road stretched before the nation. Nevertheless, it was full of hope.

A Return to the Nation's Original Challenges

UNO's platform called for progress in addressing the original challenge posed by increasing modernization, which had been frustrated by the Somoza and Sandinista dictatorships. This continuing challenge is to bring about democratic change and national development.

There were many opportunities to move toward both democracy and development in the domestic arena. The large majority of Nicaraguans were weary with frustration after many years of mistakes, disorder, and misery. They longed for order. The popular consensus was to avoid class struggle; rather, the "solution" required harmony among all of the social forces in the country. The people were convinced of the value and importance of the democratic process, which could only be nourished by tolerance, respect, participation, dialogue, and compromise.

The democratic fever encircling the globe, exemplified by the spectacular changes in Eastern Europe and the demise of the Soviet Union, reaffirmed the existence of new and challenging opportunities in Nicaragua to push forward the democratic program. Absent were the threats and complications of the Cold War. Likewise, the collapse of a dictatorship backed by foreign supporters and its replacement with a government seeking to evolve toward a democratic system ensured opportunities to advance democracy in Nicaragua.

The major threats to reform that existed in Nicaragua were the political and economic interests spawned by the dictatorship and the concomitant economic shock of the 1980s. These forces showed tenacious resistance to change. The indiscriminate abuse of foreign resources and replacement of market forces with government forces fostered rent-seeking attitudes among broad sectors of the population. People became accustomed to living without working and to exercising their rights without worrying about fulfilling their obligations.

The trend toward government monopoly and bureaucratization of the economy had created a rent-seeking structure based on political status and the ability of groups to generate political pressure. Nurtured by expanded public spending, subsidies, and nationalization of the economy, certain interest groups emerged with substantial benefits, not because of their productive capacity but because of their ability to generate political pressure and to traffic in influence with government administrators who managed the economy and public resources. These rent-seeking sectors were the Sandinista leadership and government bureaucracy; those businesses benefiting from production subsidies; working-class elites who were linked to state enterprises and unions; and the military apparatus.

The economic reforms that were set in motion early on by the Chamorro government meant substantial losses in economic rents for these interest groups. Reforms reduced the margins for decision-making discretion among officials, reestablished market laws, privatized state enterprises, substantially reduced public spending, reordered credit, stabilized the monetary system, liberalized domestic and foreign trade, and reduced the size of the state. The sectors that had formerly enjoyed privileged status under the Sandinistas, holding speculative, monopolistic, or oligarchic positions or dedicated to industrial activities that were overprotected by excessive tariff rates, saw their privileges and perquisites fade away.

The continuing resistance and threats to democratic transition in Nicaragua did not have ideological roots, as the Sandinistas would have people believe. When the Sandinista leadership and the rent-seeking sectors resisted economic reform in the name of "defending the revolution's gains," they were simply trying to defend political privileges and power and to maintain the distortions induced when government controls are substituted for market forces. This structure and the mentality behind it are among the greatest obstacles to economic reform wherever reforms seek to establish a market economy—not only in Nicaragua but also in Poland, Czechoslovakia, Hungary, and the former Soviet Union.

Pacification and Stabilization

The two immediate mandates that the National Salvation government received from the Nicaraguan people on February 25, 1990, were to end the civil war and to stop the further deterioration of the national economy, which was being suffocated by hyperinflation. During the first year of its administration, the new government concentrated all its efforts on fulfilling the first mandate by demobilizing the contra forces, repatriating 250,000 Nicaraguan refugees, and reducing the Sandinista army from 90,000 to 28,000 troops. At the same time, it greatly reduced the military budget.

As the pacification process moved ahead in early 1990, hyperinflation shot up to a rate of 30,000 percent annually because, in the run-up to the elections, the Sandinista administration had abandoned fiscal discipline to appease its political clientele. Upon losing the elections, the Sandinistas inflated salaries and public employment, presumably to leave behind a difficult situation for the new government, to vent the frustration of their followers, and to avoid desertion within their ranks. Other powerful debilitating influences on the economy were the boycott, strikes, and demonstrations organized by Sandinista sectors in opposition to early efforts to stabilize the government. If emergency measures were not taken to stop deterioration of the economy, the new government ran the risk of entering the eighth consecutive year of declining GNP, with all its attendant consequences.

Because of all of these problems, in March of 1992 the government launched an aggressive stabilization plan. It was of critical importance to retain credibility in the eyes of the electorate, international financial agencies, and friendly governments, without whose assistance stabilization could not be fully implemented.

There was a heated debate over whether gradual or shock therapy was needed to stabilize the economy. The new leaders ultimately realized that a gradual approach would mean the death of the "patient." The Nicaraguan economy had been in a state of shock for the previous ten years so that, when the Chamorro government took power, the economy was in a truly disastrous condition. Government leaders believed that it was necessary to administer not a shock but intensive care to get the patient out of its comatose state. This meant adopting drastic measures. Fortunately, most people understood the need for such measures; they knew that such a strategy was the best of the alternatives and represented the last resort for a sinking economy.

The therapy consisted of changing the currency, establishing an exchange rate of five to one in relation to the dollar, reducing the fiscal deficit, establishing discipline in lending practices, and eliminating the exchange-rate uncertainty that had upset prices and wages and fed hyperinflation.

Prices were also stabilized by sharply increasing the supply of basic goods through the efforts of the state trading enterprise, ENABAS, and the government supermarkets. Donations of basic goods from friendly governments helped this effort. Military spending was reduced, and a social safety net for society's most vulnerable sectors was created by the Emergency Social Investment Fund (FISE) with the support of the U.S. Agency for International Development.

Launching the stabilization plan required a well-coordinated strategy of social communication designed to obtain the support of the population. This strategy was of critical importance to the success of the plan. Its first stage consisted of a compromise agreement for implementing the plan among the diverse branches of government and an intense lobbying effort targeting the country's most influential sectors, such as unions, business organizations, the Church, the army, political parties, and opinion makers. At the time the plan was announced, the second stage of the strategy was launched, an intensive social communication campaign. Cabinet ministers participated frequently in media programs for a month, explaining the scope of the plan and responding to questions and concerns from the people. During this stage, a direct telephone line was established for the public to use to express opinions and suggest solutions to economic problems.

The new government at first forged alliances with the labor, business, and popular sectors to confront the coalition of groups that had benefited from the previous disorder and hyperinflation—namely speculators, the aristocracy, union leaders, some managers of state enterprises, and the government bureaucracy and politicians from the old regime. It was also necessary to neutralize the influence of the Sandinista unions grouped into the National Workers' Front (FNT) by agreeing to a sixty-day truce under the assumption that the workers' real wages would not be substantially affected by the stabilization plan. Hopes were that alliances among three such diverse groups as the popular sectors, who benefited from the new economic stability, a business community willing to invest and produce, and small businesses and peasants would resuscitate the economy and put it on the road to growth.

As in all democracies, especially incipient ones such as Nicaragua's, differences of opinion arose within the UNO coalition over the pace of democratic change and what sort of relationship there should be between the executive power and the opposition Sandinista party. Nevertheless, contrary to much that was written in the domestic and international press, domestic political forces generally supported the stabilization plan and the government's economic reforms. Stabilization of the economy created new bases of support to continue economic and political reforms. The very fact that polarized ideological debate existed in the early 1990s demonstrated the possibility of forming coalitions and alliances across the whole Nicaraguan political spectrum and of implementing concrete reforms and action plans.

One fundamental objective of the Chamorro administration was to reestablish financial flows and Nicaragua's access to credit. Her government inherited a bankrupt and debt-ridden public administration. The country's foreign debt was approximately $11 billion, which meant that the previous administration had exceeded the country's debt capacity many times over. The debt figure is stunning when compared to annual exports that barely reached $300 million. The previous government's inability to manage finances ended in default and the cutoff of credit from private banks and the international financial agencies. In addition, the credits were used for unproductive investments and subsidies.

To ensure the success of the stabilization plan, the government had to achieve, at a minimum, immediate productive investments, reconstruction of the country's infrastructure, and renewal of credit to finance production. It was imperative to obtain the support of both the international financial agencies and friendly governments. Only then could we resolve the problem of a matured debt of $365 million, which the previous administration had contracted with the World Bank and the Inter-American Development Bank (IDB).

The new government obtained financing of $180 million from the governments of Spain, Mexico, Colombia, and Venezuela. The United States, France, Taiwan, Sweden, Norway, Finland, Denmark, Korea, Holland, Italy, Switzerland, and Canada contributed $149 million in grants. Japan, Germany, Switzerland, the World Bank, the IDB, and the International Monetary Fund agreed to a cofinancing operation of $430 million, permitting a positive cash flow at the beginning of 1992 to reactivate the economy.

The Structural Adjustment Plan

Once foreign resources were committed to help stabilize the economy, the major challenge was to create a stabilization program sustained by the country's own resources and not dependent on foreign credits and grants. To achieve that objective, a second-stage structural adjustment plan was launched. The state apparatus was reduced and transformed to make it more manageable and efficient. Additionally, profound reforms were launched in the fiscal, financial, foreign trade, industrial and agricultural sectors. It was hoped that this plan, implemented with the assistance of the World Bank, would generate resources for credit, private investment, and maintenance of the productive infrastructure that the economy required to function.

Reestablishing the Market Economy

Stabilization and adjustment had to be accompanied by the return of true market forces. Government leaders believed that the only healthy linkage was the one between the market and private enterprise; that between the state and public enterprise was weak and had generated many distortions.

The new government initiated the privatization of public enterprises in an orderly and sustained manner. As the first step, businesses confiscated by the old regime and those managed by the government were moved to the Nicaraguan Public Sector Corporation (CORNAP), which was responsible for temporarily managing these businesses and deciding how best to transfer them to the private sector.

The National Assembly also approved a broad and nondiscriminatory foreign investment law, a law creating a Superintendency of Banks, a law on financial institutions authorizing the reestablishment of private banking and insurance companies, and an export development law. Simultaneously, steps were taken to deregulate domestic and foreign trade, to free exports and imports, reduce paperwork, eliminate price controls and public and private monopolies and oligopolies, reduce highly protectionist tariffs, and to implement programs to foster small industry.

Reintegrating Nicaragua into the Hemisphere and the Global Market

The government sought to integrate Nicaragua fully into the region, the hemisphere, and the world from which it had been isolated for over a decade. The prolonged economic crisis the country experienced over a number of years showed that small, developing economies like that of Nicaragua are not viable in an international system characterized by large economic and trade blocs; thus, integration is a must for our countries to survive in the twenty-first century.

For reintegration into the world market, the economy had to be based on the principle that growth needs to be congruent with its competitiveness. Basing the economy on import substitution—thereby developing highly protected and thus inefficient production sectors—does not suit the country's needs. A fundamental challenge was to use our competitive advantages to the fullest. Negotiations were begun for free-trade agreements with Mexico, Venezuela, Colombia, and the United States.

Political Democratization

The government's strategy of democratization was to change the country's political culture. Ever since the colonial period, a certain set of political attitudes had accounted for the idiosyncrasies and behavior of the Nicaraguan people and their governing elite. Those attitudes and values include devotion to the ruler, the cult of force, systematic elimination of opponents, the idea that citizens have no rights and must beg the ruler for favors, an arbitrary exercise of power that does not recognize human dignity, the idea that the state and public resources are the victor's booty, a contempt for institutions, and the personalization of political projects. These values are profoundly rooted in the population and the elite; they are a type of historical "unconsciousness" that guides political behavior.

During the Sandinista dictatorship, the leadership's Leninist values and the authoritarian values of Nicaragua's historical consciousness fused perfectly: The vanguard concept combined easily with *caudillismo;* Leninist "statolatry" fit the concept of state patrimony for the ruler and the ruler's clique; and arbitrariness and disrespect for law and order meshed readily with "establishment of the dictatorship of the proletariat" because, according to the Sandinistas, the proletariat made "the revolution a source of law." In addition, the Sandinistas' relationship with contemporary dictatorships in the Soviet Union and Cuba provided them with highly efficient technology for the administration of power. The Sandinista dictatorship reproduced Nicaragua's past political style to its advantage, deeply frustrating legitimate aspirations among Nicaraguans who, after the fall of Somoza, justifiably hoped for qualitative change in the social, political, and economic life of the country. People wanted a definitive break with the past—replacing exclusion with participation, arbitrariness with law, dictatorship with democracy, state ruler patrimony with a republic, and exploitation with justice—and they wanted engagement in international relations with dignity.

The Sandinista experience shows the surprising continuity and persistence of our society's authoritarian political culture. Even a revolutionary takeover of power was unable to change this political culture. In a vicious cycle, Nicaragua's political structures nurtured and maintained an authoritarian political culture which, in turn, could not transform those structures. That is why the democratic transition in Nicaragua required political intervention geared to break down this process of mutual reinforcement and to make it possible to change both the political structure and culture profoundly.

The Chamorro government fostered reconciliation, dialogue, harmony, transparency in government acts, respect for the independence of state powers, the rule of the law, and civic education—all cultural factors. The government attempted to break down the executive's centralized control over the public sector. The government aimed to rid the culture of its legacy from the authoritarian past, which is that public administration is concentrated and centralized in a powerful executive. Sandinismo consecrated this centralization from the Somoza period at the constitutional level by granting the president unrestricted powers and expanding central government functions. The transition to democracy is incompatible with such structures. It requires, instead, that they be replaced by a more equitable distribution of power among branches of government; administrative decentralization and deconcentration in favor of municipal governments; reduction of the public administration's discretion; reapportionment of government functions to intermediary organizations in civilian society; abolition of the army and all vestiges of militarization; and refinement of the electoral process.

The integration of the Nicaraguan economy into the economy of the democratic countries of the world should also stimulate a surge within Nicaragua in the interests and values on which a democratic community can be consolidated, helping to change the existing political culture.

Economic Development

The Chamorro government turned toward a national development plan. The challenge lay in making democratic political development and income distribution plans compatible with investment processes, opportunities offered by outward growth, the development of human resources, and the conservation of ecosystems. There were several goals.

The first goal was to recapture our traditional productive capacities, reactivating the production of cotton, coffee, sugar crops, livestock, and fishing. There had to be initiatives to maintain the production infrastructure, still in a lamentable state; achieve food supply self-sufficiency by reviving basic grain cultivation; and promote microenterprises and industrial free trade zones to combat unemployment, the black market, and informal economic activities.

The second goal centered around the rational and intensive exploitation of natural resources (forests, mines, marine resources) and the introduction and expansion of nontraditional crops and industries to our competitive advantage. To accomplish this goal, Nicaragua had to substantially expand its economic and social infrastructure and overhaul its obsolete technology and equipment.

The resulting demands for the development of human resources would be the central axis of the third goal. Education and training would help to develop agroindustrial activities and raise the value added to our export products.

Economic stabilization and adjustment, social peace, and the implementation of these development goals would brighten the outlook for Nicaragua's renewed economic growth.

CONCLUSIONS

The process of change begun with the Sandinista revolution has been difficult. The attempt to make a transition to socialism failed. That economic strategy rested on the use of foreign resources, not upon a viable economic model. The political strategy of increasing centralization proved inappropriate. The conflict with the United States and the disintegration of the Sandinistas' international supporter, the Soviet Union, heightened the contradictions and contributed to Nicaragua's economic collapse. Under these circumstances the Sandinistas had to attempt a political opening through elections they believed they would win. Both international circumstances and internal conditions made it necessary for them to cede power when they lost the presidential election in 1990.

The opposition coalition led by President Chamorro did not inherit an easy task. The economic and political transition unfolded in a tense environment. To the credit of all groups in Nicaragua, the nation and its political actors backed away from policies of extreme confrontation. It is impossible and unsatisfactory for all groups to return to the past. The first difficult steps in a democratic opening were taken. But the process remains fragile.

NOTES

1. Samuel P. Huntington, *Political Order in Changing Societies* (New Haven: Yale University Press, 1968).

2. In 1979, before the fall of Somoza, three different currents of thought circulated within the FSLN concerning the best strategy for gaining power. The Front had three groups: The Tercerista group advocated insurrection; the Proletarian Tendency group advocated popular struggle, and the GPP (Prolonged People's War) advocated protracted warfare.

3. The FAO was an organization encompassing the majority of the Nicaraguan democratic opposition forces in 1978. Prior to the fall of Somoza, the FSLN divided the FAO by creating the National Patriotic Front (FPN).

4. The National Directorate was the FSLN's supreme governing body. It was made up of nine commanders representing the three different groups within the Front.

5. The mass organizations were groups created by the governing party, among them unions (Sandinista Workers Front, Association of Rural Workers), trade guilds (National Confederation of Hero and Martyr Professionals), business organizations (National Union of Farmers and Ranchers), neighborhood organizations (Sandinista Defense Committees), women's organizations (Luisa Amanda Espinoza Women's Association), youth organizations (Association of Sandinista Youth), and military organizations (Sandinista Popular Militias).

6. COSEP is the peak business confederation, encompassing most chambers of agriculture, commerce, and industry, as well as trade guild associations in Nicaragua's private sector.

7. Central Bank of Nicaragua, *Annual Report 1991* (Managua, 1992).

8. The relationship between the Sandinista regime and organizations such as COSEP, the Roman Catholic Church, the unions, the newspaper *La Prensa*, the National Confederation of Professionals (CONAPRO), and the political parties are examples of this procedure. For a more in-depth analysis, see José Luis Velázquez, *Nicaragua: sociedad civil y dictadura* (San José, Costa Rica: Editorial Libro Libre, 1986).

9. Central Bank of Nicaragua, *Annual Report 1991*.

FIVE

POLITICAL TRANSITION IN GUATEMALA, 1980–1990: A PERSPECTIVE FROM INSIDE GUATEMALA'S ARMY

HÉCTOR ALEJANDRO GRAMAJO MORALES

Over time, most societies change the ways in which they manage social conflict. Prior to 1982, however, Guatemala was an exception because free competition was not allowed, and the state suppressed political activity. Yet Guatemala faced complex social and economic tensions that required urgent attention.

In the early 1980s, the political power structure impaired the social and economic order and, consequently, failed to manage effectively the social tensions increasing within Guatemala. In 1982, the army (Guatemala's army includes land, sea, and air forces within the same institution) seized control of the government. As Professor Caesar Sereseres, a long-standing observer of Guatemala and its army, boldly noted immediately after the coup, it was "not just another coup."[1] The Guatemalan army turned quickly to the task of governing the country amidst severe social tensions.

In this chapter, I describe and analyze Guatemala's political transition during the 1980s. The chapter examines the army's plans for, and performance in, promoting democratic politics and considers the actions of, and reactions to, the early years of civilian democratic rule. I also speculate about Guatemala's future in the 1990s, focusing on how to consolidate democracy and bring about a better future for all Guatemalans. I have served in the army as director of the National Defense Staff and army inspector general (1982–83); as zone commander for the Guatemala City Military District and as adviser to the head of state as a member of the Council of Commanders (1984–85); as chief of the National Defense Staff (1986); and as minister of national defense (1987–May 1990).

BACKGROUND

Guatemala's people speak twenty-three languages and dialects. Its society, its economy and, to some degree, its politics have changed little since the times of the Spanish colonial empire (1524–1821). In 1871 a reform movement created a small middle class; decades later, in 1944, a revolution introduced social, economic, and political changes that expanded the size of this middle class.

Guatemala's recent history was shaped to a large degree by the Cold War. During this time, the United States and Western Europe opposed the Soviet Union and its Eastern European allies militarily and politically, seeking ideological allies against communism. The national defense policies of Western European countries and the United States were based on a national security doctrine that asked the state to protect society and to provide for its citizens a secure physical and psychological environment. Within the state's established economic, social, and political order, citizens worked for their own welfare.

In the early 1950s, Latin America felt the effects of the Cold War ideological struggle. Initially, many nations were surprised and caught unprepared; they lacked their own coherent national defense doctrine. For ideological reasons, most of Latin America aligned with the democratic countries, adopting the same national security doctrine of protecting national achievements. In the Guatemalan case, this "protection of achievements" translated into protection of the long-standing status quo.

In 1954, motivated by the national security doctrine of defending the world from communism, the United States and the Roman Catholic Church in Guatemala supported a counterrevolution aimed at ending the democratic gains reaped from the 1944 revolution. Motivated by the same doctrine, the new economic and political elites changed the constitution to exclude certain groups from politics.

The newly evolving Guatemalan power structure was the product of the national security doctrine. In the name of this doctrine, the development of civilian political institutions was curtailed; manifold crimes and abuses were justified; politics relied on violence, rigged elections, and armed confrontation; and special economic privileges were granted to some while participation was denied to others. The government paid little attention to the need for social change.

By 1981, there were numerous indications at home and abroad that Guatemala was on the brink of a major crisis. Within the army, our diagnosis was that Guatemala was in the throes of a strong Marxist-Leninist insurgency. Political violence was widespread. The armed conflict took its toll on important sources of foreign revenue, such as agriculture and tourism, and was leading to increased unemployment. The fighting also cut off government services to, and harmed health conditions in, rural areas. These factors in turn spurred increased migration from rural areas to the cities. The only positive news in the rural areas was improved literacy as a result of a campaign that relied on the radio.

Beginning in the 1970s, the Roman Catholic church faced a profound internal dilemma. Having long been prominent in national affairs, its influence was declining. Within the church, a rivalry arose between conservative bishops and community activists influenced by liberation theology. Especially in Guatemala's northwestern highlands, some priests (none of them native-born Guatemalans) left their pastoral work to become guerrilla commanders. Other priests did not take up arms but worked indirectly with the insurgents, serving as their key contacts in parishes while still acting within the framework of "the popular church."

In 1980 Guatemala's economy entered a recession that lingered and then worsened in the next year.[2] While gross domestic product (GDP) rose slightly in 1981, GDP per capita fell by 2.1 percent, signaling a decline in employment and in real income. In U.S. dollars, 1981 GDP per capita was $549; the trade balance was -$510 million. Traditional exports grew slowly while the unit price of imports rose at a greater pace. Trade with other Central American countries fell because of a regionwide contraction in demand, a regional rise in political and social tensions, and an acute shortage of external financing. Capital flight siphoned off domestic savings, furthering the country's economic decline. Guatemala's economic future was uncertain. Some feared a domino effect: a spread of political and social tensions throughout the Caribbean Basin, especially within Central America. Also, a financial scandal erupted; associates of the president, General Fernando Romeo Lucas García, were found to have gained access to international credit backed by the Guatemalan Central Bank for up to 90 percent of each loan's worth.

General Lucas was the second consecutive military candidate to win the presidency through rigged elections, and in July 1978 he replaced General Kjell Laugerud. The country was governed through an entrenched bureaucracy under an authoritarian political framework, which did not distinguish clearly among the state authorities, the army hierarchy, and the political leaders. Allegations of government ineptitude and corruption abounded. There was very little room for participation by popular organizations—few of which remained active, much less militant—toward the end of General Laugerud's four-year term.

Internationally, Guatemala was isolated. Because of Cold War alignments, countries of the Soviet Bloc and of the nonaligned movement opposed the Guatemalan government. The Guatemalan government also faced opposition from several Western countries led by the United States because of Guatemala's dispute with Belize over the latter's independence and territorial boundaries. The United States and other countries once allied with Guatemala distanced themselves because of Guatemala's poor reputation on human rights issues—a consequence of political violence and of the methods employed to confront the Marxist insurgency.

In 1977, U.S. President Jimmy Carter declared that the defense of human rights would be the centerpiece of his foreign policy. Thus, he voiced indirect support for various movements favoring redemocratization. With the U.S. government's support, political regimes similar to Guatemala's were toppled in Nicaragua (General Anastasio Somoza Debayle's, July 1979) and El Salvador (General Carlos Humberto Romero's, October 1979), thereby applying additional psychological pressure to Guatemala, where the government again feared that the domino effect might be at work—that the regimes would all tumble. Guatemala's armed opposition, too, promoted polarization, applied pressure, generated fear, and eventually provoked panic within the government and the Guatemalan business community.

Foreign currency reserves plummeted; production dwindled to dangerously low levels. The government's anticommunist policies remained inflexible and repressive, adding to polarization. Isolated nationally and internationally, the government saw its legitimacy founder. It turned toward a totalitarian style of rule. Politicians who would not join the government were forced into exile. The government was so rigid that even its old allies on the extreme right deserted it and began to plan its overthrow.

In May 1980, the Sixth Command and General Staff course at the army's Center for Military Studies appraised the national situation and presented its findings unofficially to President Lucas in a document, "Strategic Appraisal." One recommendation stated: "To convince citizens to vote, it is necessary to guarantee that their political will, expressed through the ballot, is a powerful democratic instrument that will be respected. It would also make things much easier if a military officer were not to participate as a presidential candidate in the next elections." Unable to find a civilian candidate loyal to him, General Lucas asked the Institutional Democratic Party (Partido Institucional Democrático—PID) and the Revolutionary Party (Partido Revolucionario—PR) leaders to identify and present to him three prospective civilian candidates from among whom he would choose one to run for the presidency. The party leaders came up with just one name: General Angel Aníbal Guevara, minister of defense.

Under Guatemala's constitution, military officers are not allowed to vote, a prohibition remaining to this day. Many hoped that Guevara would lose, fearing that the insurgents would be the main beneficiaries of a Guevara victory. Some officers even believed that the insurgents were pressuring rural voters to vote for General Guevara. When Guevara was declared the winner of the March 7, 1982, elections, the three opposition candidates joined forces and led an uprising to protest the electoral fraud. Donaldo Alvarez, eight years the interior minister and secretary-general of the PID, called on his efficient director of the national police to crush the uprising. The three opposition candidates were jailed, along with many Guatemalan and foreign journalists.

The military knew that the prevailing political, economic, and diplomatic circumstances made it more difficult for the army to suppress the insurgency. The army was suffering significant losses in field combat and was surprised by the extent to which the insurgents had organized and achieved control over the civilian population in the central and western highlands. Terrorist tactics such as the use of Claymore-type mines damaged army morale, but the government's neglect of and lack of commitment to meet the basic needs of the population in the highlands damaged army morale more. The army cared deeply about the importance of addressing such basic needs. The sense of dignity among Guatemalans was also low: to them, General Guevara's victory signaled more of the same. Keeping a military man in the presidency made the war against the communist insurgency more difficult to conduct. Guatemalan society and the military institution were both in peril.

To prevent the government from falling to the rebels, some officers responded to the overtures of the conservative economic groups. Earlier in the election campaign, these rightists had supported Mario Sandoval for the presidency while they conspired to prepare for a possible military coup if their candidate were to lose the election.[3]

THE MILITARY GOVERNMENTS
The 1982 Coup d'État

Several elements set the background for the coup d'état. First was the government's tough response to the broad protests against the results of the March 7, 1982, elections. Second was the imprisonment of many national political leaders and Guatemalan and foreign journalists. Third, there was a general sense of societal alienation. And, lastly, army morale was low; the army was concerned about the deteriorating military and economic situation.

The week before the coup, the head of military intelligence supplied the president and the army's high command with the details of the conspiracy. President Lucas disregarded the information, reaffirming instead his belief in his personal good luck. General Benedicto Lucas, the president's brother as well as chief of the army's general staff, also rejected the information, which he considered exaggerated, and accused the head of intelligence of being under stress and therefore of thinking irrationally. Benedicto Lucas was overconfident because he enjoyed good relations with air force junior officers and thought highly of his own personal leadership qualities. The defense minister, not a Lucas relative, remained silent.

On March 23, 1982, President Lucas was overthrown in a bloodless coup. The new junta consisted of nine military officers, two of whom were generals. One was General Efraín Ríos Montt, a member of the army's "active reserve."[4] He had connections with two political parties, the National Liberation Movement (Movimiento de Liberación Nacional—MLN) and the Authentic National Center (Centro Auténtico Nacional—CAN), as well as with junior military officers. The other was General Horacio Maldonado, a close friend of President Lucas and commander of the Honor Guard, a major military unit in the capital city. Another junta member was Colonel Luis Gordillo, who likewise had close ties to President Lucas and who served as commander of the headquarters garrison in the capital city; he represented army hard-liners allied with ultraconservative economic groups. Also in the junta, in an advisory role, was a member from each command level of the military rank structure: a battalion commander and the chief of intelligence from the Honor Guard; a battalion commander and an infantry company commander from Mariscal Zavala, the other major military unit in the capital city; a lieutenant fighter pilot from the air force; and a second lieutenant from the air force's security troops.

During the negotiations leading up to the coup, the most important conspirators were the battalion commander, the chief of intelligence of the Honor Guard, and the infantry company commander from Mariscal Zavala. They had wanted Ríos Montt alone to be president but could not rally enough support behind him. Instead, they settled for the formation of a junta. They never gave up hope of fully controlling the government, however.

Confusion reigned after the collapse of the Lucas government. On one side there were the army hard-liners, the powerful economic interests, and the leaders of the political parties of the right. Uncommitted were the urban middle class and the lower and middle classes of the rural areas. The leaders of the political parties of the left were still in exile in neighboring countries. The armed insurgency endured, exercising some control over rural ethnic groups and enjoying international political and logistical support from the Soviet Union, Cuba (whose government admitted it publicly), and Nicaragua and unofficial support from Mexico.

The insurgents still pursued the revolution. From exile, the parties of the left urged democracy. Ill-organized and fearful of repression, the urban and rural middle classes remained on the sidelines. For the first time ever, representatives of the largest Indian ethnic groups were offered membership in the new State Council. For the first time in twenty-eight years, the powerful economic interests soon switched to support the opposition, although they did not clearly understand their new position nor did they attempt to understand or accept the army's new approach to the nation's problems. Leaders of parties of the right were puzzled by the attitudes of their long-time partners in the army.

The junta itself soon developed its own internal problems. General Maldonado was accused of protecting officials from the Lucas government and interfering with efforts to punish those accused of corruption and violation of human rights.

In a swift palace coup, on June 9, 1982, General Ríos Montt ousted General Maldonado and Colonel Gordillo. It was a moment of glory and vindication for the politician-general, who had been the Christian Democratic candidate in presidential elections in 1974 and who probably won them. At that time, Ríos Montt, a victim of postelection fraud, had been denied the presidency. The "establishment" had given the presidency to General Laugerud instead. Now, Ríos Montt could enjoy the satisfaction of ordering Laugerud to relinquish the presidential sash he had used during his term to the captain of Ríos Montt's body of advisors (*la juntita*), who then presented the sash to Ríos Montt at the inaugural ceremony where he took the presidential oath of office.

Pacification, June 1982–August 1983

While the predictable power struggles and uncertainties followed in the wake of the coup, under specific orders from General Ríos Montt the National Defense Staff joined forces with the Center for Military Studies (CEM) to choose the members of the Secretariat for Social, Economic, and Development Planning (SEGEPLAN). They would update and revise the 1980 CEM "Strategic Appraisal," creating a strategic plan for the military government. Any army's basic mission is to protect and preserve the nation's independence, sovereignty, domestic and international security, and peace. For that reason, the National Defense Staff was given cabinet rank under the new military government and, along with the CEM and SEGEPLAN, it was charged with the task of assessing the country's social, military, economic, and political situation as well as the strategies of the state's opponents—of determining the strengths and weaknesses of the army and government.

Those of us in the Defense Staff saw a problem in using repression to bring peace to Guatemala. Although wracked by political violence and armed insurgency, Guatemala had other, deeper problems. Peace had to be promoted by means other than war, means that would be more complex and time consuming but also more humane and likelier to resolve or ameliorate the obstacles to pacification. Guatemala's problems had deep roots in the nation's inflexible traditional agro-export production model, its maldistribution of wealth, and its social conditions. Guatemala also faced new short-run problems. When the international prices for coffee, cotton, and sugar fell in 1981, the economy had to absorb the loss. When the price of petroleum and other imports rose, the problem became acute. In 1982 we concluded that we had to address the long-standing ills of the social and economic system inherited from the Spaniards in colonial times. That task would not be easy.

We identified thirteen clusters of national problems requiring action. In May 1982, the president of the junta and the advisers approved our scheme, although they added a fourteenth issue so that the number would not be thirteen, which they believed was unlucky. These clusters were called the "actual national objectives" to achieve the hopes of Guatemalans; it was understood that there could be no short-term, solely military solutions to the problems. This realization led to drastic changes in the military doctrine and strategy embodied in the National Security and Development Plan.

The plan's general proposition was that the Guatemalan state should promote and implement legal as well as managerial, structural, and functional reforms to change existing institutions in the executive branch and the courts; the legislative branch was suspended. The state would also develop and coordinate counterinsurgency programs to include political entities; the goals would be to ensure the economy's proper operation, giving priority to social and economic problems, the achievement of a sense of nationhood, and the preservation of national traditions. The structure and operations of the army and other security forces would be improved so that they could face the insurgency effectively. Programs would be adopted to improve the living conditions of the less privileged, to reactivate national production, and to bring about greater equality of opportunity in access to national wealth. The plan called also for steps to be taken to reconcile Guatemalans on opposite sides of the conflict and to promote security, peace, and dignity based on the full respect of human rights. We would try to improve the country's image internationally through a well-coordinated and well-implemented diplomatic plan. A war would have to be fought on all fronts: military, political and, above all, social and economic. The people's minds and hearts were our targets.

This developmentalist, reformist national strategy replaced the prior doctrine of national security that had emphasized a policy of mere coercion. We sought, instead, to implement national objectives to overcome the country's problems. This strategy would later come to be known as the "Thesis for National Stability."

To implement the army's strategy, the new government needed an array of decisions and programs. The underlying approach of the strategy was to mobilize all national resources to address the country's problems. The strategy required everyone's political participation; armed with the legitimate exercise of power and within the framework of democracy, the necessary economic changes would be made to improve the general welfare and to solve Guatemala's chronic social problems. The top priority would focus on political issues, to be followed by economic and social issues.

On June 9, 1982, new Legal Codes for the Nation were promulgated. They had been drafted by a team of lawyers headed by Air Force Colonel Manuel de Jesús Girón Tánchez, a distinguished, moderate, and sensible lawyer who served as the president's secretary-general. Girón Tánchez was the architect of the legal changes implemented under both General Ríos Montt and his successor, General Oscar Mejía Víctores (Girón Tánchez would serve also as the liaison between the head of state and the National Constituent Assembly while the latter drafted the new constitution). Girón Tánchez performed tasks that resembled those of a British prime minister or those of a White House chief of staff in the United States. His clever yet humble common sense was a great asset for the government and for the army at such a difficult time in their history.

A state of siege was declared; political party activities were prohibited. Politicians were unhappy but the majority felt relief because it was thought that political violence stemmed from political competition. To achieve democracy in the end, the government had to proceed step by step, eventually seeking freer expression and freedom from repression and fear under the rule of law. Although a state of siege suggests that the prevailing laws are set aside, its actual implementation did not detract from the new breath of freedom that the country felt in comparison with the experiences of the immediate past.

The political scenario featured a polarized people. The army and the armed insurgents stood on opposite sides, while most ordinary people did not participate in politics. The military's campaign was called "Victory in 1982 by beans and bullets"; it emphasized civic actions (the beans) instead of merely fighting the armed guerrilla bands with bullets.

The insurgent movement had become even more active. To achieve democracy, however, the country would first have to be at peace. Hostilities had to cease to bring peace. In a dramatic change of policy, in order to save lives and resources, the military government sought to engage in a kind of dialogue with the insurgents through the diplomats of governments known to have open communications with the representatives of the insurgency. The insurgents haughtily and openly rejected this bid.[5]

The president decreed an amnesty program to benefit both the insurgents and those members of the security forces who were believed to have committed crimes during the armed conflict. This was an effective policy. Special courts were also set up to protect witnesses and judges in the administration of law, especially with regard to cases of insurgency or organized crime.

The president decreed a general mobilization to authorize the army to draft at once into military service those public employees who abandoned their place of work and used the pretext that the armed conflict excused them. The army further drafted medical doctors, teachers, and agricultural advisers, who were all sent to remote regions of the country to provide services to the population. The mobilization decree also permitted calling up experienced and well-trained veterans. Naval and air reserves were created. Along with support from community self-defense organizations, these measures bolstered the army's personnel and other capabilities quite quickly. To be sure, to enlist the support of a people tired of abuses and terror, the most important factors were good motivation, clear commitments, and open cooperation.

General Ríos Montt's outgoing personality contrasted sharply with the shyness and awkwardness of General Lucas. Every Sunday, Ríos Montt's own evangelical religious radio programs served as a psychological and moral campaign. He was a good communicator of the army's internal consensus and of its ideas for change. He understood the importance of communication and he played his role very well to win the hearts and minds of the people in the cities, while the National Reconstruction Committee and the army's units did their part in the rural areas.

Headed by Jorge Serrano (a subsequent president, who had just recently entered politics), a thirty-four-member State Council was established to advise the president. Among others, there were four representatives from the powerful economic groups; seven from such national institutions as the university, the press, the municipalities, and the bar association; one from each of the five legally registered political parties (except for the National Unity Front [FUN], the parties refused to take their seats); and ten from ethnic Indian groups. One of the State Council's most important achievements was the design of a new, independent, and capable Supreme Electoral Tribunal and the selection of its members.

In 1976, the National Reconstruction Committee had been created to coordinate reconstruction efforts after a major earthquake. In 1982, its executive director was Air Force General Federico Fuentes Corado. The committee was well staffed with able, nationalist civilian technocrats. This agency was given the task of coordinating all the relief plans for civilian communities, delivering government services and embodying the "beans" part of the military campaign.

To address economic issues, taxes were lifted on agricultural exports. Import permits were given for fertilizer, pesticides, and other agricultural and industrial inputs. The most difficult decision was to maintain parity between Guatemala's currency, the quetzal, and the dollar (one quetzal equaled one dollar). A great many firms queued at the Central Bank to request access to scarce foreign currency. International financial institutions pressured the government to adopt an economic stabilization program and to devalue the quetzal.

President Ríos Montt informed the army commanders that he had changed priorities. Economic problems would be addressed first and political problems later. He would give immediate priority to implementing a value-added tax, deferring national elections for the time being. He said that he expected it would take him at least seven years of hard work to solve the economic problems.

At about the same time, the evangelical church to which the president belonged, the Church of the Word, began to take control of various national government agencies, especially those at the Office of Social Welfare which had been staffed heretofore by relatives of army officers. These actions added to disaffection with Ríos Montt among the officers.

The army's judgment was that the strategy agreed upon at the outset should be continued. Pressures from powerful economic groups and conflicts between the Church of the Word and the military over the government's social welfare programs were also among the reasons why the officers would oust Ríos Montt. With the help of the military high command, Ríos Montt successfully resisted an ill-planned and poorly executed coup attempt on June 29, 1983. Some had the impression that this attempt sought to test his reactions. On August 8, 1983, the army high command and the field commanders relieved Ríos Montt of his duties as head of the military government. Force had to be used; in exchanges of fire around the National Palace between army rebels and Ríos Montt's personal guard, a lieutenant was killed and several soldiers were wounded.

Political Liberalization, August 1983–January 1986

General Mejía, minister of defense and the army's senior officer, was appointed head of state by the "Council of Commanders." The very concept of this council was developed by General Mejía, who used it widely whenever he announced to the nation decisions that he had reached with his closest associates. The council included the secretary-general of the Office of the Presidency, the foreign minister, the colonel who was chief of General Mejía's personal staff, and sometimes General Rodolfo Lobos, chief of the National Defense Staff. These five people and the four most outspoken military commanders would be the key strategists for this period of liberalization in Guatemala's politics. The Council of Commanders also raised the status of the garrison commanders, who became "advisers" to the head of state (although he rarely sought their advice). The council replaced Ríos Montt's "little junta," thereby symbolizing renewed respect for the principle of military hierarchy according to which lower-ranked officers should have no role in making high-level political or military decisions. In his inaugural speech, General Mejía stated that his "government was provisional and of short duration" and that his "mandate was to hold elections and return the responsibility for the government to civil society."

In late 1983, the process of liberalization began. The state of siege was lifted, signaling respect for individual and civil liberties. The special courts were disbanded. The president of the Supreme Court was replaced; the court system was revamped. Stricter laws were enacted to regulate the army itself, to streamline personnel, and to bring younger officers into the upper echelons of the military hierarchy.

The military pacification campaign proceeded according to the 1982 Security and Development Plan. Results surpassed expectations; it was time to move to the next phase: to heal the nation's deep wounds, paying special attention to the people in the war zones and to the army itself. Thus 1984 was declared the year of reconciliation. Programs were also to be implemented within the army's officer corps to heal the wounds opened by the coups of March 1982 and August 1983.

More important for the process of democratization were policies to mitigate the pain of years of armed conflict. New windows were opened to allow for freer expression of views and of criticism. In the rural areas an effort was made to provide the population with a safe and secure environment to live and work. "Development poles" were created throughout the countryside centered on rebuilt villages. The program's hallmarks were its "three t's": *techo, tortilla, trabajo* (shelter, food, work).

Most foreigners did not understand these concepts and saw them in quite superficial terms, especially if they had a clear ideological bias; through ignorance or malice, most made no distinctions between the military operations conducted by the Lucas presidency prior to 1982 and the army's military campaign after March 1982. The international press mistakenly compared these rebuilt villages with the U.S. army's concept of strategic hamlets devised during the Vietnam War. This international and intellectual misperception, however, framed the Guatemalan experience for much of the world and turned it into a cliché; only derogatory terms were used to describe what I believe were the army's successful humanitarian efforts to foster participation and human development in the rural areas.

General Mejía's mandate had politics as the first and only priority but he was not able to isolate the country from Latin America's widespread economic structural crisis of the 1980s. Excluded from access to international financial institutions, Guatemala had borrowed from commercial banks to meet its obligations. In 1984, for the first time in its modern history, the problem of the external debt surfaced as a serious issue even though Guatemala's debt was small compared to those of other countries in the region. In November the government announced a "parallel" exchange rate; for the previous fifty-five years there had been parity between the quetzal and the dollar. Overnight the quetzal's value against the dollar dropped to a four-to-one exchange rate. This change shocked everyone. Time would be needed to learn how to manage in the new environment. Four times during 1985, exchange rate shifts reduced the central bank's capacity to manage external transactions. In addition, although foreign currency was scarce, it was auctioned to import items not of the highest priority, such as remittances to pay for education abroad, spare parts for vehicles, and so forth.

Because of collective bargaining or the decisions of individual firms, wages rose slightly; labor union activity remained minimal. Inflation accelerated, however; in 1984, its annual rate rose to 31 percent, compared with more typical increases of 18 percent in previous years. The rapid rise in prices coupled with a modest wage increase led to a loss of purchasing power in real terms. During the last three years of the military government, moreover, government expenditures were cut. According to data from the United Nations Economic Commission for Latin America, GDP per capita fell each year from 1982 through 1986.

In 1985 the politics of economic policy were intense. The military government tried but failed to implement a tax reform package and other economic initiatives. Despite all the powers of the bayonets, General Mejía could not even raise the cost of an urban bus ticket by five cents Guatemalan (just over one penny U.S.). Although the military government enacted a consumer protection law, this effort to protect the population went unrecognized. By carrying out a well-orchestrated and well-funded media campaign, groups that opposed the military's economic policies—the powerful economic groups with vested interests—succeeded in portraying themselves as "defenders of the people" and made the military look foolish and ignorant. The army could not implement economic reforms and felt humiliated. To save face, the government called for a national dialogue among different groups; the powerful economic bodies participated along with a few labor unions, consumer organizations, and other small interest groups. There was agreement to impose a small tax on travelers and to exempt transportation from the value-added tax. These events clarified and confirmed the judgment that army planners at the Center of Military Studies had reached in the strategic plan for 1982: "Without political legitimacy, no government can initiate economic policy changes; it is even worse if the government launches an initiative but lacks popular support for it." In future years, the military would recall the experience of these events.

Demilitarization was an important part of the liberalization process. The army viewed this policy as its disengagement from civilian public sector duties. To govern the country was difficult and complicated; it diverted the best officers to performing civilian tasks. The disengagement program also served a psychological purpose. It accustomed the officers to doing without preferential treatment from or access to the bureaucracy. Except for General Mejía, by May 31, 1985, no military officer (retired or on active duty) held a civilian government post.

The Rules of the Game

A newly created, genuinely independent Supreme Electoral Tribunal replaced pre-existing entities and was given the task and the resources to prepare new election rules and to call for elections for a National Constituent Assembly, which were held in July 1984. For the following months, its one hundred representatives worked busily on a new law on habeas corpus, on new electoral laws, and on a new constitution; having done its job, the assembly was disbanded. Except for the new constitution, the laws were put immediately into effect.

In July 1985, general elections were announced and free political competition began. For the first time in Guatemalan history, the military did not back, favor, or support a particular political party or candidate. The army wanted to be a problem solver, not add to the country's problems. This political opening unleashed popular participation. It extended to all Guatemalans the full rights of their citizenship. Leaders of the parties of the left returned from exile to participate in the elections. Long-suppressed popular organizations re-emerged. New labor unions were organized, as were new militant and outspoken human rights groups. The Roman Catholic Church had kept a low profile during the military governments; the bishops had avoided speaking out in a deliberate effort not to validate the regime's actions. A few of the Catholic clergy cooperated discreetly with refugee groups on the Mexican side of the border; some worked with the "people in arms" movements, and some provided occasional logistical support and resources to the insurgents.

Given the changes in the rules of the game and the new political opening, a transition to democracy began. From the March 1982 coup that overthrew General Lucas to the inauguration of a democratically elected civilian president in January 1986, it had taken nearly four years to prove that the March 1982 military movement, as noted at the beginning of this chapter, was "not just another coup."

LEARNING TO LIVE IN A DEMOCRACY (1986–1991)

In early 1986, the political situation was as follows: the Christian Democratic Party won the national elections, capturing the presidency for Marco Vinicio Cerezo Arévalo as well as gaining a majority in Congress. The Marxist-Leninist insurgency—small but armed and well connected internationally—remained in the field; for them this democracy was a sham—at best a well-conceived army counterinsurgency program to install a puppet president.

The political parties of the left remained in the opposition but adopted a wait-and-see attitude. As usual, rural Indians were skeptical. So too was the urban middle class, wondering how long this new government would last and whether it would remain in power long enough to make a difference; the urban middle class feared retaliation from the right if the Christian Democratic government were to fail. The rural middle class remained uncommitted to democracy, relying instead on community rule, self-defense, and community vigilance, aware that the insurgency remained active and aggressive and also suspicious of the ever-present army. The newly organized human rights groups were in the opposition; they asked for punishment for the leaders responsible for repression during the authoritarian governments. The Roman Catholic Church remained neutral. The evangelical church, a new social actor, was very active, summoning up its congregations and participating in national political discussions.

Mass media leaders remained the same for the most part, with a few new voices added. All major mass media organs opposed the Christian Democratic government. The second largest daily newspaper belonged to the second runner-up for president, who was already giving signs of becoming a candidate for the next elections. The owner of the television news program with the largest audience had also been a losing candidate in the presidential election. Most of the press and the television outlets were owned by members of the most powerful economic groups.

Bureaucrats expected many dismissals. Military leaders were uneasy at the disorder and the prospect of more; because of the politicians' rhetoric and the provocations of human rights groups, army officers feared retaliation and loss of petty privileges. The parties of the right were in the opposition and in a minority in the Congress; they had done badly in the elections and they feared major economic and political changes. The major economic groups were also in the opposition. Despairing that they lacked congressional power, they began to prepare their organizations to confront the government to defend their interests and the status quo even by means of street demonstrations. In his inaugural address, President Cerezo referred to the fact that the country was in turmoil but indicated that the Christian Democrats had come to power to reorder the nation's affairs and to correct the past abuses and misbehavior of the authoritarian governments. It was a good speech, brimming with rhetoric and promises.

The Army under the Constitution

During the military governments, commanders had been lax in order to remain on the job and to gain obedience and loyalty from their subordinates. In those days, they owed their positions to the approval of their subordinates. With few exceptions, they had not enforced military discipline; most had delegated disciplinary responsibilities to a second in command. The commanders spent most of their time on other duties, such as working with government officials and the civilian population in development projects in each commander's zone of responsibility. In early 1986, some still believed that the Council of Commanders had the right to address national political issues, especially those related to military policy and foreign relations. It had been much easier for the officers to speak of democracy, liberties, and military professionalism when the head of state and commander in chief was also an all-powerful general who served simultaneously as defense minister.

After the political transition, circumstances changed. The president and commander in chief was a civilian. Elected civilian government officials led the country. The minister of defense and the chief of the National Defense Staff were both generals, but they had been appointed by civilian authority, and they dealt mainly with politico-military affairs; both derived their authority from the laws. The military high command and the army itself were legitimate institutions under the law. The law stipulated that all soldiers owed subordination to the state. Army officers became nervous and had second thoughts about the timing and extent of the democratic opening when they listened to the fresh expression of the long-suppressed voices of the parties of the left and to the claims and threats from human rights groups.

At the National Defense Staff, I chose a bright and even-tempered colonel to serve as vice chief and assigned him the task of recruiting a hardworking staff. All of the highest-ranking officers immersed themselves in seeking to understand the army's new institutional role in order to come up with suggestions and guidelines to manage the challenges of adaptation.

Professionals chose the approach called "military fundamentalism," an effort to depoliticize the army, to comply with the law and, at the same time, to affirm military authority from above rather than from below. The army needed a strong internal authority. Professional leadership meant a depersonalized authority, without personal privileges or commitments; officers had to obey and to enforce obedience to rules and regulations without questioning.

Through these measures we hoped to strengthen the military institution, to prepare it to persevere, and to adapt it to its new challenges in helping the country prosper.

The minister of defense accepted the concept of military fundamentalism (or "pure professionals"). Then the president as commander in chief did so as well, adding that the joint effort to move Guatemala forward along the path of democracy would benefit from this "alliance of professionals," given that he considered himself a professional politician.

The strategy and the ensuing orders to implement it were made known to the officer corps by directives and speeches. The orders were also discussed in retreat-type seminars, so as to complement the written orders with an intensive educational process at the high and middle levels of command. Most of these seminars were limited to officers; sometimes professors, politicians, and retired generals were invited to give lectures to cover the same topics but from their own different perspectives. The following summarizes the tenets of military fundamentalism.

The army's external strategy to adapt to national challenges had three elements:

1. The army as an institution, and its leaders, would withdraw from routine government activities and from participation in politics. In order to create the space to allow the institutions and groups of civil society to participate, the military would not take sides in national discussions of economic matters.

2. The officers would behave as professional soldiers. They had to obey and support the nation's laws and the legally established authorities. They should not criticize publicly either the government as a whole or individual government officials. They should set the example for the rest of the nation about how to live in a democracy.

3. The minister of defense was to be the only active-duty officer charged with communicating with political leaders and institutions. Let the politicians fight the political battles. Let the economic groups fight their own economic battles. Let civil society grow. The army should not and would not attempt to redeem the nation from social injustice.

The army's internal strategy to adapt to national challenges had two elements:

1. The army would strengthen its own institution by depersonalizing authority at all levels; by obeying and complying with the laws and with all rules and regulations and enforcing these across all levels of command; by managing efficiently; and by educating and training officers to improve

their job performance. Maintenance of existing equipment would be improved to the utmost.

2. The army would maintain pressure in the field on the insurgent groups to ensure peace, while its actions would also emphasize the concept of the role of the army in a democratic state in the curriculum of military schools, updating the curriculum of the Military Academy and of the CEM to adjust them to the nation's new social and political realities. The army would improve military discipline and behavior and would use financial resources efficiently.

The Christian Democratic Government's Strategy

I have not carried out a detailed study of the Christian Democratic government's strategy or of its real plans for government (in contrast to its electoral slogans). For the purpose of this analysis, I will endeavor to show what the strategy seemed to be as observed in the actions and policies adopted at the outset and later implemented; I will rely on observations based on my service as defense minister.

An early event that I am certain had a negative impact on the performance of the Christian Democrats in government was the fatal air accident of a Guatemalan commercial plane on January 16, 1986. The airplane carried Dr. Arístides Calvani, a renowned Venezuelan Christian Democratic ideologist, and other Venezuelan Christian Democrats. I witnessed the sorrow and despair, the sense of loneliness and helplessness in the leaders of Guatemala's Christian Democratic Party, especially President Cerezo and Alfonso Cabrera, who was president of the newly installed National Congress. From their evident despair, I concluded that Calvani had been a mentor, guide, supervisor, director, and source of inspiration for them. The man who died had been tutor to the politicians who had just taken charge of leading Guatemala toward a better future; they were now on their own.

1986: Mobilization and reorientation. In 1986, there was much social mobilization—many demonstrations, strikes, walkouts, and protest marches. The president often said: "This is the strategy. This year we have to open the pressure valves in order to sense how high the pressure is and then release most of it."

There was a reorientation of the economy. The installation of the new civilian government, along with some improvement in foreign trade, generated an optimistic outlook on the economy. At the outset, the government sought to liberalize prices to spur production and to ensure the supply of mass consumer goods. The central government's budget was cut and a prudent monetary policy adopted. The government designed a short-term Economic and Social Reorganization Plan, which took effect in July and was to be applied for a year. The plan sought to ease inflationary pressures and to help raise the level of employment. The government sought to lower the fiscal deficit, restrain the money supply, and reduce pressures on the exchange rate by creating a controlled exchange rate of two and one-half quetzals to the dollar for most external trade transactions. The government imposed a new tax on exports and on international telephone calls. It increased public service rates and fees, especially for water and electricity. It granted some subsidies. It implemented a program designed to create 40,000 jobs.

By the end of 1986, the parallel market exchange rate was only slightly above the controlled exchange rate, leading to the virtual disappearance of the parallel market. In contrast to that success, the fiscal deficit rose and inflation accelerated sharply (although the rate slowed down by late 1986). Unemployment rose and real wages fell. Private investment reacted timidly but it was stimulated by the rapid growth of in-bond (*maquiladora*) industries.[6]

1987: Three learning experiences. In 1987, three major events influenced politics and gave Guatemalans a good learning experience on the concept of democracy.

On August 7, the government's foreign policy of active neutrality in the Central American conflict began to prove its value in the results of the Esquipulas II accords. These accords resulted from several rounds of meetings of Central American presidents, held at Esquipulas, Guatemala, intended to bring peace to all of Central America. The accords called for the establishment of a National Reconciliation Commission in each Central American country to seek a political solution to the existing conflicts. This required dialogue among different groups and also direct talks between the governments and the armed insurgents.

On August 12, at a hotel in Guatemala City, I, as minister of defense, the chief of the National Defense Staff, and members of the defense staff made a public presentation to the nation. In attendance were representatives of every economic, social, and political group as well as foreign diplomats, government officials, and members of the national and international press. Based on the terms of the army's external strategy as conveyed to the president in January 1986, our public presentations stated the army's position on current issues and events. Reactions were mixed; questions arose.

The International Monetary Fund (IMF) and the World Bank required that Guatemala adopt a stabilization and structural adjustment program before they would assist its government financially; these were the same requirements that the previous military government had been unable to implement. Knowing of the strong business opposition to these policies, in

April 1987 the government began negotiations with the powerful economic groups to reach a mutually beneficial agreement. Each proposal was analyzed at length; various statistical sources were consulted. After a long delay, it became evident that the economic groups were strongly opposed to any changes in the current laws and rules that governed the economy. Although some government negotiators had had strong ties with some of the economic groups (some members of the cabinet believed that the government's negotiators were in fact the representatives of those groups inside the government), negotiations broke down in mid-August. In mid-September, the Congress enacted a tax reform package consisting of sixteen new laws or changes to existing laws.

The powerful economic groups reacted quickly. Relying once again on a well-funded and aggressive mass media campaign but lacking political support in the Congress, the groups took the struggle to the streets. As in 1985, they portrayed themselves as defenders of the people. This time, however, they faced a government that had been elected by the people.

In the second week of October 1987, seven government representatives (including three active-duty officers) met with members of the armed insurgency in Madrid. This event was added to the media campaign against the government: "The government is communist," they said, using the familiar cry to attract support from conservatives, from democrats, and from the United States. The private business sector organized a general lockout for the third week of October, but it only lasted three days. It was called off because of terrorist actions committed by the extreme right, which was not under the control of the business leaders.

1988: The first coup attempt. Unable to force the government to cancel the tax reform, the economic groups turned to politics to show that the government had become unpopular. They planned to win the April 1988 mayoralty elections; much time and effort was spent to unite the opposition to the Christian Democrats. The election results surprised the economic groups as well as politicians on both sides of the spectrum. To the opposition's despair and panic, the Christian Democrats won the majority of municipalities. Even if the entire opposition had been united, they would not have reached a majority. The Christian Democrats rejoiced. At the highest levels of party authority, some became overconfident, arrogant, and too proud of their unmatched political skills.

Politicians from the right and the economic power groups (which together controlled the mass media) joined a conspiracy with some army officers to organize a coup. The planning for the coup was monitored by government agencies from the outset. Although the active-duty officers who were engaged in the conspiracy were warned by the General Staff that the government knew about the plot, the coup attempt was launched on May 11, 1988. Without a shot being fired or anyone being hurt and without any concessions being made, the coup attempt was suppressed after five hours of communication with the rebels. The attempt failed because the garrison commanders of the capital city and its surroundings (including the elite airborne unit), the navy, the intelligence services, and the army's high command remained loyal to democracy.

Because they expected adherence to the guidelines agreed upon in January 1986 and embodied in the internal and external strategies to manage the challenges facing the army as it sought to live in democracy, the army's high command, the members of the National Defense Staff, and the Ministry of Defense were disappointed that the civilian government did not use its full legal powers to punish the officers who participated in the coup attempt. Either for lack of experience or because of a lack of will, the attorney general, the military court system, and the civilian courts failed to prosecute those who had acted against democracy.

The coup attempt had to be dealt with solely by administrative actions within the army. It was labeled an act of military undiscipline. Thus the army had an opportunity to play down the significance of the attempt and to lessen the damage to the institution's prestige as a promoter of democracy. The situation also gave President Cerezo the opportunity to discourage public demonstrations that might have damaged the army's prestige. The failure of the courts to act and the lack of public demonstrations of support for democracy created dangerous perceptions and had a great impact on the aftermath of this first coup attempt.

I promised myself and my fellow officers that there would not be another coup attempt. I worked hard on this. In the army, I gave lectures, proffered advice, wrote warning letters to individuals, ordered transfers, organized seminars, and took many administrative and educational measures to ensure that the army remained loyal to democracy. Special attention was given to the garrison and zone commanders and members of the intelligence service. I also spoke at universities, private clubs, labor union halls, diplomatic receptions, and meetings of the economic associations and chambers. I addressed all of Guatemala, except the politicians. I wanted to avoid "being penetrated by politicians" and I wanted to persuade army officers that there was no chance of the defense minister making an alliance with politicians. I even avoided the Christian Democrats, who were in power. History will have to judge whether I made a mistake in avoiding direct communication with the Christian Democratic leadership.

Because of the army's past and present weight in national affairs, the army and the government were partners, sharing interests in the unfolding of the democratic process. It was tempting to say: "We are the military professionals; you, the civilian politicians, have to mind your own business." But that view was wrong. Its effect was to prevent the army from better understanding the party in power. By letting the politicians mind their own business, by acting coolly and professionally, by setting the example of how to live in democracy, by providing the space to be filled by civil society, and by not criticizing the government, the army became unable to assess the politicians' despair, their inefficiencies, and their general attitudes, which ultimately would invite another coup attempt.

Did we shirk work? Were we excessively concerned with opening up space for civil society? I think not. Instead, the army's stance was pure down-the-line compliance with the existing military orders. It was pure military orthodoxy. My strict adherence to institutional norms, on the one hand, and the arrogance and overconfidence shown by the Christian Democratic leaders, on the other hand, were the key factors that prevented constructive communication and cooperation at the highest levels of government.

President Cerezo was under enormous pressures from many quarters. His party associates in the government were avoiding hard work, using the excuse that another coup was imminent. They failed to show up to work, traveled abroad, or generally wasted time. The government almost ceased to function. To defense staff analysts, it appeared that the president had either abandoned his initial plans and strategies or had changed his priorities and was simply reacting to the issues of the moment.

1989: The second coup attempt. On May 9, 1989, officers cashiered from the army after the first coup attempt, in alliance with politicians and some members of the powerful economic groups, bribed army officers at two military installations in the capital city; the key plotters were the same people who had supported the successful 1982 coup but had failed to control the government installed by that coup—and who had supported the failed May 1988 coup attempt. The forces supporting the 1989 coup seized the air force base in the capital city, held it for four hours, flew two fighter planes over the city, and threatened to bomb the National Palace and the official residence of the defense minister. For three hours, they neutralized the key garrison, the Honor Guard, where one battalion commander with his own commander's consent had maintained contact with the plotters. On the day of the coup attempt, the battalion commander prevented loyal troops from taking action against the revolt, but he was not able to mobilize those troops to act against the government. The rebel leaders also kidnapped my family, held them for three hours, and threatened to kill them if I did not surrender. I did not surrender. Instead, the kidnappers surrendered without a fight; they were outmaneuvered by

Mariscal Zavala Brigade troops. The rebel leaders were captured by the defense minister's personal guard.

The second coup attempt unleashed a series of cabinet changes in an attempt to correct matters and especially to address the economic and fiscal problems better. In fact, the changes presaged pre-election campaign activities. These cabinet changes worsened government inefficiency. The cabinet was quite different at the end of Cerezo's presidency than at the beginning; in the end, the cabinet included mostly the president's personal friends, second-class politicians, and bureaucrats.

Assessment of the Christian Democrats' Strategy

I believe that the Christian Democrats had a strategy for governing when they first came into power, but they were overwhelmed by events: the air accident; the intense political struggle over economic policy and the strong coordinated opposition from powerful economic groups; talks with the insurgents in Madrid; two coup attempts; the complexities of local politics, especially the Christian Democratic attempt to strengthen their labor union allies; the arrogance and overconfidence of Christian Democratic leaders after the April 1988 elections; and above all, the unceasing political campaigning from the very outset until the end of the administration. These cumulative events wore down the president's image and discredited the party. They made it impossible to maintain a steady course in the early stages of Guatemala's experience with democracy.

The Christian Democrats had a good foreign policy, however. President Cerezo's European tour was a political success, as was his Esquipulas initiative. Guatemala had to pay a high price in forgone economic aid and in other political pressures from the United States because it adopted a policy of active neutrality in the Nicaraguan conflict, at odds with the other Central American governments, which were aligned with the United States. Dr. Mario Quiñónez, Cerezo's first foreign minister, mastered the art of explaining how this innovative and independent Guatemalan policy would enhance democracy and save lives in the region, as it ultimately did.

In the administration's early days, Central Bank President Dr. Federico Linares was considered the superstar of the economic and social reorganization. Vice President Roberto Carpio showed his clear purpose and commitment with regard to three well-defined projects: the creation of a Central American Parliament, the promotion of microenterprises, and the "Trifinio" (a program to develop the area where Honduras, El Salvador, and Guatemala share borders).

The Christian Democrats also had a strategy for leveraging development, the Guatemala 2000 plan, the Social Investment Fund (FIS), and other initiatives that never took off. The government used memoranda to make its strategy known, but it seemed that these and other documents were either in-dividual initiatives or small-group projects. They did not reflect a coordinated effort and felt unreal. Current events were often not considered in the formu-lation of those programs, as was evident in the failure of the 500 Days Plan, which was a last attempt to get a grip on the government, though to no avail.

The Election Campaign

It has become common for well-known chief executive officers, for the owners of large and important firms, for certain public officials, and for some mem-bers of the diplomatic corps to be surrounded with bodyguards. For some of the nouveau riche and for some petty politicians, having bodyguards is a symbol of status. Guatemala's bodyguard industry has transcended the country's borders; it became fashionable to hire foreign bodyguards. Foreign or national, most bodyguards—though unfortunately not all—are profes-sionals who provide a specific service. Some bodyguards, however, came to be used to open car doors, to carry packages, or to fix drinks. Other bodyguards were employed to kill a foe. Bodyguard services must be regulated: their legit-imate services must be spelled out, and some services must be declared illegal.

During the election campaign many bodyguards were hired from the pro-tective services of factories and farms or from the security services of the En-ergy Institute or the Port Authority. Politicians' sons or government officials with bodyguards and personal weapons proved deadly at times during the election campaign.

The national campaign opened in April 1989 with the murder of Danilo Barillas, a prominent Christian Democratic leader. It ended one day before the runoff election on January 5, 1991, with the murder of another prominent politician, Marco Tulio Collado, mayor of Escuintla, the country's second most important commercial and communications center. Many other assassi-nations occurred in between.

Political methods did not change from 1986 to 1991. Guatemala lost the opportunity to make a real transition and to advance toward democracy. Un-solved political assassinations are still a major feature of the electoral process, along with a clear absence of democratic principles and procedures inside the political parties. Politicians did not learn any lessons. At least a new president was elected, which was a remarkable achievement for the system.

THE CONSOLIDATION OF DEMOCRACY

In the future, the first democratic presidential period will not be seen as having produced great material advances for the country, but the unseen foundations for a true democracy were laid. We began to practice and to learn how to live in a democracy.

We have discussed many of the factors that brought Cerezo to the presidency. An analysis of the outcome of the 1985 elections, and also of the lack of subsequent support evident during the Cerezo administration in the actions of the different parties and interest groups, suggests that his election was not a vote for the Christian Democrats but rather a vote against the military and the conservatives. In 1990, in another free and democratic election, once again most voters were not committed to any particular ideology. Again they voted against the government (this time in the hands of the Christian Democrats); it was more this than a vote in favor of Jorge Serrano, a civilian who represented moderate conservatives.

The new constitution's Article 186 effectively prevented repetition of the past pattern whereby a military leader would succeed the first civilian president, as had happened in the cases of Juan Arévalo (1951) and Julio Méndez (1970). Article 186 prohibited election to the presidency or vice presidency of any person who had led a coup to change the constitutional order as well as prohibiting the election to those offices of any army officer on active duty; five years had to elapse between an army officer's decommissioning and his eligibility to run for election to the presidency.

At the beginning of the 1990s, there was a fair amount of political reconciliation, thanks in part to Serrano's active participation as a member of the National Reconciliation Commission (created by the Esquipulas II accords) prior to his election as president. Unfortunately, the talks between the government and the armed insurgency soon lost their focus when both sides began to use the talks to make short-run gains in national and international fora.

The political parties should learn from past experiences and introduce democratic practices and procedures into the life of each party. This will improve representation and reduce the frustrations and abuses that have contributed to use of violence as a means to achieve political ends. Democratization of the parties and effective implementation of a new gun control law would reduce political violence.

The army's strategy of eschewing participation in party politics and not registering opinions over economic issues has permitted greater social and political activity. More interest groups have come to be represented in the Congress through their own leaders, not just through politicians. Discussions over national issues are more likely to occur in Congress than in the streets or in the mountains. As time passes, the likelihood of an insurgent victory becomes unthinkable. A clear understanding of the country's social, economic, and political dynamics will give the army a greater capacity to maintain its professionalism and to resist the pressures from some popular groups led by opportunists who have the same short-run objectives as those of the Marxist-Leninist armed insurgency. Such understanding will also allow the army's hierarchy to adjust the institution to a freer society, one that has come to enjoy more civil liberties thanks to the very same army's actions and beliefs since 1982.

The courts have just begun to flex their weak muscles. They must be strengthened. There must be a strict standard of ethical conduct for judges and also better security and protection for them. The courts and the executive branch have accused each other of inefficiencies that have hindered the application of the law in connection with executive branch fact-finding activities in criminal cases. Having responsibilities for crime fighting shared between executive and judicial branches has resulted in evasion of responsibility by the courts, which shirk their work. The courts need their own resources to prosecute criminals, especially in politically related crimes in which the executive may be involved or may face a conflict of interest.

During this first democratic presidency, business executives, industrialists, farmers, and other entrepreneurs as well as politicians and bureaucrats learned much about free market micro- and macroeconomics within the context of democratic politics. Laws were enacted but they were not truly effective. People depend on the efficiency and flexibility of the government's tax structures in order to benefit fully from the political battles fought over economic policy in 1968, 1983, 1985, and 1987.

From the early 1960s, following the Soviet strategic goal that has now failed, Guatemala's social and economic problems were magnified by the international Marxist-Leninist movements, which sought to create another Vietnam in the backyard of the United States—a proposition made famous by international revolutionary Che Guevara, who had worked in Guatemala for about a year in the early 1950s. Although Guatemala achieved a military victory over the insurgency, its remnants still operate in small terrorist bands, which have reacted senselessly and in rage, destroying infrastructure and killing innocent people.

In the Cold War struggle between East and West, the Eastern Bloc has decomposed. Communism has failed as a means for national development. The Cold War national security ideology, therefore, is no longer pertinent. But Guatemala's social and economic indicators still portray the underdevelopment of a large proportion of its population, with people still living at seventeenth-century standards on the eve of the twenty-first century. Since the mid-1970s, the army has understood and articulated well the real concerns over underdevelopment. In the early 1990s, however, public officials and the bureaucracy still ignore or give too little attention to these circumstances, while powerful economic groups continue to benefit from them.

Communism has been defeated in Guatemala and in the world, but

Guatemala's variant of capitalism has not succeeded. Social, political, economic, and military indicators do not identify a clear winner. Although the country has acquired a democratic structure, it has yet to forge a democratic culture. The democratic political system is too formalistic; there is much to be done to replace the institutions that wield actual power with others that would be more efficient as well as democratic according to the laws and procedures identified in the constitution.

Because of ideological conviction and not because of economic interest, the army defends a free market economy. Mercantilism and closed micromarkets remain in place, however; large sectors of society lack access to money markets. Many wages are unfair both because their purchasing power is weak and because they are not as high as the market might set. Inequality, illiteracy, and illnesses are some of the social indicators that portray how weak Guatemala's human development remains.

The United States will remain the external actor dominating Guatemala's international environment, but security is no longer the central U.S. concern in Guatemala. The United States has become more concerned over immigration and the transshipment of drugs. Moreover, the economic dynamism evident in Asia and in Europe has forced the United States to see its southern neighbors in pure economic terms. I hope that in this new approach the characteristic arrogance of the United States will not prevent it from seeing Guatemala's internal realities and idiosyncrasies and will not lead it to impose solutions conceived and crafted in air-conditioned rooms miles away from the object of its interest. I also hope that its close geographic proximity to this megapower will be good for Guatemala, enabling the nation to find joint interests with the United States through wise leadership in both countries.

Freed from ideological concerns and with the virtual disappearance of Cold War communist movements, Guatemala can demonstrate that its leaders have a clear vision about how to achieve the goals of various organizations active in the country, rather than merely witnessing perpetual fights among those organizations. Guatemalans must demonstrate solidarity and cooperation toward one another. We cannot continue to be divided, practicing selfish and self-destructive behavior. In the 1980s the country experienced a democratic transition. I hope now that all sectors within Guatemala understand the need to honor the national interest. Through this national interest, group and individual goals will be achieved more quickly, and there will be a better shared future for everyone.

NOTES

1. Caesar Sereseres, "Guatemala: Not Just Another Coup," *Los Angeles Times*, March 31, 1982.

2. Data from United Nations, Economic Commission for Latin America, *Preliminary Overview of the Economy of Latin America and the Caribbean*, various years.

3. Interview with army officers connected to the National Liberation Movement (MLN) party, Guatemala City, February 1982. See also Lic. Danilo Roca's television interview, April 1982.

4. *En disponibilidad.* In such a situation an officer is neither retired nor on active duty. He has no military duties but remains under the military code of conduct and is paid a military salary.

5. *Prensa Libre,* June 1982.

6. Data from United Nations, Economic Commission for Latin America, *Preliminary Overview of the Economy of Latin America and the Caribbean*, various years.

SIX

GUATEMALA, 1978–1993: THE INCOMPLETE PROCESS OF THE TRANSITION TO DEMOCRACY

RODOLFO PAIZ-ANDRADE

Guatemala is a nation of many different cultures, where citizens of European, Indian, and mestizo origin must continually search for ways to coexist peacefully. There is also a sharp contrast in living conditions between the capital city and the villages and communities of the country's interior. Within the capital itself, the gap widens dangerously between the higher socioeconomic groups and the living conditions of people in marginal urban areas.

Historically, Guatemala has been rooted in culture and tradition, yet it struggles to modernize. We aspire to move beyond our traditional modes of production toward global integration. We are questioning our religious affiliations. We have begun to contemplate the ill effects of the military's prolonged presence in our politics. We continue to struggle to overcome the anguish of poverty. These various issues become manifest, one way or another, in the instability and violence plaguing our nation at every turn, giving foreign observers the impression that Guatemala is in continual chaos.

The question arises: Is a transition toward democracy taking place in Guatemala? And, if so, in what way? I believe it is and that in some respects significant democratic achievements have already been accomplished. However, progress has not been consistent in all areas, and the lack of integrated progress makes the transition process vulnerable. The most glaring results of this phenomenon are the chronic lag in social development and the political events of 1993, which threatened a setback for the process of consolidating democracy initiated in the 1980s.

My analysis does not attempt to retell Guatemala's political history. Rather, I hope to extract lessons from our nation's past that can contribute best to evaluating the future of democratization. I find that there has been progress in fostering political and economic openings but a delay in addressing the social agenda. The slow pace of institutional transformation fosters instability and creates uncertainty about the future. Guatemalans need to understand the transition process and seek to open a window to the future.

This chapter is divided into four sections. The first discusses the extent to which Guatemala's recent regimes have allowed various groups to participate in the political process and to exercise their influence. This section describes the four sectors of influence on the government: military, economic, political, and social. Each sector of influence is composed of differing organizations, ideas, interests, and agendas. From 1978 to 1996, Guatemala had a military government headed by three successive military leaders followed by three civilian presidents: Marco Vinicio Cerezo Arévalo, Jorge Serrano (whose administration ended in mid-1993 when a civilian movement thwarted his own coup against Congress and the Supreme Court), and Ramiro de León Carpio (who replaced Serrano on an interim basis for the remainder of Serrano's term). The civilian presidencies are analyzed separately because they had distinct makeups, support bases, and goals. At times I employ a personal narrative style because I was involved in many of the events described or because I have drawn personal conclusions based on my experiences. (I served as finance minister from January 1986 to October 1989.)

The second section of the chapter discusses the conditions and characteristics of traditional Guatemala and the most important changes wrought by the transition process. These characteristics range from the country's moral and institutional values to its relations with other nations. A "transition map" illustrates how the democratic system is gradually being shaped by processes of which the outcomes remain uncertain.

The third and fourth sections employ the image of a bridge still under construction as a metaphor for the transition process. Each beam of the bridge represents a different element of the democratic transition. Though intimately linked to one another, the seven beams span at different rates the gulf separating Guatemala's past authoritarian history (the old paradigm) from a future consolidated democracy (the new paradigm). Readers can then reach their own conclusions as to how each of these varied elements is affecting the transition to democracy by consolidating, advancing, paralyzing, or reversing the process.

In the fourth section, I apply the transition map to Guatemala from 1978 to 1996 and show that in the transition toward the new paradigm, social reform has been postponed. There is an obvious link between crucial government decisions and probable options emerging from the transition process. Personal experience illustrates the various elements that oppose completion of this bridge to democracy. The section concludes with a discussion of the prevailing uncertainty that plagues Guatemalans and leads them to view the immediate future with cautious optimism.

SIX PRESIDENTS IN EIGHTEEN YEARS (1978–1996)

The six governments that ruled from 1978 to 1996 have been incapable of counteracting the instability that has prevailed throughout Guatemala's recent history.

General Fernando Romeo Lucas García (1978–1982)

General Lucas rose to power through elections widely recognized as fraudulent. He presided over a corrupt regime that squandered millions of Guatemala's international reserves; his rule was characterized by violence, guerrilla warfare, and counterinsurgency operations. He was overthrown on March 23, 1982, in a coup led by General Efraín Ríos Montt, after yet another fraudulent electoral process threatened to impose the presidency of General Angel Aníbal Guevara on the populace.

General Efraín Ríos Montt (1982–1983)

With a strong and charismatic leadership style, General Ríos Montt attempted to bring fundamental change to the Guatemalan economy. He created the Land Fund and implemented tax reform, including introduction of a value-added tax and removal of export taxes. His adjustment policy and an agreement signed with the IMF in 1983 led to the issuance of "stabilization bonds" worth $400 million to subsidize the payment of the private foreign debt at an exchange rate of one quetzal to the dollar.

In August 1983, Ríos Montt was overthrown in a coup led by military commanders. They opposed his efforts to remain in power rather than return to democracy, his open propagation of fundamentalist evangelical doctrine, and his lack of respect for the military's institutional hierarchy.

General Oscar Mejía Víctores (1983–1985)

General Mejía should be given credit for speeding the electoral process. Under his rule, the National Constituent Assembly, which drafted the current constitution, was installed by free elections. Furthermore, he convened general elections for president and vice president, Congress, and for mayors of all of the country's municipalities.

In spite of political progress, economic recession and financial imbalances reached alarming levels during Mejía's government. The foreign debt grew in 1983 to $2.4 billion, compared with $391 million in 1978; debt service represented 40 percent of exports. In 1984, the multiple exchange rate market was established and, because of the effects of devaluation, the consumer protection and foreign exchange crime laws were decreed.

In April 1985, Mejía confronted the private sector opposed to the selective consumer tax package and reestablished export taxes on coffee, meat, cotton, sugar, shrimp, bananas, and cardamom. However, buckling under pressure, Mejía eventually backed off, repealing the offensive decree laws and replacing his ministers of finance and economics.

Marco Vinicio Cerezo Arévalo (1986–1991)

A lawyer by profession, Cerezo assumed the presidency on January 14, 1986, with 68 percent of the popular vote. The Guatemalan people had demanded and received a civilian government. Cerezo's party, the Christian Democrats, obtained a congressional majority (51 out of 100 representatives) and won 182 of the country's 330 municipalities.

The civilian government had an auspicious beginning. It boasted broad domestic support that carried with it the expectation that Guatemala's social and economic crisis would be overcome. Likewise, the government enjoyed strong international support, which would help to improve Guatemala's international standing. Indeed, in retrospect, Cerezo's government should be recognized for its vigorous promotion of openness on all political, civic, economic, and international fronts.

Cerezo's presidency lost popularity, which resulted ultimately in defeat at the polls for Christian Democrats in the general elections of 1990. A dark horse candidate, Jorge Serrano Elías, won the presidency.

Jorge Serrano Elías (1991–1993)

An engineer by profession, Serrano headed the second elected civilian government, marking yet another important watershed in Guatemala's modern history. In the first months, his government's economic and foreign policies were hindered by a limited capacity for political maneuvering; he was unable to meet the promises delivered in his inaugural speech. Because it had neither a government plan nor a consistent majority in Congress, the Serrano government had to put more effort into confronting immediate problems than into resolving Guatemala's more profound dilemmas. The one exception came about in May 1991 when his government embarked on negotiations with the United Guatemalan National Revolutionary coalition (URNG), encompassing the country's four guerrilla movements. Nevertheless, Serrano should be credited with increasing popular participation and, initially, with consolidating civilian government in Guatemala. His clumsy coup attempt, on May 25, 1993, against the Congress and the Supreme Court, amidst widespread accusations of corruption, stemmed in part from his own political failings. On June 5, the Congress elected Ramiro de León Carpio as president of Guatemala. The failure of Serrano's coup attempt can be attributed to a civilian movement committed to peaceful change guided by constitutional precepts.

Ramiro de León Carpio (1993–1996)

A lawyer with political experience, de León Carpio was designated president by Congress in 1993. In 1984–85, he was cochairman of the National Constituent Assembly; in 1985, he was a candidate for the vice presidency for the Unión del Centro Nacional (UCN) and on March 25, 1993, when the Serrano coup occurred, he was the ombudsman for the office of the human rights prosecutor. His courageous resistance and criticism of Serrano's authoritarian style gained him praise and popularity. His designation was well received by all sectors.

Notwithstanding his positive beginning, early on his administration ran into problems with all sectors because of the lack of a government plan and of a team of experienced people to implement one. To improve his rapidly deteriorating public opinion ratings, he embarked on a crusade against Congress and the Supreme Court, thereby making the already difficult transition process worse. Arguing that corrupt practices were prevalent in these institutions, he attempted to persuade all members of Congress and Supreme Court justices to resign. Because of his weak leadership style and the lack of experienced politicians around him, he failed and had to negotiate a constitutional reform to elect a new congress by the end of 1994. Although this process allowed him to save face, he nevertheless wasted most of his first year in office in squabbles, forgoing the opportunity to pursue actively the nation's socioeconomic transformation.

PREVAILING INFLUENCES ON THE VARIOUS GOVERNMENTS

There are three clearly distinguishable stages to the democratic transition in Guatemala over the last two and a half decades.

1. Military rule (1978–85). The army sought cultural and ideological control. The regimes of this period are properly called authoritarian.

2. Democratically elected governments (1986–93). This stage saw the first transition from military to civilian government and, with it, the opening of democratic opportunities. This stage marked the first transfer of power

from one democratically elected civilian to another. In the end, however, President Serrano's actions yet again threatened civilian rule.

3. A new temporary government (1993–96). The defense of constitutional democracy depended on Guatemala's civil society in the years between the foiled coup of May 25, 1993, and the installation of a new government in 1996.

Areas of Influence

Some generalizations serve to compare the regimes and the various interests they served; figure 6.1 diagrams the prevailing influences. Under each regime heading are listed the key political actors in Guatemala; the actors holding the most sway over the regime are listed first, those with least sway last.

The diagram's indication of military influence includes military rulers and the army as an institution. The reference to economic influence is shorthand for business organizations; they do not express an explicit wish to govern but rather seek government protection to defend their interests. Political influence refers to political parties. Social influence alludes to sectors such as the urban and rural middle and lower classes, with all their economic, cultural, and social organizations; these groups tend to organize around unions, cooperatives, and private development organizations.

When looking at the diagram, the reader must be aware that the level of influence a group has on a regime is a measure of the degree to which the group lends support to the regime and is allowed in return to organize and reap benefits. Groups further down on the diagram tender relatively less support, or are in opposition to, repudiated by, and even persecuted by the government. The purpose of this diagram is to visualize analytically the realignment over time of the actors influencing government and public policies.

Figure 6.1 indicates that the military, supported by the economic sector (particularly the traditional agro-exporters), exercised the prevailing influence from 1978 to 1985. During these years, high-ranking military commanders became landlords and businessmen under military protection. Meanwhile, political groups were dismantled or persecuted, except during the Mejía period. Social movements were repressed and fundamental human rights were violated repeatedly, thus harming the country's international reputation. Some of the military regimes' detrimental effects on Guatemala can be seen in figure 6.2, which charts the leading economic and social indicators of the period.

Cerezo's five-year term marked the rise of political parties as the agents of government decision making. This occurred because the military high command supported democratization, and Cerezo retained that support

| 1978–1985 | 1985–1991 | 1991–1993 | 1993–1996 |
Military	Cerezo	Serrano	De Léon Carpio
1. Military	1. Political	1. Economic	1. Military
2. Economic	2. Military	2. Military	2. Economic
3. Political	3. Economic	3. Political	3. Social
4. Social	4. Social	4. Social	4. Political

Fig. 6.1. Guatemala: political regimes and prevailing influences. (Shaded areas indicate groups that were influential; rank order indicates relative strengths of each group.)

throughout his term. In the early stages, the economic groups supported his administration, but because of ideological and political differences, they eventually withdrew their support in 1987, halfway through the administration's term. This withdrawal was in reaction to tax reforms implemented that year. Although the Cerezo regime's "opening" included new rights for all social sectors—which allowed the formation of new organizations—such social groups exercised the least influence on the regime's political decisions.

As finance minister, and earlier as president of the Christian Democratic Party's Technical Council, on several occasions I coordinated the task forces responsible for drawing up national programs, following up on strategy, and implementing policies. To understand the Cerezo administration's opening process, the military high command's support for this process, and the fluctuating influence wielded by the political and economic sectors, it is important to understand Cerezo's programs. Below I describe the programs that were carried out and discuss the reasons why the private sector and its Chamber of Agricultural, Commercial, Industrial, and Financial Associations (CACIF) broke with the government and joined the opposition.

The Socioeconomic Reordering Program was launched on June 6, 1986, to carry out short-term (one-year) tasks to stabilize prices, the exchange rate, and public finances. At the same time, it sought to reactivate private and public investment under a consensus approach. Under this program, public-investment projects in infrastructure, road repair, terrace construction for agricultural sowing, and other social benefit projects ultimately boosted employment and income to compensate for the effects of currency devaluation. These macroeconomic adjustment effects were intermediate in nature—somewhere between "shock" and "gradual." The official exchange rate that had remained unchanged for sixty years prior to implementation of this program was suspended and the quetzal was devalued 150 percent: from parity with the dollar, the exchange rate shifted to two and one-half quetzals to the dollar. Shocking as this change may seem, I call it an intermediate adjustment effect because the unofficial exchange rate on the black market had been at

Item	1978	1979	1980	1981	1982	1983	1984	1985
Percent growth in GDP	5.0	4.7	3.6	0.9	3.5	2.7	0.6	1.7
Investment as a percent of GDP	16.8	13.9	11.4	13.1	11.0	9.2	9.0	9.0
Tax burden as a percent of GDP	10.2	9.0	8.6	7.5	7.2	6.3	5.3	6.2
Fiscal deficit as a percent of GDP	1.1	2.6	5.6	7.4	6.0	3.9	4.2	2.7
Current account deficit	4.3	2.6	2.2	6.5	4.6	2.5	3.3	3.0
International monetary reserves (US$)	792	777	527	347	318	408	446	390
Foreign Debt (US$)	391	514	819	1202	1490	2076	2258	2400
Inflation rate	9.1	13.7	9.1	8.7	−2.0	15.4	5.2	31.4
Unemployment rate	—	—	35	24	29	32	34	37
Number of displaced persons/refugees	—	—	—	—	—	6300	—	250,000
Number of troops	14,500	—	14,900	—	—	—	—	51,600
Number of armored personnel carriers	—	—	75	—	—	—	—	155
Number of combat aircraft	—	—	60	—	—	—	—	125
Number of political assassinations	—	—	—	—	—	3573	1564	993

Fig. 6.2. Guatemala: economic, social, and military indicators. *Source: Centroamérica: La Crisis en Cifras* (Guatemala: Instituto Interamericano de Cooperación Agrícola, FLACSO, 1986).

four quetzals per dollar at the outset of the Cerezo administration. The private sector reacted favorably to these policies and Congress approved export tax surcharges and windfall profits taxes on a sliding scale that would reach zero within three years. Public finances were strengthened because, in the first year of the Reordering Program, government income increased by Q400 million, amounting to 1.5 percent of the gross domestic product (GDP).

The National Reorganization Program initiated in June 1987 had two objectives: to introduce tax reforms to strengthen the government and to promote economic growth through innovative public investments such as the National Council for Export Promotion (CONAPEX), which united all the country's sectors under a new economic strategy. The underlying strategy of the National Reorganization Program lay in applying the successful framework of CONAPEX to other problems. For example, CONAGUA was founded to facilitate access to running water and CONATIERRA was created to purchase and reallocate land. Similar reorganizations were applied to other problems such as irrigation (CONRIEGO), literacy (CONE-DUCA), citizen security (CONSEGURA), housing (CONAVIVE), roads (CONCAMINOS), food and nutrition (CONALIMENTOS), and health care (CONSALUD).

A new investment mechanism was sought to encourage greater participation from citizens of all sectors to address the nation's outstanding problems. Thus, CONAS (Consejos Nacionales, or National Councils) were organized to provide an arena for equal participation of every sector. The state's interests did not take precedence. Because CONAS projects required hefty investments, the Cerezo government felt justified in pushing for the tax reform that Congress approved in September 1987 over CACIF's steadfast objections. The passage of the tax reform put to rest the myth that widespread strikes, promoted by the private sector, signaled the fall of ministers and even of governments.

From the point of view of the social sector, tax reform was part of a new political concept: the payment of the social debt. CACIF refused to accept the concept of a social debt or that new taxes were one way to compensate, in part, for the accumulated poverty of the poor. The tax reforms were followed by creation of the Social Investment Fund (FIS) which, along with the Export Fund (FODEX), was to balance the development strategy.

This development balance—as a goal—is very important to Guatemala. Anyone visiting the country will observe three Guatemalas: a major city that in some respects rivals any modern metropolis; rural areas; and marginal urban areas. The last two suffer from poverty and misery. The purpose of CONAS and FIS was to save these two Guatemalas.

Once stabilization had been achieved, public finances strengthened, and with an abundant portfolio of projects in hand, the government sought support from the international community. Within the World Bank framework whereby countries bid for support, Guatemala presented its case at the bank's consultative group meeting (Paris, April 1989), backed by IMF support and working papers produced by non-Guatemalans attesting to the success of Guatemala's new program. The Christian Democratic government presented its projects under the concept of "leveraging development," alluding to the fact that it sought support to complement efforts already initiated to fight the poverty afflicting over 70 percent of Guatemala's population.

Guatemala's development projects were so well received internationally that over the next five years the government could have obtained more than $1 billion in additional support. However, endless clashes between the private and public sectors prevented the receipt of this assistance and also diverted attention from CONAS. The private sector even fomented demands led by schoolteachers for public sector wage increases. The government prevailed, but there remained a sense of perpetual crisis. The result was paralysis and loss of the momentum generated under the National Reorganization Program.

Neither the Guatemala 2000 Plan nor the 500 Day Plan—part of the leveraging development strategy—was as fruitful as the two preceding programs. Besides problems with the business sector and lack of participation from the social sector, there was deep division among cabinet members, which further impeded the team efforts witnessed during the Reordering Program. In 1989, for political reasons the ministers of economy and agriculture as well as the secretary for economic planning opposed the adjustment measures called for by the Ministry of Finance and the Guatemalan Central Bank. The bank had taken a stance favoring programs oriented toward international trade, especially export promotion, as opposed to social investment and inwardly oriented economic programs. As finance minister, I firmly supported the export program but insisted that it be balanced with more social investment and domestic economic development.

Indeed, there had been continuity between the Reordering Program and the Reorganization Program. Ultimately it broke down when challenged by historical barriers to social investment and domestic development, chiefly a centralized social structure resistant to institutional changes. Society at large was also disinclined toward such social investment because it raised wages principally in health and education while promising only long-term rewards.

When Serrano's government assumed control, it faced a vulnerable, risky, and potentially explosive situation. The Movement for Social Action (MAS), the party that had carried Serrano to power, was weak in Congress. A mere eighteen MAS representatives faced two opposition parties: the UCN and the Christian Democratic Party (PDC), with thirty-nine and twenty-nine representatives respectively. Upon assuming power, the president indicated that he would not negotiate a power-sharing agreement with either party in exchange for their support in the legislature. He maintained that he would try to achieve consensus on a project-by-project basis. However, this approach failed. Instead of negotiating parliamentary alliances to give him more latitude to govern, Serrano tried and failed to shut down the Congress and, instead, was forced to leave the presidency.

As for Serrano's relations with the military, officers were initially surprised by the lack of respect he showed for the military hierarchy when he made appointments to top positions. The president's first speech at the Military Academy also created unease among some officers. However, five high-ranking officers participated in peace talks with the URNG, suggesting that the army might support President Serrano's efforts to end thirty years of armed confrontation. Yet this apparent harmony contrasted with the inability of the courts and public prosecutors to shatter the wall of impunity protecting the military. Social sectors continued to lack influence at the government's highest levels; there was a lack of political will to follow through with social programs. Consequently, the only major influence on the government was the business sector, which exercised its influence mainly through the most important economic agencies: the Ministries of Agriculture, Finance, Economics, and Public Works, and the Central Bank.

Arrangement and Rearrangement of Influences

The shifting of influence by sectors is represented in figure 6.1. Two consistent trends can be observed: postponement of the social agenda and competition among the military, economic, and political sectors. The loss of political party influence compared to during the Cerezo regime was counteracted by the stronger political institutions, such as the Supreme Electoral Tribunal, by laws such as the Law of Political Parties, and by the political maturity of parties and their leaders. These institutions successfully joined forces with the media to resist Serrano's coup attempt in May 1993.

President Serrano identified more with political parties than with economic groups, but because he had no economic team ready to govern he was forced to "borrow" staff from the private sector, relying on the best-educated, albeit nonpolitical, people whom he could find. Nevertheless, he failed to create a formal alliance with the CACIF; hence their relationship remained fragile. In the end CACIF, too, opposed Serrano's coup attempt in May 1993. On the other hand, President Serrano was socially progressive in areas such as education and had been a religious leader prior to becoming president. His apparent desires for national change ultimately were subordinated to an arrogant and ambitious personal agenda.

Figure 6.1 illustrates the apparent isolation of the economic group and the weakening of the political parties and the military. By the end of President Serrano's rule, his capacity to govern had eroded. The military initially supported Serrano's coup attempt but, within days, acted to depose him. The parties resisted the attempt, thanks especially to the rapid mobilization of mass social protests spurred by media resistance to Serrano's censorship.

President de León Carpio created a power vacuum when, in 1993, he repudiated political groups and sought to gather support from the social sectors. Given their lack of organization and credible leadership, the effect was to leave only the military and economic elites as the prevailing influences. The continuous realignment of sectors that influenced his government, along with the lack of direction of President de León Carpio's government, rendered the transition to democracy vulnerable again.

THE PARADIGM TRANSITION MAP

Democratic transition can be understood as a shift from military governments, which have limited legitimacy, to civilian-run, liberal-democratic governments with a high degree of legitimacy. Such a transition poses the challenge of changing traditional power structures while maintaining the ability of various social groups to settle their conflicts within the framework of political institutions. The transition begins with the "old paradigm," which is my term for Guatemala's traditional model of society. The old paradigm was best exemplified in all its crudeness by the government of General Fernando Romeo Lucas. His was a centralized military regime unable to control violence; it favored protectionist measures for privileged sectors whose priority was rent, but it lacked international support.

The "new paradigm," to which Guatemalan society aspires, aims at the formation of a democracy characterized by grassroots decision making achieved through local government engagement. It must be built upon an institutional framework of both political and socioeconomic participation, focused domestically on human development and internationally on effective engagement. The movement toward this paradigm should occur peacefully.

The transition from the old to the new paradigm will require a great deal of conflict management to channel and resolve disputes among groups. Although in many ways Guatemala still remains underdeveloped, there are some areas where change has occurred and where development can be ascertained. These key dimensions are listed down the left-hand side of the paradigm transition map in figure 6.3.

	Old Paradigm	Characteristics of Transition	New Paradigm
National values	Traditional values	Disposition to opening	Transformative values
Politics	Militarism	Civilian government	Democracy
Institutional framework	Centralized	Institutional reorganization	Local government participation
Macroeconomic orientation	Protectionism	Trade opening, modernization	Outward orientation and internal change
Social orientation	Profitability	Solidarity	Humanism
Societal environment	Violence	Respect for human rights	Peace
International situation	Isolation	Negotiation	Globalization

Fig. 6.3. The paradigm transition map.

The Four Degrees of Progress

Each of the seven regions on the paradigm transition map has witnessed a different degree of change away from the traditional model. At this point, I would like to introduce the metaphor of a bridge to assess the pace of change in Guatemala. As illustrated in figure 6.4, the dimensions of the transition to the new paradigm can be compared to the beams of a bridge. There are four terms I use to describe how far along the transition has progressed.

If change has been firmly established for a specific region on the paradigm map, the transition there is described as *consolidated.* Consolidated developments—such as those accomplished by the Supreme Electoral Tribunal and the Office of the Human Rights Prosecutor—help to form a new and transformative Guatemalan society.

Advancing changes are those which, while showing positive progress, still require Guatemala to make extraordinary efforts to reach a new society. The circumstances of macroeconomic policy are a good example.

Paralyzed changes are those initiated but, over time, unable to continue. An example is the reform of state institutions.

Developments are said to be *regressing* when performance worsens enough to endanger advances achieved in other areas. Because of their magnitude, the problems described here should not be ignored. Nevertheless, they have been put aside. One example is the lack of social policies to solve problems in health, education, employment, and training.

TRACING DEVELOPMENTS IN THE SEVEN AREAS OF THE PARADIGM: TRANSITION MAP ACROSS REGIMES

National Values: From Tradition to Transformation

When examining national values, the first category on the paradigm transition map where democratic development can take place, I assess whether new values representing a break with past corruption have emerged in Guatemala. Given that Guatemala is a culturally divided society (half mestizo and half Indian), I also ask whether positive steps have been taken toward respecting cultural pluralism or whether cultural barriers and discrimination remain entrenched. Finally, I ask whether a democratic political culture is possible in Guatemala.

The values held by the three military governments were different. Lucas's regime was characterized by corruption, fraud, and violence. In short, it projected an image of Guatemala as a society without principles. Ríos Montt launched a campaign to restore ethics to government. He spoke often in public to promote ethical values. The credo of the time became "I don't rob, I

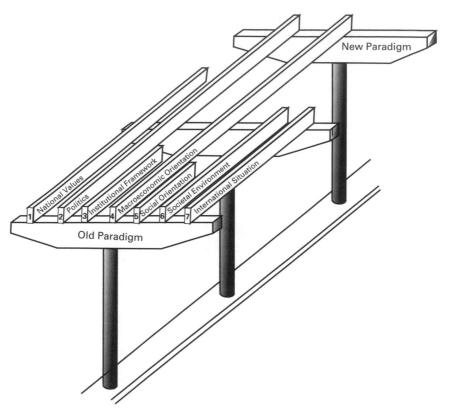

Fig. 6.4. From the old to the new paradigm.

don't lie, I don't cheat." General Mejía broke with Ríos Montt's moralizing policies; his government fell back into a moral vacuum. When Cerezo came to power, the recovery of moral values had come to a standstill.

Cerezo placed more emphasis on political values such as building consensus, participation, and pluralism, than on moral issues such as honor and personal integrity. He made positive attempts to deal with the instability stemming from social and cultural diversity. He created the Ministry of Culture and the Ministry of Urban and Rural Development, to provide opportunities for development for different ethnic groups.

The Cerezo government's first years in power passed without corruption being the focus of popular criticism. However, as his term expired, there was substantial evidence to support charges of corruption in the executive and legislative branches of government. Funds donated by the U.S. Agency for International Development (AID) were subjected to various audits. The audits disclosed poor management in the purchase of medical supplies. Different congressional factions accused each other of corruption over the approval of a number of ethically questionable laws (nationalization of foreign investments and regulation of ocean freight and cable television).

The Indian communities, which had given a majority vote to Cerezo in 1985, continued to support his interests during the mayoral elections in mid-1988 but conspicuously withdrew their support in the 1990 elections. This change can be explained by the following: (1) the national bilingual education program (PRONEBI) was limited to levels up to the fourth grade and went no farther; (2) the project to help widows and orphans who were victims of the violence came too late; (3) the Ministry of Culture curtailed some urban projects and neglected rural areas; (4) the Ministry of Development was more engaged in political proselytism than in straightforward development activities; and (5) cultural and ethnic problems were neglected, although the greatest threat to Guatemalan democracy was precisely cultural divisiveness. After a promising start, Cerezo left the government with a poor image because the trend toward forging new social values had simply halted.

In 1990, a substantial portion of Serrano's votes came from evangelical groups and followers of General Ríos Montt. (Ríos Montt tried to run for the presidency but was prevented from doing so by a law disallowing leaders of coups to run for this office. Using evidence from public opinion polls, many political analysts assert that, had such a law not existed, Ríos Montt would have won the elections.) Once elected, Serrano did not establish a cooperative relationship with Indian groups, nor did he promote the concept of a multicultural nation, or of a civic culture to challenge individualism, corruption, social division, and excessive pragmatism. Moreover, with Serrano in power, public opinion became more concerned with questions of morality because of increased levels of corruption in his regime.

I have characterized the change on this front as advancing. Evidence to support my affirmation is that Serrano's own demise was caused partially by the spread of democratic values that inspired many Guatemalans to resist the coup attempt and to espouse a return to constitutional government. Despite a leadership vacuum, Ramiro de León Carpio's government was in fact inspired in transformative values. Consequently, I ratify the characterization of this front: advancing (see fig. 6.4).

Politics: From Military Regimes to Democracy

The second category on the paradigm map is political power. It covers the transition from military governments toward civilian government. I ask whether this change toward democracy is permanent.

The democratic regime is a form of state that, to assure the common good, provides for frequent transfers of power. Lucas tried to keep power in the hands of the military when he chose General Angel Aníbal Guevara as his successor. Through fraudulent elections, Guevara would have become the fourth consecutive military officer in power in fifteen years; the young officers of the March 1982 coup d'état carried Ríos Montt into power instead. At first, Ríos Montt gave the impression that he was presiding over a transitional government, to be followed up by popular elections. He quickly shattered that illusion by displaying dictatorial inclinations shortly after beginning his term. The military replaced Ríos Montt with General Oscar Mejía Víctores, then minister of defense, who was expected to organize an authentic transitional government to turn power over to the civilians. Mejía fulfilled this expectation.

Cerezo, too, fulfilled his role by being the first civilian president to turn power over to another civilian. While in office, Cerezo allowed his political opponents plenty of maneuverability. In the new climate of openness and popular participation, the parties of the traditional right lost their near monopoly on national politics. Cerezo never bowed to conservative pressures; not once did he turn to the military or proclaim a state of siege in order to end strikes and popular demonstrations.

With repeated free democratic elections, the Supreme Electoral Tribunal triumphed for a second time since the era of General Mejía. Guatemalans regained confidence in the electoral process. The Supreme Electoral Tribunal now stands as one of Guatemala's clearest and most encouraging examples that there has been a genuine transition toward democracy. In fact, the tribunal evolved from a corrupt body to one of the most honored and respected institutions in Guatemala, along with the Constitutional Court. These two institutions played a key role in halting Serrano's coup attempt. The Constitutional Court's ruling against Serrano's attempt was obeyed by the military, thus consolidating the democratic forces against Serrano. Another highly regarded institution created during Cerezo's period is the Office of the Human Rights Prosecutor, which was occupied during Serrano's presidency by Ramiro de León Carpio, who also adamantly opposed the coup attempt; as a result, he was appointed by Congress to replace Serrano as president.

Cerezo withstood two attempted coups. In spite of those attempts, the professional military officers unquestionably backed the democratic process as never before and, upon Serrano's inauguration, there was an anticoup atmosphere among the general population as well as within the army. This trend was established as a new national guideline. Although the military at first supported Serrano's coup attempt in May 1993, they soon abided by the Constitutional Court's ruling and acted to preserve constitutional government.

Despite vulnerabilities, as past events would suggest, Guatemalans have defended constitutional government successfully. Therefore, it is fair to say that the transition from military to democratic rule is consolidating. In figure 6.4, the political beam has completely traversed the chasm across the bridge separating Guatemala's old paradigm from the new. This phenomenon is evidenced by the fact that faith has been restored in institutions responsible for the electoral process, while the army has remained in the barracks; civilian presidents have governed Guatemala since 1985. It is unlikely that this well-entrenched and positive trend will be reversed. If it is, the reversal should be attributable to other factors.

The Institutional Framework: From Centralization to Participation by Local Government

The third category on the map refers to changes in the reorganization of state institutions. Are these institutions socially cohesive and efficient?

Each of the generals leading Guatemala's last three military regimes chose a different way to organize his government. Lucas chose "administrative centralism." The country was governed by an elite group of corrupt politicians whose power depended on privileges granted to powerful economic groups; meanwhile, civil unrest was pervasive. Ríos Montt broke from that elite, centralized system by placing decision-making power in the hands of a Council of State and regional "inter-institutional coordinating mechanisms." Community-based civilian self-defense patrols were organized, and in most of the remote areas he established development poles—or model towns—which centrally organized the disparate mountain populations and isolated the guerrillas. General Mejía preserved Ríos Montt's institutional system and counterinsurgency tactics but dispensed with the council.

The 1985 Constitution sought to decentralize power and redirect it toward municipal governments. However, Cerezo achieved little progress in that direction. For example, the Constitution called for the formation of urban and rural development councils. These councils were to create opportunities for citizen participation at the municipal, departmental, regional, and national levels. Rather than follow this policy, Cerezo placed power into the hands of Development Council presidencies appointed by the president of the republic. Guatemala thus lost an opportunity to open up new means for participation by social sectors in the country's interior.

Even though Cerezo's administration every year poured more than $100 million into the municipalities for development (about 8 percent of the national budget), the investments did not achieve better results because they were not channeled to support regional and local administrative structures. Serrano also failed in supporting measures to dilute the state's central power. Instead, his advisors favored a secondary role for participatory organizations.

The problems arising from Guatemala's neglected administrative apparatus cannot be solved simply by selecting professionally qualified ministers, as was Serrano's policy. Rather, state institutions themselves must be reformed extensively. I often use the story of a school bus as an illustration. A bus is halfway to school when the engine blows. The vehicle loses its steering power and is in danger of catching fire. What should be done? Simply changing the driver leaves the problem unsolved because the solution lies in replacing the bus. In Guatemala's present case, if intransigent government structures are not replaced by new, participative democratic institutions, I fear (though I hope to be wrong) that the national bureaucracy will burden a frustrated population more and more, and the state will eventually lose all capacity to govern efficiently.

The language of President Ramiro de León Carpio in the first months of his government was appropriately participative, signaling the importance of moving toward local government. Yet his actions were not congruent with his words. The institutions of government remained centralized. Consequently, the transition to decentralized, local government participation remained paralyzed.

Macroeconomic Orientation: From Protectionism to Global Integration

The fourth category alludes to the modernization of the economy and contrasts differences in economic management by the military governments and the civilian governments.

The three military regimes that ruled Guatemala from 1978 to 1985 shared a number of economic characteristics. Each promoted protectionist trade policies and import substitution industrialization. Also, each concentrated political power in the hands of a closed circle of ruling elites and favored certain well-organized business sectors at the expense of the majority of the population. Despite Guatemala's inclusion in the U.S. government's Caribbean Basin Initiative, the three military governments remained relatively isolated internationally, with little access to development funds.

By investing in huge state projects, General Lucas tried to address the financial speculation, the drain on capital, and the drop in private investment that plagued his administration. However, this move only caused an unprecedented fiscal deficit in 1981, amounting to 7.4 percent of the GDP. General Ríos Montt followed with an unsuccessful attempt to strengthen public finances, which included a fervent austerity and morality campaign and incoherent applications of exchange controls, interest rates, imports, and price caps. General Mejía worsened the situation. For political purposes, he ventured to overprotect the parity of the quetzal against the dollar to the point of subsidizing importers by overvaluing the quetzal. He left the country bankrupt, with inflation spiraling over 30 percent and with a black market exchange rate of four quetzals to the dollar.

The military realized that their political power was not solving Guatemala's macroeconomic woes. Instead, the 1985 per capita GDP dropped to levels registered twenty years earlier. While in 1978 each Guatemalan bore a burden of $100 to repay the foreign debt, by 1985 the burden had risen to $331. Many other indicators, such as real income and employment, fell to 1960 levels.

The Cerezo administration sought to balance its production diversification and export promotion policies with those of macroeconomic adjustment. As a result, nontraditional exports grew at an annual compound rate of over 20 percent. The economy began showing signs of recovery. Also, free trade zones were established, the in-bond assembly industry was given support, and advances were made in foreign trade mechanisms, laws, and development institutions.

Exchange rate adjustment—unifying the various markets and types of exchange—remained realistic until it began interfering with vested political and business interests. The same occurred with fiscal, monetary, and credit policies. The resistance of some sectors to tax reform, liberalization of interest rates, and exchange rate readjustments once again ushered in financial instability. Inflation had been contained at 10 percent in Cerezo's third year; it rebounded to 60 percent by the end of the term. By 1990, the black market quoted an exchange rate of six quetzals per dollar. Gone was the capacity to collect taxes. The country was insolvent, unable to service its foreign debt. Varying exchange rate systems were introduced (lasting on average one month each) but the economy was again left in the hands of speculators.

In terms of commercial activity, Cerezo began the process of breaking with tariff protection and of ending fiscal privileges; these trends are difficult to reverse. Moreover, there seems to be a national consensus, as never before, that Guatemala should seek outward-oriented economic development and make a concerted effort to modernize its economy.

Supported by Guatemala's organized private sector (headed by nontraditional exporters), Serrano's government believed in an economic future founded on an outward-oriented strategy. The adjustment program he implemented in his first year stabilized the nation's economy and achieved macroeconomic balance. Three challenges remained for Guatemala to meet. First, the government must strengthen public finances—the most difficult task before it. Second, it must meet obligations to international creditors to keep open Guatemala's relations with the international financial community. And third, it must use to its advantage the General Agreement on Tariffs and Trade (GATT), which Guatemala joined in April 1991.

After the downfall of the Serrano regime, de León Carpio retained the finance minister and sought to keep in place the stabilization and economic modernization programs. Fiscal and monetary policies remained the unsolved problems.

Macroeconomic management, which has the potential of affecting all aspects of the transition between paradigms, has had its ups and downs. However, at present, it should be classified generally as consolidating.

Social Orientation: From Interest in Profitability to Interest in People

The fifth category refers to Guatemala's dichotomy of wealth and poverty. It requires an analysis of the advance, or in some cases the reversal, of social programs promoting a more just distribution of wealth and cultivating social solidarity.

When modern economic literature approaches the subject here labeled as domestic social orientation, it treats this as the change from a production-oriented growth economy to one based on humanistic-oriented "people-centered" development.

Under the three military governments, the traditional agro-export model was at work. That model is not concerned with modifying the concentration of income, property, and wealth, nor with attending to people's basic needs. To be sure, Ríos Montt's moralistic messages criticized the rent-seeking orientation of the traditional economic model. Other than using such rhetoric to defend Guatemalan communities for the purpose of combating guerrillas, however, Ríos Montt did not invest in ventures that would promote equality and human development.

The Cerezo administration, too, put forth good proposals and projects but in the end had little to show for it. According to a World Bank report, poverty in Guatemala spread from afflicting 60 percent of the population in 1985 to 80 percent in 1990, while a 1989 survey by the National Institute of Statistics proclaimed a more dire situation, classifying 89 percent of the population as poverty stricken. Because the state's inefficient public services do little or nothing to halt these ills, it seems senseless for people to comply with their civic duty to pay taxes. Furthermore, honest government efforts to improve on tax collection ultimately clash with the organized private sector.

In 1987, Cerezo proposed a tax reform plan to redirect some public funds into social programs. While this forced a break between the government and CACIF, the program signaled an attempt to foster social-oriented development, introducing the concept that a social debt had to be paid. The majority of the population with their scarce resources accepted the concept; the private sector, however, stood vehemently opposed, denying the very existence of such a debt.

Cerezo's government had inherited a tax burden equal to 6 percent of GDP, the lowest in Latin America. It raised this to 9 percent in 1988, only to see it fall again to just 6.5 percent of GDP in 1991. The tax issue continues to be a key factor in the country's social situation. In 1990, Guatemala saw more widespread illiteracy, more malnourished children, fewer medicines, fewer schools, and fewer health care centers. In fact all social indicators reveal that Guatemala's social ills continue to mount.

Besides Cerezo's tax reform plan, in 1990 an attempt was made to create the Social Investment Fund (FIS), with resources from international loans and donations (more than $100 million). Even though work had begun on the fund as far back as 1987, the FIS was labeled a last-ditch effort. The fund proposal also suffered because it ran the risk of being used to buy votes for the government's party.

Cerezo ended his term without tending to the country's tremendous social needs and without leaving the resources the FIS needed to aid poor communities to resolve, on their own, their most urgent problems.

Because many members of President Serrano's economic cabinet came from the organized private sector that had opposed the tax reforms, neglect of social concerns prevailed. Investment in social programs requires strengthening state finances through better and greater tax collection; this situation did not exist in Guatemala. In all probability, such a policy would still meet serious resistance. Moreover, the mentality of the Serrano government team dictated that social problems not be addressed through direct investments. Rather, the solutions to social problems were supposed to arise automatically as a consequence of reduced inflation and a favorable investment climate.

Ramiro de León Carpio appointed a cabinet more attuned to social concerns but without a program, without a team, and without leadership. Therefore, not only was the social agenda postponed, but in fact it is regressing.

Societal Environment: From Violence to Peace

The sixth category deals with human rights and how respect for those rights leads to justice, peace, and stability.

The state of social coexistence under the military regimes can be summed up as follows: General Lucas created conditions that set the stage for a nationwide war. Through civilian patrols whose members were recruited from the communities themselves, Ríos Montt repressed the insurgency; no respect was shown for human rights (for instance, under the Special Jurisdiction Courts, court-martial executions by firing squads were above the law). General Mejía inherited the problem of violence and passed it on directly to the Cerezo government.

President Cerezo gave this problem his personal attention; his approach was successful. He chose to address Guatemala's domestic violence at the regional Central American and the wider international levels, even though in doing so he faced negative pressure and opposition from the U.S. government. At the Esquipulas II talks, the outcome of his policies broadened the search for peace beyond Guatemala's borders into El Salvador and Nicaragua. The National Reconciliation Commission—created to follow up on Esquipulas II and composed of representatives from the social sectors—successfully established reconciliation mechanisms between the government and the guerrillas, culminating in the signing of the 1990 Oslo Agreements. In 1986 Cerezo created the Special Commission to Attend to Repatriated and Displaced Persons. Also, by constitutional mandate, the Office of the Human Rights Prosecutor was established. And a framework for seeking peace and social integration was institutionalized in the Central American Parliament.

Serrano should be given credit for being part of the National Reconciliation Commission while Cerezo was president. Later, during Serrano's first months as president, he showed a great deal of concern for dialogue with the guerrillas, calling on all Guatemalans to unite for what he called "Total Peace." In his first presidential year, he also sent an official delegation to initiate direct talks with the URNG. Talks were stalled, however, when Serrano left the presidency in May 1993.

President Ramiro de León Carpio also took steps to activate those talks, although success has yet to be reached. Internal urban violence erupted. Nonetheless, there is a continuous effort and some progress in maintaining a dialogue, institutional mechanisms have been strengthened, and the climate created by the end of the Cold War is more favorable. Therefore, I would say that the nation's trend toward peaceful coexistence should be classified as advancing.

International Situation: From Isolation to Globalization

The seventh category refers to relations with the international community. Guatemala moved from international isolation during the military regimes to a position of acceptance evident when the Cerezo government began widespread negotiations seeking international cooperation. The question of international support for the Serrano and de León Carpio governments is also examined. At issue is the desire to involve Guatemala in a world favorable for development and justice.

General Lucas's government used foreign financing to the tune of millions of dollars for short-term objectives and to benefit companies involved in corrupt practices with government officials. For example, projects to harness hydroelectric energy, to build a highway network, and to start a giant wood and paper industry cost millions but were never finished. In addition to excoriation for his poor use of foreign resources, Lucas and his military successors were condemned internationally many times for their violations of human rights.

When Cerezo assumed the presidency, the international community strongly supported Guatemala. However, that situation changed later. In the last year of Cerezo's administration, the country suffered international isolation again. I believe this was a consequence of the government's failure, for purely political reasons, to make the necessary economic adjustments. The administration's inaction led to increased inflation, a lack of foreign currency, noncompliance with debt payments, internal disorder, and general socio-economic and political chaos.

In the view of many bilateral and multilateral organizations, Guatemala had intentionally allowed its approximately $200 million debt to accumulate. Observers noted that it had had the repayment capacity from funds in its portfolio. Both the Stand-by Agreement with the IMF in 1988 and the Consultative Group Meeting convened by the World Bank in 1989 to coordinate support from the international financial community favored financing investment projects of over $1 billion. Moreover, in 1988 financial inflows from these agencies were greater than the annual debt service payments.

There was a tacit understanding between Guatemala and both the international lending institutions and other governments that, as Guatemala managed to strengthen its internal savings, it would obtain leveraging from the international community. Such an arrangement obviously favored Guatemala. Yet, during Cerezo's last year in office, progress on this front came to a halt.

Investments succeed if the government fosters a domestic climate of coexistence among the nation's varied groups and interests. Serrano happened upon a great opportunity. His goal was to reopen the doors to international financing and to provide Guatemala with the investment resources needed for several years. Both Serrano and de León Carpio had initial success in this area. As a former human rights prosecutor, de León Carpio built upon the promises of the new global community of the post–Cold War era in order to guarantee adequate, just, and equitable development. Given these circumstances, it appears that progress in that direction is still advancing.

DECISION MAKING AND SOCIAL LAGGING: APPLICATION OF THE DEMOCRATIC TRANSITION MAP TO GUATEMALA

As a civil engineer by profession, I have an unending fascination with bridges. Therefore, I have allowed myself the useful analogy of a bridge under construction to illustrate how the paradigm transition map can be applied to Guatemala. The metaphorical bridge in figure 6.4 falls short in spanning the gulf between the traditional, nondemocratic Guatemala (the old paradigm) and a new democratic nation. Seven beams make up the bridge to date, but construction has not been completed equally on each beam. The beams represent the seven distinct elements of democratic transition discussed throughout this chapter. In this section, I examine the bridge as a whole with the purpose of determining to what extent it has been completed.

Consolidating Elements of Democratic Transition

The beams representing the political dimension of the democratic transition and the macroeconomic orientation have almost reached completion. The "gap" has been crossed in these respects because there now exists in Guatemala a legal constitutional order, that is, the rule of law, accompanied by a party system that permits the orderly transfer of power from the government to the opposition. The Supreme Electoral Tribunal is a decade old, with an impeccable record of honesty and commendable management. It has handled efficiently every phase of Guatemalan elections from that of the National Constituent Assembly in 1984 to the general elections in 1985, 1990, 1994 (congressional), 1995 (presidential, first round), and 1996 (presidential, second round) as well as the transitions evolving from the May 1993 coup attempt.

Proof of Guatemala's successful consolidation of outward macroeconomic orientation lies in its more market-oriented exchange rate and foreign trade policies, membership in GATT, and more flexible price control policies. Stabilization programs have prevailed successfully during the three civilian governments from 1986 to 1996.

Advancing Elements

Beams six and seven of the bridge have also shown progress, though not as dramatic as the political and macroeconomic advances. The social environment has improved because institutionalized violence has been reduced under the civilian governments. Also, the Office of the Human Rights Prosecutor has raised consciousness concerning respect for human rights, peace, and law. Nonetheless, violence persists in cities and rural areas and the army and guerrilla forces remain at war.

Guatemala's relations with the international community have evolved favorably. No longer the victim of interventionism and paternal attitudes, Guatemala has become an engaged participant in an interdependent world, promoting a democratic society and a more just international economic order. Nevertheless, it is still too early to rely upon the international community to encourage global solidarity in order to eradicate underdevelopment entirely. This stage of development can be expected only in a more mature and balanced world society.

Elements Where Development Is Paralyzed or Regressing

Construction on beams three and five remains stalled. The political system remains centralized and inefficient, with the government showing little will toward reform. The rest of Guatemalan society so far has offered no clear program to address this problem.

The postponement of the social agenda remains a perennial problem, as reflected in the country's deteriorating social indicators. The lowest income bracket suffers the worst unemployment and underemployment. The majority of these citizens continue to be excluded from basic educational, health, and general human services required to lead a life of dignity.

From a human perspective, the regressive trend in healing social ills is the most worrisome of the bridge's weak beams. Peaceful and democratic coexistence cannot be assured if certain groups remain permanently excluded from the benefits of development.

It is well known that, in Guatemala, the subject of tax reform is taboo. Often, coups d'état are sparked by attempts at tax reform, causing the fall of either a minister of finance or the government itself. In fact, Guatemala's history of public finance will remember this author as the first finance minister who carried out tax reform (1987) to finance social policies, and survived the coup intended to topple him.

Guatemala has one of the world's lowest tax burdens. Such a situation is reprehensible when a state needs resources to satisfy the basic unmet needs of the majority of its population. I believe that sound fiscal policy and the means to tax efficiently are crucial. During my term, I received support from the AID for a project worked out jointly with Georgia State University and the consulting firm Peat Marwick to revise fiscal policy over a three-year period. However, closing the fiscal gap while simultaneously improving public welfare in Guatemala is not simply a question of technical tinkering but one of moral confrontation.

My personal experience that best illustrates this problem centers around the Guatemalan Congress' approval of the unified real estate tax. Conducting an up-to-date appraisal of all real estate property holdings would represent a significant burden on the state. Therefore, the government opted to have all property owners voluntarily assess the value of their own properties, as conscience dictated, and thus assign the respective tax to be paid. The system was called "self-appraisal" and was meant to replace territorial taxes which had not been updated since 1928. The response to the government's initiative was selfish organized tax evasion. It was not uncommon for neighbors of the same district, who enjoyed similar standards of living and property holdings, to meet to fill out the self-appraisal forms in such a way that no one's declared values would contradict anyone else's and thereby put them at risk.

Both this story and the private sector's resistance to the FIS as payments to address the social debt simply confirm the extreme difficulty inherent in organizing people to achieve shared goals, not just for their own sake, but especially for those Guatemalans barely subsisting in the nation's interior.

The Synthesis Space

The nation's will to change has broken down during periods of political and social turmoil. Beam one of the bridge, representing national values, is in many ways the synthesis of the many other varied elements that comprise the democratic transition. There has been progress, but not enough. National values are the collective creation of the nation's people and the articulation of common aspirations. This collective action "to build the bridge" is the essence of the democratic ideal. Cultural creativity and moral values are also elements of national values. The populace must reject the notion that political power is wielded only by the governing class and public officials. This mistaken notion lies at the root of Guatemala's corruption. To complete construction on beam one of the bridge also requires a change of heart from those who believe that public matters, particularly politics, are unworthy and undignified areas of personal endeavor. Continued indifference will prevent Guatemala from forging a national identity and a just society.

So far, Guatemala has taken a course of action in its transition to democracy that has favored macroeconomic and political development while neglecting institutional and social development. This uneven approach must be reconsidered. A viable democratic transition requires a more balanced, coherent, and integrated set of policies. One or two beams of a bridge can span a chasm and provide limited short-term service, but more beams will provide the long-term strength needed to withstand general passage. Analogously, the incomplete transition in Guatemala does not satisfy the citizenry's aspirations for a better life. It does not provide adequate passage from nondemocratic to democratic values. Rather, Guatemala's incomplete transition only reminds us that a bridge, when only partially completed, is fragile and vulnerable.

We must remain wary, for our social ills continue unattended. Nevertheless, I continue to be optimistic about the progress made in certain areas. This is why I view the future with cautious optimism.

SEVEN

DEMOCRATIC TRANSITION OR MODERNIZATION? THE CASE OF EL SALVADOR SINCE 1979

RUBÉN ZAMORA

Several countries in the Americas responded to the depression of the 1930s with political-economic strategies such as modernization and redistributive populist policies. El Salvador was an exception. The country's ruling elite was too weak politically to take such measures, and the subordinate classes responded too radically and intensely to the crisis to be easily assuaged, leading to a stalled economy and the assumption of power by the military, with a subsequent restriction of popular political participation and mobilization. El Salvador today still suffers the aftereffect: The military sets the boundaries for the political game and defines the game's permissible options.

SIXTY YEARS OF MODERNIZATION UNDER THE MILITARY

Since 1930, El Salvador's political development has revolved around a double axis. On the one hand, the military's political power has been institutionalized. On the other hand, a sporadic democratic struggle has sought to dislodge the military's grip on power.

There are two ways to view the military's institutionalization of its political control. In one respect, over the last sixty years there has been a transition from personalized political control, beginning with General Maximiliano Hernández Martínez's dictatorship (1931–44), toward institutional procedures. Under the latter, the whole of the armed forces came to set the political rules using standard decision-making procedures, instead of relying solely upon the will of one ruler. A second way to view the military's increasing institutionalization is to note that the political system underwent some liberalization under military dominance. Nonetheless, this change occurred at such a slow and sporadic pace that the military was able to modernize while at the same time maintaining its control over politics. Viewed either way, the military's political control had become increasingly sophisticated since the early 1930s.

Countering this pronounced trend of the last sixty years, four periods of antimilitarist, democratic struggle took top priority on the agenda of the populace and helped to open new political spaces.

The first such revolt against militarism began in 1944, when a combination of popular struggles and military uprisings toppled General Martínez's thirteen-year-long military dictatorship. Efforts to restore a one-man dictatorship failed. A coup d'état finally took place in 1948. The so-called Revolution of '48 granted the nation its first modern political constitution and installed a regime based on an official political party. The new Revolutionary Democratic Unification Party (Partido Revolucionario de Unificación Democrática—PRUD) was a creation of the military, serving as a "constitutional" procedure to retain power through controlled and fraudulent elections in order to permit the rotation of military presidents.

Eleven years later, the political system plunged into another crisis; a second democratizing opportunity opened up, lasting from 1959 to 1961. Centered around the National Civic Orientation Front (Frente Nacional de Orientación Cívica—FNOC), the new popular struggle brought down the government of Colonel José María Lemus. A subsequent coup brought forth a body called the Civic-Military Directorate, which passed a new constitution, established proportional representation in Parliament, and created a "new" official party, the National Conciliation Party (Partido Conciliación Nacional—PCN).

In 1971, El Salvador experienced the third resurgence of the antimilitary struggle. An opposition coalition called the National Opposition Union (UNO) mobilized the popular vote in its favor in the 1972 elections. There was a broad perception that UNO had won, but the military committed fraud and escalated its repressive tactics. A democratically inspired coup d'état failed; the political crisis deepened.

Finally, the years of 1979–81 witnessed a fourth attempt at democratization. The effort began with a mobilization and unification of forces under the aegis of the Popular Forum and culminated in the October 1979 coup. The coup was sparked by the Military Youth movement, a group of young antimilitarist and antioligarchical officers supported by many civilians from the political left (including myself). But this coup was also followed by another restoration of military power; changes were made to the makeup of the Revolutionary Government Junta, and the Military Youth were defeated and forced to disband. After the failure of this democratization attempt, a cycle of generalized civil war began in January 1981.

Four elements constitute the pattern of democratic struggle evident in Salvadoran society across these four episodes: the time interval separating the attempts, the degree of popular mobilization in each instance, the extent of foreign influences affecting the situation, and the nature of military involvement. Examined in light of these elements, each of the four episodes of democratic struggle shows the following:

1. Political crisis in El Salvador appears to operate on a ten-year cycle. Between each attempt at democratization and the next there was a lapse of nine to eleven years. This relatively short cycle is directly related to a structural weakness in Salvadoran society, namely, the uneven distribution of goods. A society so highly polarized at the economic and social levels tends to suffer from recurrent political crises within relatively short time frames.

2. The subordinate sectors of society were able to transcend their normal ideological divisions when they needed to mobilize politically. The degree to which diverse sectors of society were able to band together and mobilize was different each time. But, in each instance, the resulting popular front always included a broad cross section and a cohesive group of social actors, as in the cases of FNOC, UNO, and the Popular Forum.

3. There were evident changes in U.S. foreign policy toward the country or the region. In every instance, except that of 1971–72, events within El Salvador coincided with changes in U.S. foreign policy. Such changes destabilized relations between El Salvador's dominant classes and the military, spurring the subordinate sectors' expectations for change. In 1945, the New Deal and the antifascist alliance served that role. In 1959, it was the changes leading up to the Alliance for Progress. And in 1979, it was President Jimmy Carter's human rights policy.

4. The mechanism chosen to overcome militarism and democratize society was, paradoxically, the coup d'état. Civilian society, unable to overcome military power on its own, would turn to a sector of the armed forces (called "the constitutionalist sector" in local political jargon) to evict the military from power.

The outcome of all these struggles was a relative modernization but not the democratization of the political system. Thus we can say that in El Salvador "transformism," not "transition," prevailed. In the 1944–48 period, the first modern political constitution in our history was born. Then, during the second episode of democratic struggle, El Salvador acquired proportional representation in the Legislative Assembly and a system of permanent political parties. In the third period of upheaval (1971–72), there were no actual advances in the modernization of the political system. This may have been due to a peculiar combination of factors: the absence of change in U.S. foreign policy, extreme popular mobilization, and a failed coup d'état. The political crisis actually deepened. Yet for the first time there was an attempt, albeit unsuccessful, to confront the socioeconomic agrarian problem through (unfortunately, too timid) agrarian reform.

THE OPPORTUNITY FOR DEMOCRATIZATION (1979–1981)

There is no doubt that the events of 1979–81 were some of El Salvador's most tragic and traumatic. For the first time, the trends of the preceding half-century (growth of militarism and acceleration of political modernization) greatly intensified and poignantly revealed themselves to present a novel picture of Salvadoran politics. As we have seen, those trends had been proceeding hand in hand. Now they would produce a somewhat paradoxical but critical situation in which new political possibilities opened up. Like the three previous democratization efforts, this new situation can also be analyzed in terms of the effects of foreign influence, the degree of popular mobilization, and the nature of the coup attempts.

First, without doubt, President Carter's human rights policy was the most radical postwar attempt yet at redefining U.S. foreign policy toward Latin America. It went beyond the narrow confines of the Cold War framework and its containment doctrine. The human rights policy had a powerful capacity to destabilize the military's power in El Salvador. In 1977–79, during General Carlos Humberto Romero's regime, tensions between Washington and the government of El Salvador would heighten to an intensity greater than in the first years of General Martínez's dictatorship, when the United States had refused to recognize Martínez's military government. This was undoubtedly an important factor in Romero's downfall.

Second, popular mobilization reached a new level of radicalization after 1975. Increasingly, various popular organizations joined forces to confront the military apparatus in an ever more violent manner. At the same time, a broad coalition known as the Popular Forum emerged; it encompassed opposition parties, almost all the popular social forces, and even universities and churches.

Finally, in October 1979, the most radical coup d'état of all these periods occurred. The coup's goal was far-reaching demilitarization and socioeconomic reform. Its leaders within the Military Youth hoped to achieve a profound break, not only from the traditional role of the armed forces in politics—which occurred in effect when the military turned the government over to the opposition and withdrew to their barracks—but also from their historic allies, the dominant oligarchic elite.

Nevertheless, the military high command made their traditional efforts to restore their power after this 1979 coup, though this time without a countercoup. The high command began by gradually marginalizing the government's progressive civilian sectors. Marginalization was achieved through repeated changes made to the state's formal leadership, that is, to the three revolutionary government juntas (their terms were October 1979–January 1980, January–March 1980, and March 1980–82). The high command also dismantled the Military Youth movement by co-opting, assassinating, or exiling its members.

The period from 1979 to 1981 offered the most favorable opportunities for defeating militarism and achieving democratization. Once the pursuit of those opportunities failed, the reformists faced a dead end. Democratic spaces had been closing gradually since 1972. Democracy's "fighting tools" (elections, political parties, and political debate) had become more and more ineffectual, and both repression and extraparliamentary forms of popular involvement were on the rise. The democratic movement was at an impasse.

In 1979, I was a leader of the Christian Democratic Party (PDC), the largest of the opposition parties. Since 1972, we had had a political alliance with the Social Democrats and with the Communist Party of El Salvador through UNO. The regime kept us continually aware not only of the danger of our struggle but also (and this was the worst part) of its lack of practical effect. Each day, we watched as a good part of our support base, upon sensing this futility, leaned more toward the political-military organizations. Each day, it became more difficult to attract new supporters.

Under these circumstances, we democrats betrayed our ideology. I say betrayed not because I harbor guilt for what we did but to emphasize the contradiction between what we proclaimed and what we did. We accepted, supported, and collaborated with the October 1979 coup d'état. We championed not the popular will expressed at the polls but the reformist will of a group of young military officers. These officers proposed the same things we were struggling for; such convergence has justified actions in history. But by attaching ourselves to a military coup, we remained at the mercy of the military. And, as hard as we tried to subordinate military authority to civilian authority and the rule of law, we failed.

This democratic coalition's brief tenure in government from October 15, 1979, to January 4, 1980, made clear to those within the democratic movement that we were indeed at a dead end. It forced us to face a basic question that confronts all democratic movements and individuals: what to do when extreme social, ideological, and political polarization seems to cut off all avenues for compromise and democratic coexistence. With whom should we side: the armed revolution led by Marxist-Leninists or the counterrevolutionary military power, which was committing the most brutal excesses against human rights in the name of "avoiding totalitarianism"?

When the first junta collapsed with all of its civilians resigning in January 1980, we, the democrats in El Salvador, faced just such a question. What we decided to do marked the sharpest division within the democratic camp in twenty-five years.

We understood with brutal clarity that the alternatives were to confront our dilemma or to withdraw from the political struggle, go home, and grieve for a democracy that could not be achieved. Even safer than that, perhaps, we could leave the country and wait for a more propitious time to return. For those who decided to stay active, the political climate at the time required us to put on hold (at least temporarily) a great many of our convictions.

Those of us who aligned ourselves with the guerrillas put on hold our commitment to democratic practice when we attached ourselves to the armed camp. Our idea was to reinstate democratic practices later on, once the old authoritarian military order had been destroyed. We judged that we could preserve democratic freedoms in the "new revolutionary order." In the same way, those of my Christian Democratic friends who made the decision to remain as part of a government they did not control—but that needed them as an international credential—put on hold their own twenty-year-long struggle against the military regime in the hope that they could transform it from within. Both groups had justifiable motives.

In retrospect, neither group won the bet: the military officers were not converted into democrats, and no new revolutionary order came about to preserve democracy. Nevertheless, the possibility of building a political democracy is stronger today than it has been in all our modern history. The question, then, is this: Did we help, or have we been nothing more than pompous, deluded fellow travelers of one side or the other?

MODERNIZATION AND CIVIL WAR: THE EXPERIENCE OF THE 1980S

There was ample evidence in the 1980s of modernization in the Salvadoran political system. This was particularly true after 1984 when José Napoleón Duarte, a civilian leader of the Christian Democratic Party, assumed the presidency. He had been denied it in 1972 because of electoral fraud; from 1980 to 1983, he had headed a governing coalition between the Christian Democrats and the military. Yet, one is inclined to view this modernization as linked directly to the political repression of the previous five years, perhaps five of the blackest years in our history.

Most government measures taken to modernize the political system were predicated on the prior elimination of leaders of the social and political opposition and their organizational bases. At the same time, the population endured truly traumatic levels of terror, beginning with the assassination of the Roman Catholic Archbishop of San Salvador—a man extremely dear to the population—and continuing through the "corpse dumps," the death squads roaming the streets, and generalized torture.

During the years of terror, the military's war-making apparatus expanded, as did the concept that the military stood above the law and should be exempt from any future punishment. The war capabilities of the armed forces were greatly expanded by shipments of arms and equipment from the United States.

Yet, ironically, the modernization of political institutions did, in fact, parallel military expansionism. Several indications of this are evident.

1. Society experienced an important expansion of the media. In the 1980s, the number of television news programs rose from one to four, and the number of radio news programs grew to over fifty. There was not only a higher degree of media professionalism but also a proliferation of varied political points of view.

2. The political party system developed and strengthened. Parties tried to define their positions along ideological lines. They remained politically active full-time, not just during elections. They managed to act conjointly by forming an interparty coalition.

3. There were significant advances in the electoral system, such as expanded voter registration, introduction of computer techniques, and distribution of identification cards to the voting population.

4. Social organizations were given institutional recognition by further developing their ties with the state, such as by expanding popular access to state organs through institutions like the Legislative Assembly and the Supreme Court. Especially during the latter half of the 1980s, the state implemented its paradoxical policy of institutional repression and recognition, increasing formal institutional recognition while trying unsuccessfully to constrain social organizations within prescribed parameters.

In the latter part of the 1980s, little by little it became apparent that neither the governing military nor the armed opposition would be able to win out over the other. This created a stalemate or at best an unstable power "equilibrium" likely only to become more intractable over time. Some called this situation one of "mutual veto," in the sense that neither side could make headway because either could block its adversary's progress.

After 1985, this unstable equilibrium in the military arena increased. To break the stalemate, government forces launched repeated political-military offensives; so too did the Farabundo Martí National Liberation Front (FMLN) guerrillas in November 1989. Both sides failed.

An unstable equilibrium on the political level became obvious as well in the late 1980s. The PDC won clear electoral majorities in 1984 and 1985; these, however, were followed by Nationalist Republican Alliance (ARENA) majorities in 1988 and 1989. The 1991 legislative elections produced different results: the ruling party lost its legislative majority but the opposition parties still did not earn a majority, thereby consolidating a political impasse as well.

In the social arena, it is less clear that an unstable equilibrium has existed. However, since 1990 the union movements have moderated their methods of struggle; in turn, the power structure has been cautious in confronting the social movement, despite the predictions to the contrary. These trends indicate that both forces felt they could not risk testing the limits of their opponent.

The process begun in El Salvador in the second half of 1991 constituted a fifth opportunity for democratization. Several factors were responsible which, had they been present seven or ten years earlier, would not have led to the current promising possibilities for democratic advancement. External factors were quite favorable, while the various domestic stalemates fostered new forms of behavior, which also yielded positive results.

Three important factors were international phenomena. One was the end of the Cold War. To a large extent, the Salvadoran crisis was a product of the Cold War; at a minimum, the Cold War added to its severity. For example, socialist countries gave support to the FMLN, and the United States justified its involvement in the Salvadoran conflict in terms of the need to "contain Soviet-Cuban expansionism." Present political alignments within El Salvador still reflect the ideological divisions that the Cold War had produced internationally. The end of the Cold War meant disappearance of one of the most important ideological justifications for the Salvadoran civil war as well as for the stances taken by the United States and by international supporters of the revolution.

A second international factor was the changing U.S. policy toward El Salvador. The highly ideological U.S. approach to involvement in the region, typified by the policies of the Reagan administration, began to change toward pragmatism. The U.S. government began to realize that it was not "winning" the war, despite ten years of military effort, only prolonging it. The U.S. Congress became increasingly impatient. The time had come to negotiate.

The third international factor was regional in scope. Two important events changed the Central American panorama: General Manuel Noriega of Panama was defeated militarily in December 1989, and the Sandinistas were defeated in the February 1990 Nicaraguan elections. Both defeats were perceived by Salvadorans as lost support for the FMLN. These two events helped to increase doubts in El Salvador as to the necessity and appropriateness of militarism as the form of political-strategic control.

In addition to international developments, several domestic factors shaped the possibility for democratic progress in El Salvador. The 1990 national election in Nicaragua and the 1989 Salvadoran presidential election won by Alfredo Cristiani—the candidate of the most important party of the right, ARENA—demonstrated to conservative forces that retaking the government was possible via politics. This new perception gradually overtook the all-or-nothing concept of power, which had been prevalent among those on the right (the Salvadoran and Guatemalan cases being perhaps the most extreme) as well as among those on the left (the Salvadorans and Nicaraguans serving as examples). The possibility of a more pluralistic exercise of power opened up.

Some in the business class increasingly recognized the economic necessity of resolving El Salvador's civil war through negotiation. The upper ranks of corporatist organizations, especially the Chamber of Industry and Commerce and the Salvadoran Association of Industrialists, expressed publicly and with great clarity the need for negotiation. In 1990, they even established contacts and formal talks with the guerrilla leadership.

The call for negotiations caused a split within the ARENA party. One faction, centered around President Cristiani, viewed a negotiated settlement not only as a means of legitimizing ARENA but as economically necessary. Among certain other members of the bourgeoisie, the armed forces, and ARENA, negotiation was viewed as useful as "legitimizing speech" but not worthy of support. In March and April 1991, the latter groups reacted violently to the possibility of negotiated agreements concerning the status of the armed forces; they launched a furious advertising campaign that went so far as to call a president who had come from the ARENA party a "traitor." They even attempted a coup d'état.

Another factor influencing change could be seen at the level of popular social organizations. During the second half of the 1980s, the social movements reemerged, but they were divided along two axes: over ideological issues and over sources of financing. Each side denounced the other. The results were extreme radicalization along with paralyzing passivity.

After ARENA's presidential victory the situation changed. An agreement was reached; in 1990–91, groups in the popular movement came together, rising above ideological differences. The Permanent Debate for Peace played the pioneering role. Later, there emerged a coalition of social groups as well as the Peasant Democratic Alliance (ADC)—organizations that sought to unify the groups that were bickering and to forge common platforms among them.

Any general rule of "social movement development" in El Salvador would have to hinge on two conditions. First, to move toward democracy, social movements would have to act for goals above and beyond the ideological differences of its members. Second, although radical opportunities for change often present themselves in times of social struggle, it is not during these times but rather during times of united social struggle that possibilities for real democratic advancement open up. Examples in the Salvadoran experience include the sitdown strike of 1944, the struggle against Lemus in 1959, formation of UNO in 1972, and the rise of the Popular Forum in 1989.

A third domestic factor influencing democratic change was the military stalemate. As indicated, the military forces of both sides had been trapped in unstable equilibrium since the mid-1980s. This did not become clear until the November 1989 guerrilla offensive, however. The magnitude and duration of that offensive shattered claims by the regime and the United States that the guerrillas were being defeated. Yet despite their decisive show of strength, the revolutionaries discovered that they were still in a stalemate with the regime when the poor urban masses did not respond to calls for insurrection despite the military cover that the FMLN offered them. This came as a bitter disappointment to the rebels, who had hoped for a classic revolutionary triumph over the government's armed forces; FMLN leaders had thought they had more popular support. Since they evidently did not, the revolutionaries were forced to abandon the truckloads of arms that the people had not taken up to fight against the army at the FMLN's behest.

Despite—and to a large degree, because of—the immense human tragedy that took place in El Salvador, a set of factors, all indispensable to democratic transition, arose in the 1980s.

1. Authoritarian-style political and social management, which had traditionally characterized El Salvador, became obviously inefficient and outmoded.

2. There was no consensus, and consensus is indispensable for democratic pluralism within the country. It was not possible to build consensus through normal mechanisms of democracy, such as the rule of law and elections. This changed for the better in the 1980s.

3. Real development of political institutions took place, and even though this occurred under "conditional liberty," it meant that El Salvador would not have to start building institutions from scratch when democracy was finally achieved.

4. Various international actors had become favorable to democratic development in El Salvador. These forces questioned militarism as a system of exercising power.

5. Unstable equilibrium of military, political, and social forces meant that opposing groups in each category had the capacity to veto each other's actions, making it impossible for any one group to impose its will on another. This would only perpetuate conflict without the hope of resolving it.

In 1991, these conditions were evident in ways that would have been unheard of two years earlier. Dialogue changed to negotiation. The political left participated in elections, winning 12 percent in 1991, up from 3 percent in 1989. For the first time in sixty years, there was a parliament in which no political force had a majority and in which the left sat with its own legislative faction. And, for the first time, the congressional leadership was elected by agreement between the ARENA party and the Convergencia Democrática, the right and the left.

A BRIEF PERSONAL REFLECTION ON THE EVOLUTION OF THE DEMOCRATIC LEFT

There has been a strong left in El Salvador since the end of the 1920s. The first "Soviet" on this continent—revolutionary actions by workers to seize the means of production on their own—was created in El Salvador in 1930. At certain times in El Salvador's history, such as the beginning of the 1930s and the beginning of the 1980s, repressive forces made concerted efforts to kill off the left, literally. At other times, as in the 1960s, the climate was safer for leftist political movements, although they did not enjoy the full rights and guarantees necessary for normal political action.

In its own political evolution, however, for many years the Salvadoran left has also suffered from an all-or-nothing concept of power. When trying to learn how to exercise political power, the left ended up mirroring the right, learning from the oligarchy and the military to demand all power because "I either have it all or I haven't any." In response to a long history of repression and because of the deceit surrounding the failed reformist attempt of 1979, the Salvadoran left moved toward revolutionary war at the beginning of the 1980s, a war effort eventually coordinated by the FMLN. Meanwhile, some of us in the civilian left founded a political coalition that incorporated several parties and movements. We called it the Democratic Revolutionary Front (FDR) and allied with the FMLN.

The most important political decision in the history of the Salvadoran left was the decision to go to war in 1981. Nobody sat around a table and made this decision. It was a reaction to state and army action.

The war polarized society, but it also divided the nation into isolated compartments. The war generated mutually exclusive worlds—business, religious, military, and party. These worlds did not learn from one another and did not know each other. I fell into the error of living in one of these isolated worlds during my brief participation in the junta, following the October 1979 overthrow of General Romero's government. I was minister of the presidency, but I did not even know the military ranks. I lived in a compartment of society that prevented me from learning something of obvious importance: how to distinguish among military personnel. This explains my other error: trying to pit military officers against each other, particularly the youth against the high command. The result was disastrous. The high command defeated the Military Youth, thus imposing greater military cohesion. I left the government, attempting to provoke a greater crisis that I hoped could initiate some profound change—a national revolution against the military and the oligarchy. My decision to provoke a crisis was premature and not well analyzed.

Compartmentalization also had its effects on my own party. We realized that we had detached ourselves from much of Salvadoran society; we had lost our sense of reality. Our party leaders had personal friends only among party members. The sons and daughters of the leaders were also mutual friends, but they had few friends outside party circles. A history of exile and clandestine operations had transformed the party into a sect. To correct this, we made a conscious decision to deprofessionalize the party. This would allow the leaders and members to diversify their personal relationships and to free family members from the excessive burden of politics over personal matters.

Equally serious was our party's slowness to acknowledge the important political changes taking place in the country during the 1980s. We took too long to recognize the political usefulness of participating in elections. We still believed—as we had been justified in doing in the past—that fraud and abuse prevailed in Salvadoran elections. But institutional changes had reduced, though not ended, these problems. Our belated recognition of the importance of these institutional changes postponed our timely entry into the Salvadoran elections.

In 1985, we reached our first important political conclusions since the beginning of the war. We recognized three things. First, there was a military stalemate between the guerrilla forces and the army. Second, President Duarte's government was weakening, partly because it was a reformist government without the real potential for making reforms. Third, the government had worn down the Christian Democratic Party, creating a political void, which in the coming elections only the right could fill because the democratic left was not participating in those elections. The Salvadoran people wanted to vote against the government, but the absence of an electoral alternative on the left limited their protest vote to one supporting the right.

Upon realizing those three things, gradually we decided that we should build a political alternative to the right's electoral power. Several leaders of my party, myself included, returned to El Salvador between 1985 and 1987. However, we had not come in sufficient time to play a real political role in the 1989 elections. Victory went to the ARENA party and President-elect Cristiani, leaving us with a very low electoral percentage (3.8 percent).

The left's decision to participate in elections, however, had positive medium-term results. In the 1991 legislative elections the Convergencia Democrática (of which my party was a member) obtained significant electoral support (12.4 percent) and, therefore, representation in the Legislative Assembly. After the elections, we went on to assure the people that the democratic left was willing and able to participate in the pacification of El Salvador. The left and the right worked out a political agreement to choose the leadership of a Legislative Assembly with strong representation from both sides. We voted for an ARENA leader, Roberto Angulo, as president of the Assembly, and the ARENA deputies voted for me as Assembly vice president.

The most important political message to emerge was to show the army that the political left could behave responsibly and to show the guerrillas that it was possible to win and move forward on political, economic, and social grounds without continuing the war.

TRANSITION . . . AT LAST?

There are a number of similarities among the four previous efforts at democratization and the situation in the early 1990s. In the 1990s, U.S. foreign policy toward El Salvador changed. Also, there was a remobilization of social forces, unified above and beyond their ideological differences. If a coup d'état were to follow, then, this would complete the triad that has in previous instances defined democratic "surges," which have never achieved their principal objective of introducing true democracy to El Salvador.

However, this current opportunity is fundamentally different from the earlier periods of democratization. First, there is little likelihood of a military coup d'état. With the changes in the international and regional political arenas (for example, since the early 1980s, the United States had made clear that it held an anticoup policy) and the threat posed by renewed domestic guerilla war, a coup attempt would be too risky a venture.

The democratic opportunity that arose in 1991–1992 was shaped by the fact that neither the government nor the rebels could afford to continue their military strikes against each other. Fortunately, this development could be exploited positively; it did not lead to the black hole of "Lebanonization" of the conflict. Democratic political forces were already in place in the country, presenting a practical alternative to continuation of the war. To credit the democratic forces as "creators of peace" seems hyperbolic; nevertheless, both we and the Christian Democrats can take pride in having been catalysts—a more modest role than creators, but no less necessary.

There does appear to be a fundamental difference between democrats who opted to work with the government in 1980 and those who opted to oppose it. Those who worked with the government in 1980 paid the price in the 1990s of having been associated with the official corruption; they lost their political identity. In the 1990s, this was their worst political liability. On the other hand, our camp, which opposed the government in the 1980s, also paid a price in the 1990s, the price of having put our democratic practices on hold for a time. Only in the 1990s did we see that our confrontation with the regime had led us to underestimate drastically the worth of elections; it had also led us to needless and excessive sectarianism.

In the 1990s, the new and unique means for overcoming militarism and promoting democracy came about as a result of society's uniting for negotiation. This important development was born out of the depths of the war, yet it betokened a new style of politicking. Negotiation was carried out in a country that traditionally had valued coercive action, not negotiated agreements. "Negotiation" and "concession" had usually borne pejorative connotations among both the left and the right.

Through negotiation, the principal roadblock to democratization in El Salvador—militarism—was addressed. The negotiations centered around reform of the armed forces: reducing their size and subordinating the military to civilian authority, purging the army's ranks, separating the army from the police, and suppressing the paramilitary corps. Moreover, there was progress in strengthening political institutions by means of constitutional and electoral reform and the establishment of the legal safeguards of a democratic order, such as judicial reforms and human rights agreements.

These were the topics in the national accord arrived at on the eve of the new year, 1992, at the United Nations headquarters (with the mediation of the UN Secretary-General), where the government and guerrillas signed the agreements to end the war. The Salvadoran transition toward political democracy (a real possibility) accelerated in 1991–1992 but still depended upon the continuation of negotiations as a normal process in politics. The process of negotiation began only as a result of the long and painful conflict; at the same time, the negotiations were the most important means to end that conflict.

Whether we will be able to celebrate the birth and development of political democracy in El Salvador in the next few years is still an open question. But that question has increasingly likely prospects of a positive answer. What history will certainly tell us is that the war was the midwife for the birth of Salvadoran democracy. It was a difficult and painful delivery. I hope that the healthiest and strongest baby will have been born from this most difficult delivery.

EIGHT # RECENT CENTRAL AMERICAN TRANSITIONS: CONCLUSIONS AND POLICY IMPLICATIONS

MARC LINDENBERG

El Salvador's former president José Napoleón Duarte described Central Americans as "swept along in a wave of long steady economic growth and stable military rule from which they plummet into cycles of economic collapse and violent conflict."[1] The cyclic description of Central America's economic and political life is a useful point of departure for a look at the prospects for successful transitions to consolidated democracy in Central America and Panama.[2]

Since the early 1900s, during the periods of stability, Central American nations have generated impressive economic growth through the export of one or more agricultural commodities during global economic expansion. With the exception of Costa Rica, military leaders, allied with dominant business interests, controlled the region's governments. The benefits of economic growth from these boom periods were not well distributed. Furthermore, investments in human capital were rare. For example, excluding Panama since 1969 and Costa Rica since 1960, Central American governments spent less than 3 percent of their annual gross national product (GNP) on education and health combined.[3] These inequities were often masked until world economic recession sparked political and economic crisis.

Central America's crisis periods were normally accompanied by social upheaval countered with repression. During the height of the crisis, military dictators were overturned by new generals allied with dominant business leaders. The new rulers steadied the political helm while the next successful economic strategy was implemented. They often rode the wave of world economic recovery until it crested and began to slip downward. Then the process of collapse and realignment began all over again.

The task of this final chapter is to review the assessments of the actor-analysts contributing to this book, with the following questions in mind: Is the Central American turmoil that began in 1978 nothing more than a repetition of the normal vicious cycle of violent crisis and realignment? Or has a more profound democratic transition begun? To address these questions, I draw on this book's chapters and also on the discussions at a May 1991 workshop sponsored by the World Peace Foundation that gathered the authors and other participants from Central America and the United States.

CENTRAL AMERICAN TRANSITIONS IN THE 1980S: REPETITION OF A VICIOUS CYCLE OR A NEW BEGINNING?

On the surface, the crisis of 1978 in Central America looks like the beginning of the same old story. It was triggered by the worst world recession since the great depression of the 1930s and was accompanied by tremendous violence and disruption in all nations of the region.

But the responses to the crisis of 1978 have some surprising differences. Successful revolutions took place in El Salvador and Nicaragua. The U.S. military invaded Panama to overthrow General Manuel Noriega. Guatemala began a difficult transition to democracy while fighting a counterinsurgency war, and Honduras made a democratic transition with less violence. Eventually all Central American governments responded with double shock policies of economic adjustment and democratic political opening, unparalleled in the region.

An assessment of the transitions of the 1980s leads one to cautious optimism that four of the six Central American nations—Costa Rica, El Salvador, Nicaragua, and Panama—may have crossed the threshold to arrive where stronger more lasting participative governance structures can be built.

A closer examination shows three patterns of transition (see figure 8.1). The first type of transition, regime-led with a high degree of social consensus, was begun in Costa Rica. Its challenge is to define further a successful new economic strategy and to modernize Costa Rica's model of democratic participation. This modernization, however, continues to take place on a solid foundation forged particularly after that nation's 1948 revolution.

In contrast, in Nicaragua and El Salvador, new governance structures emerged through negotiated agreements among key coalitions representing a relatively broad spectrum of ideologies and social groups. Society-led movements overturned earlier governments, but no single internal group proved capable of imposing its will on the others. Power relations were altered precisely because military stalemates led to negotiated political settlements with broad support. Property relations were changed due to land reform.

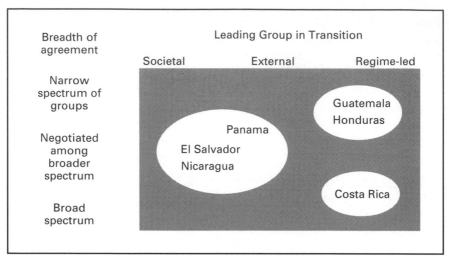

Fig. 8.1. Central American regime transitions, 1978–90. *Source:* Author's summary of participant perceptions, World Peace Foundation workshop, "Democratic Transitions in Central America and Panama," Cambridge, Massachusetts, May 1991.

Finally, the Guatemalan and Honduran transitions were military regime–led adjustments negotiated with a narrow spectrum of groups, leaving elements of the traditional business, civil elite in a predominant position. These transitions may do nothing more than repeat the old cycle of Central American military and civil realignment. For example, key participants in the Guatemalan transition of the 1980s lament that their nation again postponed social transformations.[4] Former Honduran and Guatemalan military leaders warn of the continued independence of the armed forces in their societies.[5]

Costa Rica: Fine Tuning a Transition in Process

The Costa Ricans made major headway in the economic and political transition that began in 1982. By the early 1990s, their nation had achieved successful economic stabilization and several phases of an adjustment program. The basic parameters of the outwardly oriented strategy were accepted both by major political parties and by the general population. While there was disagreement about the speed of this transition, broad consensus was built through intensive dialogue between government and business, labor, and community groups. As a result, the basic direction of economic policy has remained unchanged even though the National Liberation Party (PLN) was replaced by the Social Christian Unity Party (PUSC) in the elections of 1990. Furthermore, the nation survived the temptation to restrict basic rights and to increase drastically its police budget during the heightened tensions with Nicaragua and Panama. The main dilemma of the government of José María

Figueres (1994–98) has been to maintain a steady course in light of increasing pressures to ease some of the pains of adjustment.

The two biggest challenges to Costa Rica's continued transition are consolidating the outwardly oriented economic growth and fine tuning the democratic process. There are five barriers to consolidating the new outwardly oriented economic model. First, vested economic interests still resist opening the economy. Members of both business chambers and community groups continue to fight the reduction of specific subsidies. A second threat is the popular reaction by low-income groups to perceived losses in their real wages as a result of the new policies. A third barrier is the slow pace of transformation in the role of the state to a smaller, more dynamic catalyst of economic and social activity. This implies a reduction of the role of public enterprises and the search for new private or mixed alternatives in banking and insurance. But such systems prove extremely difficult to dismantle. A fourth dilemma is how to protect Costa Rica's human capital base during the adjustment process. The Costa Ricans want to maintain quality health and education programs without large fiscal deficits. Finally, according to leaders in both major political parties, the educational system will need to be reoriented totally to help citizens work in a competitive environment and to help public sector employees change from a bureaucratic to a service-oriented mentality.

The Costa Ricans' second major challenge is remedying the "vices of democracy," which requires creative responses to four basic problems. First, many Costa Ricans decry the excessive time and attention both parties give to political campaigning instead of to governing effectively. Often candidates begin campaigning within a year of an election. Second, both political parties need to overhaul their internal rules to permit more democratic control and participation. Third, older-generation political leaders who played important roles in the revolution of 1948 are reluctant to surrender key positions to the younger generation. Simultaneously, Costa Ricans question whether the younger generation of political leaders have the wisdom and experience to consolidate the transition. Finally, opinion polls show a public perception that there has been a serious increase in corruption in both public and private life. This may heighten cynicism about the value of democratic government.

While the potential for consolidating the change process is strongest in Costa Rica, the transition can still be weakened as a new generation of Costa Rican leaders take the helm of government for the first time.

Nicaragua, El Salvador, and Panama: Consolidating Fragile but Important Beginnings

In the late 1980s Nicaraguans, Salvadorans, and Panamanians expressed optimism about the transition process. They valued the importance of the negotiated agreements between the Sandinistas and the government of Violeta

Barrios de Chamorro in Nicaragua and between the Farabundo Martí National Liberation Front (FMLN) and the government of Alfredo Cristiani in El Salvador as first steps in setting new rules of the game. New institutions and political parties emerged, but political consolidation and the development of new dynamic institutions are important unfinished tasks.

The barriers to economic reform are formidable. In contrast to Costa Rica, which began its economic stabilization in 1982, these three nations were beginning such efforts ten years later and after a series of aborted attempts. Unlike Costa Rica, none had yet found a model that at once provided growth, employment, and substantial investments in human capital to help overcome major problems of health and education, a big factor in the region's past political instability. Panama appears to have taken larger strides in achieving an outward orientation and in achieving this balance. But its interoceanic canal provides an extra economic motor that neither El Salvador nor Nicaragua has. In the mid-1990s El Salvador has begun to experience economic reactivation while Nicaragua's economy has remained fragile.

Another barrier to economic reform was that strong vested interests opposed adjustments. Nicaraguan observers differ about whether the traditional business community presented as much of a barrier to efficient outwardly oriented production as Sandinista unions and new economic groups who, critics insist, enriched themselves through the "piñata" (the Sandinista government's distribution of public patrimony for the private benefit of its key leaders) in the last days of Sandinista rule. (The Sandinistas argue that there was no "piñata.") An additional threat is the thinness of expertise in economic policy making in new political parties, in government, and in civic groups. Furthermore, attempting to resurrect economies on a base of poverty, after war, with minimal external resources is no easy task under any circumstances. Modernizing the state and making it an efficient promoter of economic and social development will take decades.

Consolidation of a democratic transformation will not be possible without further work on the rules of the game. New legislation, pacts, and dialogues will be needed to provide the social glue to hold the transitions together. Nicaraguans lament the sporadic outbreaks of violence by what they called *recontra* and *recompa* groups—demobilized former contra and Sandinista soldiers—dissatisfied with the outcomes of the transition and backed by political extremists on both sides of the spectrum. New formal government institutions such as legislatures, executive branches, and judiciaries must build competent staff and sound procedures. The new political parties, unions, civic organizations, and business chambers need considerable strengthening to represent their constituents effectively. A deep change in political culture through massive education and through the example of efficient, fair government is needed if democracy is to have a chance. Finally, the boundaries between the military and the new civilians in government have remained ambiguous. For example, the head of the army (Jefe del Ejército) in the new Chamorro government in Nicaragua continued to be Humberto Ortega, one of the nine Sandinista commanders and brother of former President Daniel Ortega. In El Salvador it is not clear how well the agreements for establishing a new police force and civilian control of the military will actually work. While the destruction of the Panama Defense Forces (PDF) provided a real opportunity to create a new police organization under civilian control, the task of developing such a new group will not be easy. Finally, the transformations are threatened in Nicaragua, for example, by new political fragmentation and corruption, which could again sow the seeds of public cynicism. These seeds might later germinate in future cycles of violence and instability.

In summary, while the Costa Rican transition requires fine tuning of its economic strategy and its model of democratic participation by a new generation of political leadership, the Salvadoran, Nicaraguan, and Panamanian transitions demand further construction of participatory institutions and consolidation of the new institutions on a fragile foundation of radically changed political coalitions. As of the mid-1990s the Salvadoran and Panamanian cases provide cause for cautious optimism. The increasing fragmentation in Nicaragua is a more sobering example of how difficult political transformation can be.

Guatemala and Honduras: Initiating a More Lasting Transition

Most of the threats to real transition confronting Panama, Nicaragua, and El Salvador also plagued Guatemala and Honduras, but in these two countries there are two other serious concerns. Reassertion of power by traditional groups may again postpone needed social transformation. For example, according to Héctor Gramajo, the former Guatemalan defense minister contributing to this book, business pressure groups in Guatemala almost brought the government of Marco Vinicio Cerezo Arévalo down over the issue of increased taxation and social expenditures. Gramajo notes that these groups not only protested but encouraged elements within the military to try two unsuccessful coups. Postponing a social transformation may allow a bloodier transition to occur again later. The Guatemalan process continued to be punctuated by political instability into the mid-1990s.

In addition, in the absence of real contravening pressures, the military could maintain a disproportionately strong role. While civilian leadership is emerging, the Honduran military still maintains a high level of formal, structural independence from civilian control. Although Guatemala's new constitution permits executive oversight, civilians have been reluctant to take the reins fully.

IS SPEEDING UP THE TRANSITION PROCESS FEASIBLE?

For some students of democratic transitions, the changes in Central America in the 1980s might be viewed with extreme skepticism. They would assert that the process of development of democratic institutions is an evolutionary one that cannot be rushed. For example, Robert T. Putnam argues that today's relatively effective democratic infrastructure in northern Italy was built upon a base of civic organizations formed centuries earlier.[6] He believes that the lack of similar development in southern Italy can be traced to absence of this earlier civic base. Samuel P. Huntington argues that democratization is intimately related to a more complex, long-term process of economic development and modernization.[7] More recent work on the management of simultaneous economic transition and political opening in the 1980s also provides evidence for the difficulties of speeding up managed change.[8]

For better or worse, the Central American region and the world are in the midst of important economic and political transitions. Policy makers cannot afford to wait while scholars sort out exactly what might help consolidate the transition process. Recent work by the World Bank and other institutions shows convincingly that policies do matter and that economic change can be accelerated.[9] While acknowledging how little is known about consolidating democratic transitions, Graham Allison and others have attempted to identify key programmatic interventions to promote transition.[10]

There are no rules for speeding up transitions. But one can at least think about the process by first identifying barriers to it and then suggesting the policy actions that might help overcome them.

BARRIERS TO TRANSITION

Barriers to transition can be clustered into five areas based on their origin in (1) the institutional context, (2) the sphere of civic organizations, (3) political parties, (4) legislative, executive, or judicial institutions, or (5) the ministries and government programs (see fig. 8.2). Such an organizing framework is useful because it helps identify where reform programs might be more specifically directed even though each nation must find its own road to transition.

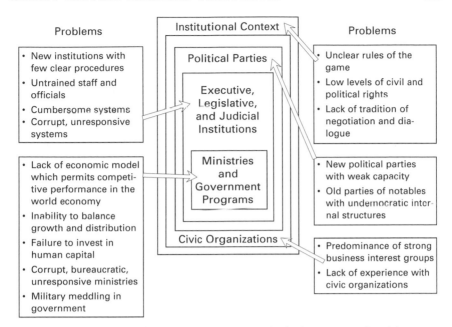

Fig. 8.2. Barriers to consolidating transitions. *Source:* Author's summary of participant perceptions, World Peace Foundation workshop, "Democratic Transitions in Central America and Panama," Cambridge, Massachusetts, May 1991.

Institutional Context

The institutional context may be thought of as the cluster of complex rules that govern the interactions among civil society, political society, and the state. Nonexistent or imprecise rules of the game continue to be a serious barrier to further transition. The presence of formal rights but the absence of real, enforceable civil, political, and economic rights results in low levels of confidence. For example, lack of clarity in property rights after a decade of revolution and reform in Nicaragua has made it difficult to attract foreign investors and even to convince Nicaraguans to invest. In addition, lack of experience with dialogue and negotiation, and much experience with regard to violence, confrontation, and repression, has made consolidating the transitions a real problem.

Civil Society and Civic Organizations

Although civil society did not flourish in Central America under authoritarian rule, citizens were able to form business, labor, and private associations to promote their civic interests. Nongovernment media were authorized as well. The terms under which civic groups were permitted to function fluctuated. Sometimes groups could operate freely until governments felt threatened, whereupon press censorship and state of siege were imposed.

Liberalization in the 1980s permitted an expansion of civil society, leaving, however, serious problems. Previously, when opposition political parties had been repressed, civic organizations such as business chambers had filled the vacuum. They not only defended specific sectorial interests but also served as the focal point for broad-based political action. With the opening of political life, it was hard for old-style leaders to accept a more restricted role and a less confrontational style.

In addition, civil society had been strongly dominated by powerful business chambers. Their resources and expertise put new labor and civic groups at an extreme disadvantage. New organizations lack the talent and expertise to develop strategies, structures, and processes to allow them to be self-sustaining and to have real impact. Finally, most civic organizations, including the business pressure groups, have yet to serve as a source of policy ideas, draft legislation, and debate.

Political Society and Political Parties

The new democratic transformations have permitted an expanded role for political parties but have also created a new set of problems. For example, in some societies where a strong political party dominated political life for a decade—as did the Sandinista National Liberation Front (FSLN) in Nicaragua or the Democratic Revolutionary Party (PRD) in Panama—it has been hard for new parties to compete on an even playing field. In addition, many of the old political groups like the National Liberation Movement (MLN) or the Institutional Democratic Party (PID) in Guatemala had been parties of notables that in effect functioned only at election time. Still others were dependent upon a single charismatic figure. Modernizing old parties has proven an important bottleneck in the transition.

Old minority parties and totally new parties have had special problems building professional organizations capable of contesting power and then staffing an effective government. For example, the Christian Democrats in El Salvador, Guatemala, and Panama had operated under severe legal restrictions in the past. Their leaders had been under constant threat, and in El Salvador and Guatemala assassinations were not infrequent. One Guatemalan participant in the workshop noted that his party had had to spend so much effort just mounting a successful election campaign that they had little chance to think seriously of what policies they would pursue if they won. He added that they had problems just staffing the new government with talented people. A final problem for all parties has been the democratization of internal procedures and the development of professional staff capable of developing policy positions.

New Legislatures, Executive Branches, and Judicial Institutions

Assignment of more dynamic roles to legislatures and the judiciary has put tremendous strains on these antiquated institutions. Many newly elected officials have had virtually no experience in legislative process, critical analysis of national priorities, or evaluation of programs and budgets. Procedures for conducting government business have had to be invented as democratization advanced. One Panamanian leader noted that in the first public legislative budget hearings, neither the legislators nor the executive officials knew quite what to do. In addition, there was no tradition of legislative staff work on policy issues. The vice president of the Salvadoran Assembly, Rubén Zamora, similarly noted that he had no staff for policy analysis. He felt it had been easier to operate clandestinely than as a key player in a legislative assembly. Many Central Americans point out that the pressures of guaranteeing a fair, open, civil, and political process have put special strains on the judiciary. Systems were cumbersome. Judges are paid poorly; they are easily subjected to threats and intimidation and are susceptible to corruption.

Ministries and Government Programs

The transitions will be only as successful as the ability of new governments to define coherent plans for economic and political development and to carry these out efficiently and fairly. With the exception of Costa Rica, the new governments have not been effective in defining economic strategies that would generate growth, employment, and income distribution. Key ministries have not had the talent to perform policy analysis nor implement programs effectively. The ministries have ambiguous objectives. They are overstaffed with underpaid and unmotivated officials. Lack of clear rules for civil-military relationships has left the door open for the return of a firm hand in government should the civilians prove incapable of providing effective government.

POLICIES FOR STRENGTHENING TRANSITIONS

There can be no single set of recommendations that will apply to consolidating transitions in every Central American nation. However, it is possible to suggest potential ways for particular barriers to be overcome when they happen to exist in a given country. The list that follows is meant as no more

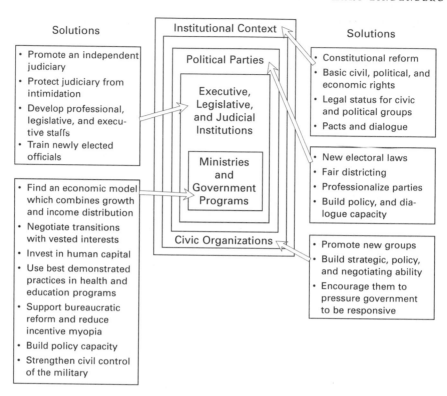

Fig. 8.3. Policies for consolidating transitions. *Source:* Author's summary of participant perceptions, World Peace Foundation workshop, "Democratic Transitions in Central America and Panama," Cambridge, Massachusetts, May 1991.

than a device to stimulate leaders and policy makers who believe their nations have particular transition problems (see fig. 8.3). Suggestions are motivated by the spirit that one should not mention problems without being willing at least to think about solutions. However, each nation must craft its own solutions based on its particular situation.

THE INSTITUTIONAL CONTEXT

1. Complete the constitutional reforms that establish the separation of powers and the basic rules for democratic government.

2. Formalize the guarantee of basic civil, political, and economic rights.

3. Insure legal recognition of new civic and political groups.

4. Promote resolution of conflicts through pacts, dialogue, and discussion rather than by violent conflict.

5. Keep international attention focused on regional advances and also on abuses.

6. Use the United Nations and regional organizations to help monitor peace agreements and the transition process.

7. Promote educational reforms that favor problem solving and awareness of basic rights. Promote basic education.

CIVIL SOCIETY AND CIVIC ORGANIZATIONS

8. Stimulate formation of new civic organizations and community-based problem solving.

9. Provide training and technical assistance to help new organizations define strategy and programs and to build their capacity to be dynamic, self-sufficient organizations.

10. Encourage civic organizations to put pressure on government to be responsive.

11. Stimulate civic and private organizations to provide programs that force government to be competitive and more service oriented.

POLITICAL SOCIETY AND POLITICAL PARTIES

12. Support new electoral laws that make the election process clear, transparent, and efficient. Rely on international experience and monitoring when fairness may be an issue.

13. Encourage redistricting to ensure fair representation of citizens by politicians.

14. Promote professionalization of political parties. Rely on world experience in party development.

15. Provide technical assistance to build capacity within the parties to define policy options and to debate these options publicly.

NEW LEGISLATURES, EXECUTIVE BRANCHES, AND JUDICIAL INSTITUTIONS

16. Use proven world practices to design executive, legislative, and judicial procedures.

17. Provide newly elected officials with training in policy design, budgeting, and program evaluation as well as in the legislative process.

18. Promote establishment of professional, analytical, executive, and legislative staffs.

19. Support an independent judiciary. Protect judges from intimidation.

20. Combat corruption.

MINISTRIES AND GOVERNMENT PROGRAMS

21. Encourage the search for economic strategies that stimulate balanced growth and employment generation and that invest in the human capital base.

22. Promote public sector reform to help develop a smaller but more dynamic and client-responsive public sector.

23. Strengthen civilian control of the military.

24. Identify and implement proven practices in social service delivery systems.

While there is no road map for successful transitions, adoption of these proposals where they apply to specific situations should increase the chances of successful transition to democracy.

CONCLUSIONS

The cycles of crisis and instability in Central America seem to deny the promise of greater social development and political participation. As indicated, however, recent studies have shown that in the last half-century several nations elsewhere have successfully managed a process of economic and political transition.

Review of recent Central American experiences provides cause for both caution and hope. On the one hand, policies that promote transition cannot even reach the agenda for approval without solid political coalitions, which may take generations to form. They cannot be successfully implemented without the institutional infrastructure necessary to make them work. On the other hand, there is evidence that from the chaos of the 1980s new coalitions have arisen which might provide a fragile but emergent base for such transitions.

Such a conclusion provides a challenge both to extreme optimists and to pessimists. Optimists who think that rapid reform through "getting macroeconomic policy right" is the exclusive leading-edge solution to the development dilemma need to take the problem of institutional capacity building more seriously. Blind macropolicy proponents appear surprised when people and institutions do not respond, for example, to market forces supposedly unleashed by their reforms. They are even more surprised when citizens throw the reform governments out of office. These advisors often blame everyone but themselves when their policies do not work. They need to incorporate into their approach to change a greater emphasis on institutional reform and political coalition building. They should not mislead others into thinking that social change is easy or that it can be imposed. They should not be misled themselves.

Yet extreme pessimism may also be an unfortunate response to insights from analyses of the recent Central American experience. Pessimists would argue that since successful reforms are so deeply embedded in the glacially slow, evolutionary development of civic culture and governance structures, nothing can be sped up. They ignore evidence that many successful governments between 1965 and 1987 as well as before this period did in fact think systematically about how to overcome barriers to more rapid change and built upon their understanding of their cultural and institutional context to speed reforms.

Pessimists need to learn more about successful mobilization of policy to promote change. They should focus on the triangle of values, coalitions, and institutional fabric providing the foundations of such change. They can identify barriers to change and suggest how to overcome them. Such an approach attempts to build upon context and culture to increase the probability that policy reform will succeed.

The authors of this book are cautiously optimistic about the region's future, believing that the balance in the region has tipped in a more democratic direction and that the phoenix emerging from the ashes of war and conflict in El Salvador, Nicaragua, Panama, and, perhaps, Guatemala just might fly.

The process of consolidation will not be an easy one. New political fragmentation and corruption in several Central American nations increase the risk of sowing the seeds of renewed cynicism and discontent. Yet there is still a disposition among Central Americans to find solutions permitting an escape from the cycles of violence and instability that have plagued them in the twentieth century. The international community can help by supporting their efforts.

NOTES

1. Author's interview with President José Napoleón Duarte, May 1986.

2. Many sources find the cyclic description of Central American economic and political life useful in discussing its dynamics. See, for example, Tom Barry, *Roots of Rebellion: Land and Hunger in Central America* (Boston: South End Press, 1987); Victor Bulmer-Thomas, *Studies in the Economics of Central America* (New York: St. Martin's Press, 1988); Marc Lindenberg, "World Economics Cycles and Central American Political Instability," *World Politics* 42, no. 3 (April 1990): 397–421; Rafael Menjívar,

Formación y lucha del proletariado industrial salvadoreño (San Salvador: UCA Editores, 1979); Fred Weaver, *Political Economy of Development in Central America* (Boulder: Westview Press, 1993); and Robert G. Williams, *Export Agriculture and the Crisis in Central America* (Chapel Hill: University of North Carolina Press, 1986). Rubén Zamora uses the cycle theory in chapter 7 of this book.

3. The International Monetary Fund's *Government Finance Statistics Yearbooks* (Washington, D.C.: IMF, 1960–90) were used to compute the annual data.

4. Comments by Rodolfo Paiz-Andrade, minister of finance during the Cerezo government in Guatemala, World Peace Foundation workshop on "Democratic Transitions in Central America and Panama," Cambridge, Mass., May 1991, discussion notes.

5. Comments by General Héctor Alejandro Gramajo Morales, minister of defense during the Cerezo government in Guatemala, and General Walter López, former minister of defense of Honduras, World Peace Foundation workshop on "Democratic Transitions in Central America and Panama," discussion notes.

6. Robert T. Putnam with Robert Leonardi and Raffaella Nanetti, *Democracy and the Civic Community: Tradition and Change in an Italian Experiment* (Princeton: Princeton University Press, 1992).

7. Samuel P. Huntington, *The Third Wave: Democratization in the Late Twentieth Century* (Norman: University of Oklahoma Press, 1991).

8. Marc Lindenberg and Shantayana Devarajan, "Prescribing Strong Economic Medicine: Revisiting the Myths about Structural Adjustment, Democracy, and Economic Performance in Developing Nations," *Comparative Politics* 25, no. 2 (January 1993).

9. World Bank, *World Development Report* (Oxford: Oxford University Press, 1992).

10. Graham Allison and Robert Beschel, "Can the U.S. Promote Democracy," *Political Science Quarterly* 106, no. 4 (1991–92).

CONTRIBUTORS

NICOLÁS ARDITO-BARLETTA has been president of Panama (1984–85), minister of planning and economic policy of Panama, and vice president for Latin America at the World Bank.

RICHARD J. BLOOMFIELD has been executive director of the World Peace Foundation and U.S. ambassador to Ecuador (1976–78) and Portugal (1978–82).

SILVIO DE FRANCO has been minister for economy and development (1990–92) and president of the Central Bank (1992) in Nicaragua.

JORGE I. DOMÍNGUEZ is the Frank G. Thomson Professor of Government at Harvard University and past president of the Latin American Studies Association.

HÉCTOR ALEJANDRO GRAMAJO MORALES has been General of the Army and minister of national defense (1987–90) as well as a candidate for the presidency in Guatemala.

MARC LINDENBERG is vice president of CARE and has been the rector of the Instituto Centroamericano de Administración de Empresas and a lecturer at the Harvard University Kennedy School of Government.

RODOLFO PAIZ-ANDRADE has been finance minister of Guatemala (1986–89) and a professor at the Instituto Centroamericano de Administración de Empresas.

JOSÉ LUIS VELÁZQUEZ has been an adviser to Silvio de Franco.

JAIME WHEELOCK ROMÁN has been a Sandinista commander, member of the National Directorate of the Sandinista Front for National Liberation, and minister of agrarian reform in Nicaragua.

RUBÉN ZAMORA has been president of the Movimiento Popular Social Cristiano, vice president of the National Assembly, and twice a presidential candidate in El Salvador.

INDEX

Agency for International Development (AID): in Guatemala, 152, 163; in Nicaragua, 105; in Panama, 55
Alfonsín, Raúl, 49
Alliance for Progress, 167
Allison, Graham, 186
Alvarez, Donaldo, 115
Angulo, Roberto, 177
Arbenz, Jacobo, 9
Ardito-Barletta, Nicolás, 2–3; declaration as traitor, 55; knowledge of allies, 29; in 1984 elections, 13–14, 38, 42–43; and Spadafora slaying, 51–52; at World Bank, 34
—, presidency, 44–53; achievements of, 52–53; cabinet of, 44, 48, 49; economic legislation, 47–48; labor legislation, 49–50; legitimacy of, 43; market policies of, 27; overthrow of, 52–53; PDF under, 45–47, 48, 49–53; professional groups under, 47; relations with business, 50, 51; social development programs of, 49, 52
ARENA. See Nationalist Republican Alliance (ARENA, El Salvador)
Arévalo, Juan, 135
Argentina, democratization in, 6
Arias, Arnulfo, 44; and Ardito-Barletta, 38–39, 42, 50; death of, 57; popularity of, 34; return from exile, 33
Arias, Oscar, 79
Arias Calderón, Ricardo, 58, 59
Asia, East: democratic transitions in, 11
Association of Business Executives (Panama), 26

Association of Rural Workers (Nicaragua), 110n5
Association of Sandinista Youth, 110n5
Authentic National Center (CAN, Guatemala), 116
Authoritarianism, 69; of Guatemala, 140, 143; Hobbes on, 6; living standards under, 10; of Nicaraguan culture, 107–8; opposition of business groups to, 24–25, 26; reformers under, 12–14; replacement by pluralism, 5; Salvadoran, 174
Axis powers, democratization of, 6

Baker, James, 49
Barillas, Danilo, 134
Barrios de Chamorro, Violeta. See Chamorro, Violeta Barrios de
Belize, dispute with Guatemala, 114
Betancur, Belisario, 49
Blanco, Jorge, 49
Bodyguard industry (Guatemala), 134
Broad Opposition Front (FAO, Sandinistas), 71, 87, 110n3
Bush administration: Nicaraguan policy of, 9; Panamanian policy of, 59
Business groups, 24–28; Costa Rican, 183; influence in elections, 21–22; role in civil society, 188; role in economic liberalization, 24, 27
, Guatemalan, 25, 27–28; influence of, 144, 156; opposition to Mejía, 123; opposition to tax reform, 130, 136, 158, 159, 185; under Serrano presidency, 148

197

—, Nicaraguan, 25–26, 74; under Chamorro government, 105; confiscation of property from, 89–90; in 1990 elections, 80; production subsidies for, 103, 184; resistance to property reform, 75; under Sandinistas, 92

—, Panamanian, 24, 60, 63; in Ardito presidency, 50, 51; influence of, 26

—, Salvadoran: in civil war, 173, 176; influence of, 26

Cabrera, Alfonso, 128

CACIF. *See* Chamber of Agricultural, Commercial, Industrial and Financial Associations

Calderón Sol, Armando, 21

Calvani, Dr. Arístides, 128, 133

Canal Zone: administration of, 40; under Delvalle government, 54; reversion to Panama, 49, 64–65; U.S. occupation of, 8–9, 33, 34. *See also* Panama Canal

Caribbean Basin, political tension in, 113

Caribbean Basin Initiative (CBI), 45, 156

Carpio, Roberto, 133

Carter, Jimmy: in Panama elections, 58

Carter administration: human rights policy of, 8, 70, 86, 114, 167, 168; opposition to Somoza, 71; treaty with Panama, 33, 35, 36, 59

Castro, Fidel, 51

Catholic Church: in Guatemala, 112, 124, 125; in Nicaragua, 71, 110n8; in 1989 Panamanian election, 58; support for UNADE, 44–45

Caudillismo (Nicaragua), 108

Central America: authoritarian states in, 6, 69; civil society in, 187–88; corruption in, 192, 193; cost of suppression in, 22; counterinsurgency in, 79, 81, 112; cycles of violence in, 180–81, 182, 192, 193, 194n2; democratic transitions in, xii, 80–84, 180; effect of depression on, 165; effect of global economy on, 180, 181; effect of Sandinista revolution on, 8; electoral

right in, 20–22; Esquipulas agreements in, 78–80; estate system of, 69; fraudulent elections in, 15; institutional change in, 14, 23–24, 192; international pressures on, 1, 5, 8–10, 22, 30n10; during Kennedy administration, 80; legal oppositions in, 15–17; National Reconciliation Commissions, 129, 135, 160; new organizations in, 188, 190; Parliament, 133; peace initiatives in, 49, 129; political coalitions in, 192; political liberalization in, 2; political oppression in, 67; political parties in, 188–89, 191; property relations in, 181; regime-led transitions in, 181, fig. 8.1; revolutionary movements of, xi, 75, 81, 136; social inequality in, 69; social movements in, 181; speed of transitions in, 186; statesmanship in, 22–24; U.S. policy on, xi, 1, 80–81, 168; use of force in, 5. *See also* Economy, Central American; Military, Central American

Central American Common Market (CACM), 69, 70, 86

Central American Management Institute (INCAE), 44; industrialization processes of, 87

Central Intelligence Agency: Noriega's cooperation with, 54; operations against Sandinistas, 75

Cerezo Arévalo, Marco Vinicio, 140, 142; and Arístides Calvani, 128; business opposition to, 185; cabinet of, 4, 133; corruption in government of, 152–53; coup attempts against, 154; economic policies of, 27–28, 128–29, 145–48, 157, 158–59; election of, 125, 135; foreign policy of, 129, 133, 161; human rights under, 159–60; inaugural address of, 125–26; Indians under, 153; institutional values under, 152–53; local governments under, 155; meetings with insurgency members, 130, 160; and 1988 coup, 131,

132; and 1989 coup, 19, 29, 133; political parties under, 144–45, 154; relations with military, 16, 17, 19, 23; respect for opposition, 22; social programs of, 158

Certainty, in transitions to democracy, 15–17, 22

Chamber of Agricultural, Commercial, Industrial and Financial Associations (CACIF, Guatemala), 27–28, 145; opposition to tax reform, 147, 158; Serrano and, 149

Chamber of Industry and Commerce (El Salvador), 173

Chamorro, Violeta Barrios de: agreement with Sandinistas, 18, 183–84; coalition of, 16, 21, 28–29, 110; disarming of contras under, 17; economic policies of, 27, 103, 104 6, 109, election of, 9, 14, 16, 17, 80, 82–83, 94, 102, 173; goals of, 108; national development plan of, 109; stabilization plan of, 104–6

Christian Democratic parties, 23

Christian Democratic Party (El Salvador): cooperation with juntas, 170, 171, 178; divisions in, 3, 12; effect on military, 13, 16; and 1979 coup, 169, 176, 178; in 1989 elections, 11, 20–21, 177; restrictions on, 188; role in democratization, 177

Christian Democratic Party (Guatemala): democratization strategy of, 128–34; Economic and Social Reorganization Plan, 129; economic policies of, 147; 500 Days Plan, 134, 148; media opposition to, 125; in 1985 elections, 28, 125–26, 135; in 1988 elections, 28, 130, 133; in 1989 elections, 134; in 1990 elections, 135, 142; restrictions on, 188; Technical Council of, 145

Christian Democratic Party (Panama), 57, 63, 66n1; restrictions on, 188

Church of the Word (Guatemala), 121

Civil society: in El Salvador, 167; evolution of, 193; in Guatemala, 127, 132, 143; in Nicaragua, 93–94; in transitions to democracy, 187–88, 191

Civil war, Salvadoran, 1, 167, 170–75; business groups in, 173, 176; end of, 7–8, 178; military in, 172, 176; role in democratization, 179; stalemate in, 176. See also Farabundo Martí National Liberation Front; Insurgency, Salvadoran

COFINA (state bank, Panama), 37

Cold War: effect on El Salvador, 172; effect on Guatemala, 112, 136; end of, 9, 10, 137; Sandinismo and, 95, 100–101, 102

Collado, Marco Tulio, 134

Colombia: military force in, 5; trade with Nicaragua, 107

Colón Free Trade Zone (Panama), 65

Colonies, Spanish: economic system of, 68–69

Communism, insurgency movements in, xi, 75, 81, 136. See also Marxism

Conflict resolution, xii; in Guatemala, 150; importance to democratization, 190

Contadora agreement, 49

Contras: CIA's assistance to, 54; demobilized, 17, 184; effect on economic growth, 81; negotiated settlement with, 101; peasants in, 100; rearming of, 83; Sapoá agreements of, 79

Convergencia Democrática (El Salvador), 16–17, 175, 177

Coordinadora Civilista Nacional (CoCiNa, Panama), 47

Costa Rica: CIA in, 75; democratic transitions in, xiii, 80, 181, 182–83; elections (1990), 182; human capital in, 183; in Sandinista revolution, 72

Cristiani, Alfredo, 21; economic policies of, 27; election of, 173; negotiations with FMLN, 184

Cuba: revolution in, 69; support of Guatemalan insurgency, 116; support of Sandinistas, 72, 74, 75, 108

Dahl, Robert A., 6, 7
De Franco, Silvio, 3, 4, 9; on economic
    crises, 11; on Nicaraguan economy,
    25
De la Espriella, Ricardo, 36, 38; coup
    against, 42
De León Carpio, Ramiro, 140, 143;
    democratic transitions under, 153;
    economic policy of, 157–58, 161; as
    Human Rights Prosecutor, 154;
    human rights under, 160; local gov-
    ernments under, 156; sectors of influ-
    ence under, 149
Delvalle, Eric Arturo, 52; presidency of,
    53–57, 62; U.S. support of, 53
Democratic Liberation Union (UDEL,
    Nicaragua), 71
Democratic Revolutionary Front (FDR,
    El Salvador), 176
Democratic Revolutionary Party (PRD,
    Panama), 36, 38; domination of po-
    litical life, 188; in Legislative Assem-
    bly, 47; in 1984 elections, 42; in 1989
    elections, 62; populist group in, 48
Democratic transitions: accommodation of
    elites to, 31n15; barriers to, 186–89,
    fig. 8.2; certainty in, 11–12, 15, 22;
    civil society in, 187–88, 191; conserv-
    atives under, 22; elements of, 2; in
    Europe, 10; executive branches in,
    186, 188, 191; fragility of, xiii;
    government programs for, 186, 189;
    institutional context of, 186, 187,
    190–91; international factors in,
    9–10, 22; judicial institutions in, 186,
    188, 191–92; legislatures in, 188,
    191; patterns in, xii, 181; peaceful, 5,
    6; policies for strengthening, 189–92,
    fig. 8.3; political parties in, 186,
    188–89, 191; rational choice in, 5, 8,
    11, 22; Reagan administration on,
    xi–xii; regime-led, 181, fig. 8.1; role
    of civic organizations in, 186; role of
    education in, 191; role of pluralism
    in, 22; speed of, 186; third wave of,
    28; use of force in, 5–6, 7, 11

Depression, Great: effect on Central
    America, 165
Díaz Herrera, Roberto: after death of
    Torrijo, 36, 38; attack on Noriega,
    55; and labor reform, 50; loss of
    power, 54; opposition to Ardito, 51;
    overthrow of Ardito, 52–53
Dictatorships: flaws in, 69; personal, 5,
    165. See also Authoritarianism
Dignity battalions (Panama), 58–59
Dodd, Christopher, 55
Duarte, José Napoleon: assumption of
    power, 170–71; on Central American
    economy, 180; overthrow of, 12; re-
    forms of, 81, 176, 182–83; respect for
    opposition, 2; U.S. support of, 13
Duque, Carlos, 58

Economy, Central American: agro-export
    models of, 69; in colonial period,
    68–69; crises in, 1, 5, 10–11, 22, 67;
    cycles in, 180, 193n2; free market in,
    2, 103, 192; human capital in, 180;
    injustice in, 81; macroeconomic poli-
    cies in, 192; marginalization in, 67;
    recession in, 41, 180, 181;
    restructuring of, 49, 51, 52; U.S.
    policy on, 70
Economy, Costa Rican, 182, 183; organi-
    zation of, 2; stabilization of, 184
Economy, Guatemalan: agro-export
    model of, 118, 144, 158; black
    market in, 145–46, 157; under
    Cerezo government, 27–28, 128–29,
    145–48, 157, 158–59; Christian
    Democratic Party's policies on, 147;
    crises in, 10; currency of, 121, 122,
    129, 145, 157; under de León Carpio
    157–58, 161; effect of insurgency on,
    112–13; exports in, 113, 129, 142,
    146, 147, 157; external debt of, 123,
    142, 161; free market in, 136, 137;
    globalization of, 160–61; gross
    domestic product of, 29, 113, 123,
    146, 156–57, 158–59; inflation in,
    129; international assistance to,

129–30; macroeconomic orientation of, 156–58, 162, 164; under Mejía government, 122–23, 141–42; micromarkets in, 136, 137; military's role in, 127, 135, 156–57; modernization of, 156, 157; and 1982 coup, 117; real estate in, 163; recession in, 113, 141; rent-seeking sector of, 150, 158; under Ríos Montt, 120–21, 141, 156–57, 158; under Serrano presidency, 157, 161; tax reform in, 123, 130, 146, 147, 158, 159, 163; U.S. policy on, 114; wages in, 123, 137

Economy, Honduran, 2

Economy, Nicaraguan: access to international credit, 92, 106; black market in, 25, 109; capital accumulation in, 91; centralized planning in, 90–91, 109; under Chamorro government, 27, 103, 104–6, 109; consumption per capita in, 98, fig. 4.7; crises in, 67, 70, 101; decrease in production, 97, 98, 101; effect of international recession on, 97; effect on Somoza's downfall, 10; exports in, 87, 99; external gap in, 99, fig. 4.9; foreign debt of, 106; foreign influences in, 69, 91–93, 101; foreign investment in, 187; free market in, 91, 101, 103, 106–7; in global market, 107; gross domestic product of, 29, 89, fig. 4.2; gross national product of, 85, 98, 104, figs. 4.1, 4.5; inflation in, 4, 92, 98, 104, 105, fig. 4.8; infrastructure of, 78; mixed, 73, 76, 91; modernization of, 86–87, 184; nationalization of banks in, 72; primary, 68; rent-seeking sector of, 101, 103; Sandinista rectification program in, 77, 81; stabilization of, 184; subsidized, 91–93; transformations in, 67–68; underground, 91; wages in, 98, 105, fig. 4.6. *See also* Transition to socialism project (Sandinistas)

Economy, Panamanian: during Ardito presidency, 45, 47–48; banking centers in, 65; crises in, 6, 140–41; domestic currency in, 41; export service sector of, 33, 40, 65; following Noriega, 60–61; foreign debt in, 33, 39–40, 41, 45, 57, 60; free market in, 63; freezing of assets, 56, 57, 60–61; goals of, 64; gross domestic product of, 29, 57, 60, 65; gross national product of, 47; importance of canal to, 66; international, 27, 32, 65; monetary system of, 61; recession (1983), 38, 42; recovery of, 41, 52, 54, 62–63, 184; "stagflation" in, 39; tariffs in, 41; transition in, 39–42; unemployment in, 41

Economy, Salvadoran: crises in, 10; gross domestic product of, 29; stabilization of, 184

Ecuador, peaceful transition in, 5

Eisenmann, Roberto, 26

Elections, competitive, 29–30, 191; defeat of incumbents in, 28; in Guatemala, 135; U.S. influence on, 81

Elections, fraudulent, 15; in El Salvador, 171, 176; in Guatemala, 5, 14, 112, 113, 115, 141, 153–54; of Panama, 28, 43, 55, 58; right-wing belief in, 22

Elites: accommodation to democratization, 31n15; economic, 2; Guatemalan, 25, 112, 155, 156; Nicaraguan, 85, 103, 107; Panamanian, 16; pressure of business groups on, 24–25; rational choices of, 8; role in democratization, 6; Salvadoran, 165; social debt of, 29

El Salvador: Association of Industrialists, 173; Chamber of Industry and Commerce, 173; CIA in, 75; Civic-Military Directorate, 166; civil society in, 167; coalitions in, 169, 181; conflict settlement in, xii; consensus-building in, 174; coup (1948), 166; coup (1979), 12, 166, 168–69, 176;

El Salvador (*continued*)
democratic left of, 175–77; democratic transitions in, xii, 2, 80, 81, 98,
168–70, 177–79, 183; democratization by force in, 5, 166; economic liberalization in, 27; electoral left of, 28;
electoral right of, 21, 22; elites of,
165; foreign influence in, 167, 175;
institutional change in, 14, 15, 185;
Legislative Assembly, 167–68, 171,
177; "Leviathans" in, 7; media expansion in, 171; modernization in, 168,
170; National Civic Orientation
Front, 166, 167; National Conciliation Party, 166; pluralism in, 173,
174; political assassinations in, 188;
political left of, 177; political parties
of, 166, 169, 171, 175; popular mobilization in, 167; reformist movements
in, 12, 13, 175, 176; reliability of opposition in, 16–17; revolutionary
juntas in, 1, 166, 169; social
movement organizations in, 17, 171,
173–74, 177; society-led transitions
in, 1; strike (1944), 174; Supreme
Court, 171; terrorism in, 171; "transformism" in, 167; union movements
in, 172; U.S. influence in, 13, 167,
171, 172–73, 177–78. *See also*
Business groups, Salvadoran; Civil
war, Salvadoran; Economy,
Salvadoran; Insurgency, Salvadoran;
Military, Salvadoran
—, elections in, 169; (1972), 12, 171;
(1989), 11, 20–21, 173, 174, 177;
(1991), 177; (1994), 21
Emergency Social Investment Fund
(FISE, Nicaragua), 105
ENABAS (trading enterprise, Nicaragua),
104
Endara, Guillermo, 58; government of,
60–64; U.S. support of, 59
Entrepreneurs: Central American, 22;
Guatemalan, 136; Nicaraguan, 92, 93
Esquipulas talks, 78–80, 101
Esquipulas II accords, 129, 135; Cerezo
in, 133, 160

Europe, Eastern: collapse of Soviet bloc
in, 101; democratic transitions in, 10,
11; electoral right in, 20
Evangelicalism, in Guatemala, 120, 121,
125, 141, 153
Export Fund (FODEX, Guatemala), 147

Farabundo Martí National Liberation
Front (FMLN), 9, 26, 95, 175; and
defeat of Sandinistas, 173; and
Democratic Revolutionary Front,
176; negotiations with Cristiani gov-
ernment, 184; 1989 offensive of, 174;
socialists' support of, 172. *See also*
Insurgency, Salvadoran
Flores, Florencio, 36
FMLN. *See* Farabundo Martí National
Liberation Front (FMLN)
Ford, Guillermo, 58, 59
Freedom of expression: in Guatemala,
122; in Nicaragua, 68, 71, 79, 82, 94;
in Panama, 62; role of business
groups in, 24
FSLN. *See* Sandinista National Liberation
Front
Fuentes Corado, General Federico, 120

García, Alan, 49
General Agreement on Tariffs and Trade
(GATT), 157, 162
Georgia State University, 163
Girón Tánchez, Colonel Manuel de Jesús,
119
Glasnost, 97
González, Felipe, 36
Gorbachev, Mikhail, 101
Gordillo, Colonel Luis, 116, 117
Government Junta for National
Reconstruction (Nicaragua), 72
GPP (Prolonged People's War)
(Sandinistas), 110n2
Gramajo Morales, Héctor Alejandro, 4,
185; after 1988 coup attempt, 131;
career of, 111; as defense minister,
19, 128, 129; in Guatemalan military,
25, 126; knowledge of allies, 29;
during 1989 coup attempt, 132–33

Greece, democratization in, 6

Guatemala: accords with insurgents, 7–8, 178; bilingual education program (PRONEBI), 153; Central Bank, 113, 121, 148; civilian government of, 4, 98, 143–44; civilian political institutions of, 112, 122, 132, 136; civil society in, 143; conflict management in, 150; constitution, 112, 114, 135, 185–86; Constitutional Court, 154; corruption in, 113, 152–53, 164; cost of suppression in, 6–7; Council of State, 117, 120, 155; counterinsurgency policies of, 112, 118, 125, 141, 155, 181; coup (1982), 13, 111, 115–17, 122, 124, 132, 154; coup attempts (1983), 121, 122; coup attempts (1988), 19, 29, 130–31; coup attempts (1989), 19, 29, 132–33; coup attempts (1993), 7, 14, 19, 20, 140, 143, 144, 149, 154; court system of, 136, 143, 154, 159; degrees of progress in, 151; democratic transitions in, xii, 2, 5, 80, 81, 125–37, 139, 161–64, 181; democratization by force in, 5, 7; Development Council of, 155; development projects of, 146–48; dispute with Belize, 114; earthquake (1976), 120; economic liberalization in, 27–28; electoral right in, 21, 22; ethnic composition of, 112, 139, 151; evangelicalism in, 120, 121, 125, 141, 153; foreign aid to, 160, 161; in GATT, 157, 162; gun control in, 135; human rights in, 16, 114, 118, 125, 126, 151, 159–60, 162; infrastructure of, 136, 145; institutional reorganization in, 14, 145, 155–56; international relations, 122, 162; isolation of, 10, 16, 113, 114, 160–61; labor unions in, 123, 144; Legal Codes for the Nation, 119; "Leviathans" in, 7; literacy in, 113, 159; local governments in, 155–56; mass media in, 125, 130; middle class in, 116, 125, 144; Ministry of Culture, 152, 153; Ministry of Defense, 127, 131; Ministry of Finance, 148; Ministry of Urban and Rural Development, 152, 153; modernization in, 139; National Constituent Assembly (1984), 14, 124, 141, 143, 162; National Council for Export Promotion, 146; National Councils (CONAS), 147; National Institute of Statistics, 158; National Reorganization Program, 146–47, 148; new paradigm of society, 150, 151, 155, fig. 6.4; Office of the Human Rights Prosecutor, 151, 154, 160, 162; paradigm transition map of, 140, 150–61, 161–62, fig. 6.3; political assassinations in, 134, 188; political legitimacy in, 25, 28, 114, 123–24, 150; political liberalization in, 121–24; political parties of, 114, 125, 144–45, 149, 154, 162; public sector of, 124; Reform Movement (1871), 112; regime-led transitions in, 1, 7, 182; revolution (1944), 112; sectors of influence in, 140, 144–49, fig. 6.1; social conflict in, 111, 115, 136, 162; Social Investment Fund, 133, 147, 159, 164; social mobilization in, 128–29, 144, 148; social reform in, 140, 158–59, 163, 164, 182, 185; Socioeconomic Reordering Program, 145, 146, 148; as Spanish colony, 112, 118; Special Commission to Attend to Repatriated and Displaced Persons, 160; Special Jurisdiction Courts, 159; state of siege in, 119, 122; terrorism in, 115, 130, 136, 162; traditional society in, 150; transshipment of drugs through, 137; 2000 plan, 133, 148; U.S. influence in, 9, 112, 114, 133, 137; value system of, 140, 151–53, 164. See also Business groups, Guatemalan; Economy, Guatemalan; Insurgency, Guatemalan; Military, Guatemalan
—, elections in, 20, 162; (1978), 113; (1982), 5, 114–15; (1984), 124;

Guatemala, elections in (*continued*)
    (1985), 14, 21, 124, 135; (1988), 28,
    130; (1990), 21, 135, 142; (1994–96),
    21
Guerrillas, Guatemalan. *See* Insurgency,
    Guatemalan
Guevara, Che, 136
Guevara, General Angel Aníbal, 5,
    114–15, 141, 153–54

Hobbes, Thomas: *Leviathan,* 6, 7
Honduras, 30n2; CIA in, 75; civilian gov-
    ernment in, 98; military influence in,
    182, 185; regime-led transitions in, 1,
    5, 80, 81, 181, 182
Human rights: under Carter admin-
    istration, 8, 70, 86, 114, 167, 168; in
    Guatemala, 16, 114, 118, 125, 126,
    151, 159–60, 162; U.S. policy on, 81
Huntington, Samuel P., 7, 186

Illueca, Jorge, 42
Indians, of Guatemala, 125, 139; under
    Cerezo presidency, 153; in State
    Council, 117, 120
Industrialist Union (Panama), 44
Institutional Democratic Party (PID,
    Guatemala), 114, 188
Insurgencies, xi, 75, 81, 136. *See also*
    Sandinista revolution
—, Guatemalan, 1, 112–13; after 1982
    coup, 116–17; after 1985 elections,
    125; meeting with government, 130,
    135; military suppression of, 115,
    128; in National Security and
    Development Plan, 118, 119; objec-
    tives of, 136; Ríos Montt's suppres-
    sion of, 159; and Serrano govern-
    ment, 135, 142, 148
—, Salvadoran, 1, 9, 170; accord with gov-
    ernment, 7–8, 178; 1989 offensive of,
    174. *See also* Civil war, Salvadoran;
    Farabundo Martí National Liberation
    Front (FMLN)
Inter-American Development Bank
    (IDB), 106

International Monetary Fund (IMF): aid
    to Guatemala, 129, 141, 161; aid to
    Panama, 41, 54, 56, 63
Isthmus of Panama, 33, 61

Justine (Panamanian commander), 38

Kennedy administration, 80

Labor Party (Pala, Panama), 57
Land Fund (Guatemala), 141
Latin America: democratic transitions in,
    11; effect of Cold War on, 112; elec-
    toral right in, 20; financial restruc-
    turing in, 49, 51, 52; recession in, 41;
    view of Panamanian crisis, 56–57
Laugerud, General Kjell, 113, 117
Legal Codes for the Nation (Guatemala),
    119
Lemus, Colonel José María, 166, 174
Lewis, Gabriel, 56
Liberation theology, 113
Linares, Dr. Federico, 133
Lindenberg, Marc, 30n6
Lobos, General Rodolfo, 121
Lucas, General Benedicto, 115–16
Lucas Garcia, General Fernando Romeo,
    5, 122, 141; economic policy of, 156;
    election of, 113; foreign aid to, 160;
    and Guevara candidacy, 114, 153; in
    1982 coup, 115–16; overthrow of, 8,
    116, 124; protectionism under, 150
Luisa Amanda Espinoza Women's
    Association, 110n5
Lusinchi, Jaime, 49

Madrid, Miguel de la, 49
Maldonado, General Horacio, 116, 117
Managua, earthquake (1972), 85
Manfredo, Fernando, 38
Manley, Michael, 36
Manzanillo talks, 79
Maquiladora industries (Guatemala), 129
Martínez, General Maximiliano
    Hérnandez, 165, 166; U.S.
    opposition to, 168

Marxism: in Guatemala, 112–13, 136; in Panama, 33–36; of Sandinistas, 89, 94–95. *See also* Communism

Media: business's use of, 24; in El Salvador, 171; in Guatemala, 125, 130

Mejía Victores, General Oscar, 14, 119, 141–42; and Council of State, 155; democratic transitions under, 154; economic policies of, 25; as head of state, 121–22; human rights under, 159; political goals of, 122

Méndez, Julio, 135

Mexico: in Sandinista revolution, 72; support of Guatemalan insurgency, 116; trade agreements with Nicaragua, 107

Military, Central American: constitutionalization of, 17–20, 24, 192; effect of economic cycles on, 180; failure of coups, 30; prerogatives of, 31n15

Military, Guatemalan, 81; Academy of, 128; active reserve of, 116, 138n4; Center for Military Studies, 114, 117, 128; and civil society, 127, 132; constitutionalization of, 19–20, 124, 126–28; Council of Commanders, 121–22, 126; in economic affairs, 127, 135, 156–57; fundamentalism of, 126, 127; governments of, 115–24, 140, 143, 144; Honor Guard of, 116, 132; human rights under, 160; independence of, 182; as institution, 127, 128; isolation under, 160; legitimacy of government, 150; Mariscal Zavala Brigade, 116, 133; National Defense Staff, 111, 117, 121, 126, 131; National Security and Development Plan of, 118, 122; in 1988 coup attempt, 131–32; pacification campaign of, 117–21, 122; professionalism in, 127, 135; response to business groups, 25; under Serrano presidency, 148–49; "Strategic Appraisal" document, 114; transfer of power from, 4, 23, 153–55; values of, 151

Military, Nicaraguan: constitutionalization of, 17–18, 109; Jefe del Ejército of, 185

Military, Panamanian, 3; constitutionalization of, 18; in 1984 election, 43. *See also* National Guard, Panamanian

Military, Salvadoran, 81; after 1979 coup, 169, 176; in civil war, 172; constitutionalization of, 19, 169, 178, 185; effect of civil war on, 176; governments of, 165, 168; institutionalization of, 165–66; U.S. aid to, 13, 171

Military Youth Movement (El Salvador), 166; defeat of, 169, 176

Movement for Social Action (MAS, Guatemala), 148

National Bank of Panama, 47; liquidity of, 54, 56

National Civic Crusade (Panama), 15–16, 55–57; after Noriega, 62

National Civic Orientation Front (FNOC, El Salvador), 166, 167

National Conciliation Party (PCN, El Salvador), 166

National Confederation of Hero and Martyr Professionals (Nicaragua), 110n5

National Confederation of Professionals (CONAPRO, Nicaragua), 110n8

National Council for Export Promotion (CONAPEX, Guatemala), 146

National Democratic Union (UNADE, Panama), 39; in Ardito presidency, 44–45; in Legislative Assembly, 47; in 1984 elections, 42, 43; reform measures of, 49

National Guard, Nicaraguan, 69, 72

National Guard, Panamanian, 35–36; budget reductions for, 47; rise to power, 36–37. *See also* Military, Panamanian; Panama Defense Forces

Nationalist Republican Alliance (ARENA, El Salvador), 16; alliance with left, 175; links with business

Nationalist Republican Alliance
(*continued*)
groups, 26; in 1989 elections, 20–21,
173, 174, 177
National Liberal Party (Panama), 39, 57
National Liberal Republican Movement
(Molirena, Panama), 39, 57
National Liberation Movement (MLN,
Guatemala), 116, 188
National Liberation Party (PLN, Costa
Rica), 182
National liberations movements, 95, 98
National Opposition Union (UNO, El
Salvador), 166, 167; coalition with
Christian Democrats, 169; formation
of, 174
National Opposition Union (UNO,
Nicaragua), 16, 82; coalitions of, 105;
in 1990 elections, 102
National Patriotic Front (FPN,
Nicaragua), 71, 73, 110n3
National Reconciliation Commissions,
129, 135, 160
National Reconstruction Committee
(Guatemala), 120
National Reorganization Program
(Guatemala), 146–47, 148
National Salvation government. *See*
Chamorro, Violeta Barrios de
National Union of Farmers and Ranchers
(Nicaragua), 110n5
National United Front (FUN,
Guatemala), 120
National Workers' Front (FNT,
Nicaragua), 105
Nicaragua: agrarian reform in, 73, 77–78,
82, 94; civil freedoms in, 78–80; civil
society of, 93–94; coalitions in, 71,
105, 181; conflict settlement in, xii;
consensus-building in, 18, 84; constitutionalization of military in, 17–18,
109; constitution of, 76, 88, 101; cost
of suppression in, 6–7; decentralization of power in, 108, 109; democratic centralism in, 93; Democratic
Liberation Union, 71; democratic
transitions in, 2, 83–84, 102–9, 183;
democratization by force in, 5, 7;
earthquake (1972), 85; effect of oil
crisis on, 86; effect of Sandinista revolution on, 76–78; Emergency Social
Investment Fund, 105; exploitation
of natural resources, 109; free-trade
agreements of, 107; illiteracy in, 70,
72, 82; infant mortality in, 70, 82; infrastructure of, 72; Institute of
Agrarian Reform, 73; institutional
change in, 14, 185; international isolation of, 97; labor organizations of,
15, 72, 82, 105; landholders in, 81;
"Leviathans" in, 7; middle class of,
87; modernization in, 86–87, 102,
184; National Assembly, 76, 107; as
oligarchy, 85; political culture of,
107–9, 184; professional associations
of, 15, 110n8; property reform in, 68,
74, 75, 77, 82, 83, 89, 187; public
sector of, 89, 107; Reagan administration policy on, xii, 12; *recontra*
groups in, 184; relations with Central
America, 79; revolution (1893), 85;
social inequality in, 69–70; socialism
in, 80; social movement organizations
in, 15–16, 70; social organizations of,
68, 72, 82; society-led transitions in,
1; socioeconomic change in, 72–73,
81–82; Soviet aid to, 9; as Spanish
colony, 85, 107; strikes in, 71, 104;
support of Guatemalan insurgency,
116; trade embargo against, 97; trade
guilds in, 110n5; U.S. occupation of,
9, 69; voting in United Nations, 95,
fig. 4.4. *See also* Business groups,
Nicaraguan; Economy, Nicaraguan;
Military, Nicaraguan; Sandinista
National Liberation Front
—, elections in: (1984), 67, 76; (1990), 9,
14, 16, 17, 80, 82–83, 94, 102, 110,
173
Nicaraguan Public Sector Corporation
(CORNAP), 107
Nicaraguan resistance. *See* Contras
Noriega, General Manuel Antonio: under
Ardito presidency, 45–46, 48, 51; as

commander of National Guard, 38; control of PDF, 54; cooperation with CIA, 54; on economic reform, 50; effect of economic crisis on, 10; as head of state, 59; illicit activities of, 46, 53, 57, 59; intelligence contacts of, 46; in 1984 elections, 3; in 1989 elections, 28, 57–58; opposition to, 6, 7, 15–16, 21, 26; overthrow of, 5, 173, 181; pact with Paredes, 36; provisional government of, 58; in U.S. invasion of Panama, 59, 60; U.S. negotiations with, 45–46, 48, 51

O'Donnell, Guillermo, 2, 20
Oduber, Daniel, 36
Oligarchies, 5; Nicaraguan, 85
Opposition Democratic Alliance (ADO, Panama), 39; following Noriega, 61; in 1984 elections, 43
Organization of American States (OAS): mission in Panama, 58; and Somoza dictatorship, 71
Ortega, Daniel, 16, 185
Ortega, General Humberto, 18, 185
Oslo Agreements (1990), 160

Paiz-Andrade, Rodolfo, 4; as civil engineer, 161; as finance minister, 140, 145, 163
Panama: civil-military administrations in, 62; constitutionalization of military in, 18; constitution of, 61; Coordinadora Civilista Nacional, 47; corruption in justice system, 37, 42; coup (1984), 42, 52–53; coup attempts (1989), 59; democratic transitions in, xii, 2, 33–36, 44–53, 60–64, 180, 183; democratization by force in, 5; electoral right of, 21; Electoral Tribunal, 37, 43–44; elites of, 16; geographical importance of, 32–33; infrastructure of, 33, 34, 40, 61, 64, 65; Judiciary Code, 45; labor legislation in, 49–50, 51; leftist influence in, 35; Legislative Assembly of, 35, 44, 47, 52, 55, 61; legitimacy of government

in, 61; "Leviathans" in, 7; National Assembly of Representatives, 36, 37; outlook for future, 64–66; political coalitions in, 38–39, 61, 63; political goals of, 64; political polarization in, 34; populism in, 34, 37, 48, 53; post-Noriega governments of, 7, 60–64; private investment in, 34, 39, 40, 41, 49; professional associations in, 21, 35, 41, 47; public investment programs in, 39, 40; public sector of, 45, 57; reformist injection into, 13–14; regime-led transitions in, 1; in Sandinista revolution, 72; social goals of, 64; social services in, 63; sovereignty over isthmus, 33; state enterprises in, 39, 41; Supreme Court, 61; tourism in, 62, 65; trade agreements of, 49; trade associations in, 41, 54, 56, 63; trade associations of, 62; U.S. influence in, 8–9; U.S. invasion of, 1, 18, 20, 59–60, 65, 181; U.S. withdrawal from, 64, 65; weakness of institutions in, 66, 185. See also Business groups, Panamanian; Canal, Panama; Economy, Panamanian; Military, Panamanian
—, elections in: (1984), 3, 13–14, 33, 38, 42–43, 55; (1989), 28, 57–58, 61–62
Panama Canal, 33; importance to economy, 66; infrastructure of, 65; modernization of, 64; revenue from, 39, 40
Panama Defense Forces (PDF), 14; under Ardito presidency, 44–47, 48, 49–53; defeat of, 20; destruction of, 59–60, 185; opposition to, 54, 56, 58–59; reorganization after Noriega, 61; and U.S. Southern Command, 58–59. See also Military, Panamanian; National Guard, Panamanian
Panamanistas Party, 34, 42, 57
Paredes, Rubén Darío, 36; candidacy for president, 38; reform proposals of, 37
PDF. See Panama Defense Forces
Peasant Democratic Alliance (ADC, El Salvador), 174

Peasants, Nicaraguan: as contras, 100; displacement of, 91; organizations of, 72; rebellion (1985), 94; Sandinista policy toward, 77–78, 82; socioeconomic power of, 3
Peat Marwick (firm), 163
People's Property enterprises (APP, Sandinistas), 92–93
Perestroika, 97, 101
Pérez, Carlos Andrés, 36
Permanent Debate for Peace (El Salvador), 174
Peru, peaceful transition in, 5
Pluralism: in El Salvador, 173, 174; replacement of authoritarianism, 5; role in democratization, 22; under Sandinistas, 76
Political liberalization, 2–3; role of business groups in, 24
Political parties: coalition-building among, 192, 193; in democratic transitions, 186, 188–89, 191; of El Salvador, 166, 169, 171, 175, 177; of Guatemala, 114, 125, 144–45, 149, 154, 162; of Nicaragua, 107–9, 184; of Panama, 38–39, 61, 63
Popular Forum (El Salvador), 166, 167, 174; scope of, 168
Portugal, military force in, 5
PRD. *See* Democratic Revolutionary Party (Panama)
La Prensa, 110–8; censorship of, 16, 75; founding of, 26, 37; reopening of, 79
Professional groups: influence in elections, 21–22; Nicaraguan, 15, 110n8; Panamanian, 21, 35, 41, 47
Proletarian Tendency group (Sandinistas), 110n2
Property: confiscation from business groups, 89–90; expropriation of, 11–12, 77, 89; relations in Central America, 181; under Sandinistas, 92–93
Przeworski, Adam, 11, 12, 15
Public sector: in democratic transitions, 192; of Guatemala, 124; of Nicaragua, 89, 107; of Panama, 45, 57
Putnam, Robert T., 186

Quiñónez, Dr. Mario, 133

Rational choice, in democratization, 5, 8, 11, 22
Reagan administration: Central American policy of, xi–xii; and Noriega, 54; opposition to Sandinistas, 8, 75, 76, 98; Salvadoran policy of, 12, 173
Republican Party (United States), 97
Revolutionary Democratic Unification Party (PRUD, El Salvador), 166
Revolutionary Party (PR, Guatemala), 114
Ríos Montt, General Efraín, 13, 141; amnesty program of, 119–20; decision-making under, 155; economic policies of, 120–21, 141, 156–57, 158; ethics campaign of, 151–52; evangelicalism of, 120, 141, 153; *juntita* of, 117, 122; legal changes under, 119; mobilization of army, 120; in 1982 coup, 116, 117, 154; overthrow of, 121; pacification under, 117–21; repression of insurgency, 159
Rodríguez, Francisco, 58
Romero, General Carlos Humberto, 5, 168; overthrow of, 8, 114, 176
Royo, Dr. Arístides, 35, 36

Salvadoran Association of Industrialists, 173
Sandinista National Liberation Front (FSLN): abuse of power, 29, 89–90; achievements of, 83; agrarian reform by, 77–78, 82, 94; agreement with Chamorro government, 18, 183–84; antidemocratic policies of, 6; breakup of alliance, 89; business organizations under, 92; CIA activities against, 54; civil society under, 93–94; commitment to transformation, 74; corruption in, 101; and COSEP, 27, 73, 75, 92, 110n8; decision-making processes of, 93; defeat of contras, 23, 101; Defense Committees of, 93–94, 110n5; demobilization of, 184; democratization under, 76; domination of

political life, 188; effect of Soviet collapse on, 101–2; factions within, 71, 87–88, 110n2; foreign policy of, 74–75; goals of, 87; intervention in production, 89; legitimacy of, 14, 71, 72, 73–74, 93; Leninism of, 108; mass organizations of, 92, 93, 94, 110n5; military budget of, 90, 92; National Directorate of, 3, 23, 75, 93, 110n4; National Reconstruction Plan, 72; in 1990 elections, 9, 14, 23, 68, 82–83, 102, 173; as opposition party, 18, 83; opposition to, 3–4, 83; overthrow of Somoza, 87; peasants under, 77–78; "piñata" of, 184; pluralism under, 76; political clientele of, 92; revolutionary government of, 72–73, 88; role in liberalization, 3; and Roman Catholic Church, 110n5; social base of, 93; social programs of, 92; Soviet support of, 74, 75, 95–98, 101, 108; Statute of Rights and Guarantees, 72; support base for, 73–74, 101; "Third Way" project, 88; U.S. opposition to, 1, 14, 74, 75, 78, 79, 97, 109. See also Transition to socialism project
Sandinista Popular Army (EPS), 93
Sandinista Popular Militias, 110n5
Sandinista revolution, 1; amnesty in, 80; credibility of, 78; effect on Central America, 8, 70; effect on oligarchy, 85; expansion of, 81; institutionalization of, 76–78; legitimacy of, 71
Sandinista Workers Headquarters, 110n5
Sandoval, Mario, 115
Sanguinetti, Julio M., 49
Sapoá agreements, 79
Schmitter, Philippe, 2, 20
Secretariat for Social, Economic, and Development Planning (SEGEPLAN, Guatemala), 117
Sereseres, Caesar, 111
Serrano Elías, Jorge, 7, 142–43; civil culture under, 153; conservatism of, 21; coup attempt, 14, 19, 140, 143, 144, 149, 154; economic policies of, 157, 161; human rights under, 160;

Indians under, 153; in National Reconciliation Commission, 135; relations with military, 148–49; social problems under, 149, 159
Singapore, British withdrawal from, 65
Social Christian Unity Party (PUSC, Costa Rica), 182
Social Democrats: of El Salvador, 169; influence in Panama, 36
Social Investment Fund (FIS, Guatemala), 133, 147, 159; resistance to, 164
Socioeconomic Reordering Program (Guatemala), 145, 146, 148
Somocistas, 71; and U.S. Nicaraguan policy, 78
Somoza Debayle, General Anastasio: corruption of, 86; exile of, 72; expropriations by, 89; overthrow of, 3, 5, 8, 68, 83, 88, 114; U.S. opposition to, 71
Somoza dynasty (Nicaragua): alienation under, 85–86; deterioration of, 70; landownership of, 70, 82
Somoza García, Anastasio, 9, 85
South America. See Latin America
Soviet Union: collapse of, 9, 101, 102, 109, 136; internal transformations in, 97–98, 101; intervention in Central America, 1, 9, 136; support of Guatemalan insurgency, 116, 136; support of Sandinistas, 74, 75, 95–98, 101, 108
Spadafora, Dr. Hugo: family of, 53; murder of, 51–52
Special Commission to Attend to Repatriated and Displaced Persons (Guatemala), 160
Standard of living: under authoritarianism, 10; Nicaraguan, 29
Superior Private Enterprise Council (COSEP, Nicaragua), 25–26, 110n6; contra connections of, 75; Sandinistas' policy towards, 27, 73, 92
Supreme Electoral Tribunal (Guatemala), 14, 120, 149; effect on Guatemalan society, 151; integrity of, 154, 162; in 1984 elections, 124

Tercerista faction (Sandinistas), 87, 88, 110n2
"Thesis for National Stability" (Guatemala), 118
Third world: democratic transitions in, 11; radical-left movements of, 89
Torrijos, General Omar, 5; business opposition to, 26; command of National Guard, 35–36; commitment to democratization, 33; death of, 36; domestic policies of, 8; economic policies of, 33–34; and electoral right, 21; foreign policies of, 36; Marxists under, 35–36; political transition after, 36–39, 60; political transition under, 34–36
Torrijos-Carter treaties (1978), 33, 35, 36, 59
Transisthmian pipeline, 39, 40, 64
Transition to socialism project (Sandinistas), 88–89; breakdown of, 97–102, 109; centrally planned economy under, 90–91; effect on population, 99–100; foreign subsidies in, 91–93; international alliances under, 95–97; nationalization of economy under, 89–90; organizations comprising, 93–94; proletarianization under, 94–95. See also Economy, Nicaraguan; Sandinista National Liberation Front
Trifinio program, 133
Turkey, peaceful transition in, 5

United Guatemalan National Revolutionary coalition (URNG), 142, 148
United Nations: in democratic transitions, 191; in Nicaragua, 17; Nicaragua's voting in, 95, fig. 4.4; and Salvadoran civil war, 178
United States: Central American policies of, 1, 80–81, 168; and collapse of

Soviet bloc, 101; counterinsurgency policy of, 81, 112; influence in El Salvador, 13, 167, 171, 172–73, 177–78; influence in Guatemala, 9, 112, 114, 133, 137; influence in Panama, 8–9, 53, 55, 56; influence on social change, 81; invasion of Panama, 1, 18, 20, 59–60, 65, 181; national security doctrine of, 112; negotiations with Noriega, 54, 56, 57; occupation of Nicaragua, 9, 69; opposition to Sandinistas, 1, 14, 74, 78, 79, 97, 109; recession (1970s), 1; support for democratic transitions, xii; trade with Nicaragua, 97, 107; withdrawal from Panama, 64, 65. See also Agency for International Development; Carter administration; Central Intelligence Agency; Reagan administration
UNO. See National Opposition Union

Velázquez, José Luis, 3, 4, 9; on economic crises, 11; on Nicaraguan economy, 25
Venezuela: military force in, 5; trade agreements with Nicaragua, 107

Wheelock Román, Jaime, 3, 14, 29; on consensus-building, 18
Whitehead, Laurence, 9
World Bank, 186; aid to Guatemala, 129, 147, 161; aid to Panama, 49, 50, 51, 53, 54, 56, 63; Ardito at, 34; loans to Nicaragua, 106
World Peace Foundation, 30n6, 181

Zamora, Rubén, 3, 189, 194n2; election of, 16; on elections, 28; on institutional change, 15; knowledge of allies, 29; participation in junta, 176